INSTITUTION BUILDING
AND
LEADERSHIP IN AFRICA

Edited by

Lennart Wohlgemuth – Jerker Carlsson – Henock Kifle

Nordiska Afrikainstitutet, 1998

This book is published with support from the Swedish International Development Cooperation Agency and in cooperation with the African Development Bank.

Indexing terms

Leadership
Institution building
Capacity building
Public administration
Private enterprises

Africa

Cover: Alicja Grenberger

Drawings: Anders Suneson, Tecknade Bilder

© the authors and Nordiska Afrikainstitutet, 1998

ISBN 91-7106-421-4

Printed in Sweden by Elanders Gotab, Stockholm 1998

Contents

Introduction

A great deal has been written in recent years about the continuing economic difficulties of most African countries. Much of the current analysis has sought to identify the factors that have held back economic recovery and sustained development in the continent. Four reasons are often advanced: the historical heritage including the colonial legacy, unfavourable external factors, poor economic policies, and increasing dependence on foreign assistance.

Although the causes for Africa's economic malaise are undoubtedly varied, the countries in the region have, in the last two decades, followed remarkably similar economic policies. These have sought to put African economies on a path of sustained growth and development. Such economic policies, which have been supported by both bilateral donors and international financial institutions, have consisted of two distinct sets of measures: stabilization and structural adjustment policies. Stabilization policies, through the adoption of prudent macroeconomic policies, have sought to restore economic stability, by reducing high inflation rates and by restoring external imbalances. And adjustment policies have sought to bring about major changes in the economic structures of African countries by re-defining and reducing the role of the state, and by promoting economic policies that are private sector-led and market-based.[1]

The economic and social impact of the stabilization and structural adjustment policies that countries have pursued over the last two decades has been a source of considerable controversy. A number of African countries have achieved some degree of economic stability, and a few have even started to record respectable rates of economic growth. Yet, it is quite evident that African countries will need to pursue a much more complex set of economic, social, and institutional development policies if they are to achieve sustained economic development and transformation. This is, of course, not too surprising. Economic development is a complex process affected by a myriad set of economic and non-economic factors. The natural and human resource base of a country, its population size and growth, the vigour and development of its public and private institutions, and the degree

---

[1] World Bank, *Adjustment in Africa*. London: Oxford University Press, 1994.

to which social values and norms are shared by the populace at large, are all important factors that affect economic development.

This book focuses on one of these factors—the capacity of a country to manage and marshal its resources in pursuit of economic development. As the experience of a number of countries has shown, there is a clear connection between a society's institutions—political as well as economic and administrative—and its ability to achieve growth and development. The economic history of Western Europe and the United States, and more recently of East Asia, bears testimony to the importance of institutional growth and efficiency for economic growth.

Remarkably, the critical role of institutional development for economic growth has only been fully acknowledged in the last two decades or so. The seminal work in this area has been that of Douglas North, who, from the perspective of economic history, has shown the strong link between the efficiency of public and private institutions and economic growth.[2]

What, then, is an institution? Does it differ from an organization—and in that case, how? Casual use of these terms, which are often interchangeably used, often gives the impression that they are one and the same thing. In this book, however, the concept of institution has a particular meaning. As Anton Johnston argues in his chapter, the most important characteristic of an institution is its strong and evident culture. An organization thus becomes an institution only when it has developed a set of values that hold it together, and whose strategic vision is guided by such a culture.

From the perspective of economic development, we are interested in different types of institutions—both public and private. Those that fulfil the basic functions of the state—such as maintaining law and order, collecting taxes, and providing defence—are of course pre-requisites for any development to take place. Other state institutions that provide essential public goods, such as education and health services, are critical for the success of the development enterprize. There are also other public institutions that perform essential regulatory functions, such as those that oversee the functioning of capital markets and ensure that agreed rules and regulations are followed. And in civil society, as well as in the private sector, there are a variety of insti-

---

[2] North, D., 1990, *Institutions, Institutional Change and Economic Performance*. Cambridge: Cambridge University Press.

tutions that create the basis for democratic development, provide social services and promote and protect the interests of different social groups.

The failure of institutions in Africa, encompassing those of the state and civil society, has been an important theme in much of the debate on African development in recent years. In a fundamental sense, the crisis of African development can be said to be a crisis of its institutions. It needs to be recalled, in this connection, however, that most African countries inherited a model of a strong and centralized state that was essentially created to fulfil two functions: upholding law and order, and collecting taxes. The experience of a large number of countries has shown the inadequacy of this model from both political and economic perspectives. It has proved incapable of providing political stability and protecting the welfare of citizens, and it has also failed to promote economic development and growth. Clearly, African countries will need to develop and nurture—as some have already started to do—new institutions of government. They will also need to create the necessary space for the evolution and development of the institutions of civil society, as these are essential for both social and economic development.

It needs to be stressed that the institutional crisis in Africa is no longer a crisis of knowledge, or the absence of educated and trained people who can man and lead such institutions. Following independence, most African countries did invest heavily in education; such that there is now a large group of highly educated people, who are, however, far from being fully used. This has, among other factors, led to a sizeable emigration of well-trained Africans. Today, it is estimated that 100,000 well-educated Africans work in OECD countries.[3] Clearly, African institutions have been unable to absorb and retain the domestic capacity that has been built up over the last forty years.

There are no simple solutions to the institutional crisis faced by African countries. Neither the wholesale import of foreign patterns of organization nor the imposition of traditional methods will work. In its study of African Management in the 1990s, the World Bank has, for example, argued that Africa needs institutions that are firmly anchored in local culture, history and tradition, but, which, at the same time, are open to new ideas.

---

[3] Berg, E., 1993, *Rethinking Technical Co-operation: Reforms for Capacity Building in Africa.* New York: UNDP.

It is evident that the economic crisis of the last decade and the policy of fiscal austerity adopted by many countries—as part of their stabilization and adjustment programmes—has undermined most public institutions in Africa. Their knowledge base has also been much weakened. These institutions have now to be rebuilt. This will require concerted action and political will on the part of governments. It will also require close interaction and consultation with civil society to enable these institutions to regain their legitimacy in the eyes of the public.

Foreign assistance can play an important supportive role in this endeavour. Yet, to be effective, it too must draw lessons from the successes and failures of the past. In this regard, it needs to be recalled that international assistance, with considerable success, initially focused on educating individuals from Africa. When it became clear, however, that limited opportunities existed for these educated people to use their new knowledge, attention was shifted to institution building which requires developing and reinforcing the capability of organizations and not simply that of individuals. This sometimes requires changing the rules and regulations that are in force. And as we noted earlier, it also requires a conscious attempt to develop a new culture that will galvanize the institution and its members. Traditionally, however, international assistance has primarily been directed at enhancing the efficiency of organizations, that is, their capacity to deliver goods and services. But in the future such efforts will need to be more comprehensive and many-dimensional if they are to succeed.

The challenge facing an outside organization, engaged in such institution building, should not be minimized. It will require extensive knowledge about the organization to be developed and built, and it will require an appreciation and respect for traditional culture and norms. An attempt will also need to be made to develop a partnership for change rather than the imposition of change that has traditionally characterized donor-recipient relations.

The purpose of this book is to increase understanding of the current management practices in Africa, and the challenges faced in building institutions. It aims to contribute to the emergence of more effective assistance in this area by the donor community. The introductory chapters are of an all-embracing nature and attempt to provide, on the basis of varied theoretical and historical perspectives, a richer understanding of the conditions faced by leaders in Africa, and the role of institutions in the process of change.

In the first chapter, Jerker Carlsson deals with the conditions for leadership in Africa and the main characteristics of African organizational structures as well as the opportunities for change and adaptation to new circumstances. In spite of the obvious need for change, there has at the same time been resistance to organizational change. The concept of the "African manager" or the "African organization" as a point of departure for understanding the problems facing the management of organizations in Africa today is not very helpful. First of all because there is no such thing as an African manager, or organization. Management practices vary throughout the continent. Second, because the "rules of the game" reward behaviour which is not compatible which organizational effectiveness and efficiency. The article argues that the current crisis of organizations in Africa is largely a reflection of a situation where institutions for historical reasons have not been able to establish an environment conducive to and supportive of development. Experience has taught us that institutional reform cannot be achieved simply by transferring institutional models from United States and countries in Europe to Africa. Neither is it feasible to build solely on the systems and principles of local society. Recent research suggests that finding ways for coexistence may be a possible option for institutional reform.

Prudence Woodford-Berger discusses the necessity of augmenting traditional approaches to organization analysis with gendered analytical perspectives and concepts for understanding the work of organizations in Africa. The significance of cultural interpretations of sex identity has been seriously neglected in organization studies. Consequently there has been faulty and incomplete understanding of how organizations actually work which has in turn contributed to the difficulty of developing effective strategies for organizational change.

Anton Johnston deals with the question of institution building and gives it an operative content. He also discusses various attempts at doing concrete work with the development of institutions and poses a question that in principle has great significance: "When can the building of an institution be regarded as complete?" This issue is further developed by Göran Andersson and Peter Winai, who present a model of how institutions can be diagnosed.

Henock Kifle addresses the challenge of capacity building in Africa both from a historical perspective and from the perspective of international financial institutions. He notes that while the importance of capacity building is now universally recognized, the record of achievement is far from satisfactory. He argues that current efforts at capacity building must take into account the considerable political and economic changes that have taken place in the continent in the last decade. He stresses that political and economic stability are essential for success in capacity building and that the focus of capacity building must be on developing capacity for capacity building. He concludes his paper by identifying a number of strategic areas for intervention and the role that international financial institutions could play in their support for capacity building in Africa.

The question of long-term sustainability has always been central in development contexts. It is particularly important for all projects that are concerned with some form of organizational development. What factors are crucial to sustainability? Apollinaire Ndorukwigira discusses what conditions are required for a capacity building project to survive and lead to lasting results, irrespective of whether it is donor-financed or not. The author's review shows that the demands on economically sound development projects are many and that they are far from always met.

Then follow two chapters which focus on financial management and personnel management. Åke Sahlin and Peter Murphy as well as Christer Wallroth start from a theoretical discussion and examine how these terms have been handled in practice. They have many years of experience from working in several African countries and give practical examples illustrating the theoretical discussions in the previous chapters.

Experiences of management, leadership and institution building have been very varied and a review of different attempts to build up institutions is a useful exercise that can lead to ideas and reflections. Therefore the book contains a number of case studies where the authors relate their own and others' experiences of capacity building projects in different sectors. Higher education and research, basic education, health, agriculture, urban development and telecommunications are included in the sectors that are analysed. Some contributions also take up the question of how one analyses the needs of the public sector for reform and discuss the potential for public sector assistance in different countries in Africa (Tor Sellström, Lais Macedo de Oliveira and Maximino Loschiavo de Barros, Dag Sundelin, Olof Hesselmark and Andreas Bengtsson).

The case studies have, naturally, different characteristics. The authors have had full freedom to interpret the concepts management, leadership and institutional development within their respective sector. The result has become an exciting mix with different angles of approach. The question has been illuminated from many and sometimes unexpected angles, from a relatively formal review of management, leadership and institutional development within a limited sector (Nils-Ivar Isaksson, Ingemar Gustafsson, Lennart Wohlgemuth) to completely new ways of thinking and posing problems (Gunilla Krantz and Frants Staugård, Björn Mothander, Anders Grettve, Ann Schlyter, Jan Valdelin, Poul Engberg-Pedersen).

Two main themes run throughout the book: one is the character of African organizations with their strengths and weaknesses, while the other is the experience of close cooperation with an African organization that finds itself in the centre of a process of change. Together, the authors create a picture of institutional development work in Africa and its enormous complexity. They emphasize the difficulties of the undertaking and the need for patience and perseverance. They also demonstrate the opportunities in, and the humility which should be a part of, beginning every task that involves international assistance.

This anthology was originally produced in Swedish. On the insistence of Klaus Winkel, Chairman of the Programme and Research Council of the Nordic Africa Institute, a partly new, partly revised, book has now been produced in English. It has been produced jointly by the African Development Institute of the African Development Bank and the Nordic Africa Institute. We hope that this anthology will also be useful for an African readership in the important and long-term work of developing good management and institutions all over the continent.

Finally, we would like to emphasize that the opinions expressed in each chapter are those of the authors. In addition to the authors, we would like to thank Madi Gray (translating), Elaine Almén (final language checking), Sonja Johansson (copy editing) and Kajsa Övergaard for their help in producing this anthology, and Sida for its generous financial contribution.

Lennart Wohlgemuth   *Jerker Carlsson*   *Henock Kifle*

Organization and Leadership in Africa

Jerker Carlsson

Introduction

Since independence, the public sector has played a central role in the state-led development of Africa. Public authorities and organizations have been the dominant actors within almost every activity in society. The reasons for this can be found in the history of Africa. Compared with other developing areas, African states are young, formed during colonial rule and taken over by the first generation of African leaders scarcely thirty years ago. The new governments embarked on institutional reform. Public organizations were established in order to manage the modernization project, in keeping with the prevailing idea that governments needed to be the catalysts, if not the engines, of their country's transformation (Brautigam, 1996:85–86).

During the last 15 years it has been made clear that the prospects for development are intimately linked to the capacity of the institutions and organizations existing in a country. Almost everyone engaged in development projects in Africa has experienced this, sometimes in a dramatic way.

> A government that is unable to harness and manage its resources effectively usually fails to identify and define its own problems and its priorities for external assistance. Unfortunately, with only a handful of exceptions in Africa, this capacity and political will are deficient. Indeed, the poverty of institutional and organizational resources available to governments in Africa probably distinguishes the region from other parts of the developing world, albeit in the context of wide intra-regional differences (Carlsson, et al., 1997:213–214).

The development process depends on the strength of the link between work carried out at the micro level and growth and development at the national level. It is not unreasonable to assume that good results at the micro-level are also reflected at the general national level (macro-level). Different organizations, private as well as public, have the task of providing resources, co-ordinating and sometimes doing the actual work. Successful development requires institutions that ensure that individual projects do not become isolated islands, but are integrated in a larger context of development work.

When all possible indicators of growth in Africa are pointing downwards, the organizations of Africa have become the centrepiece of the discussion. Most observers say that the problems of inefficient organizations have become much worse, particularly within the public sector. Public organizations seem to lack a capacity for conducting their tasks and hence become an obstacle to development. The micro-macro paradox arises from this weakness. African organizations are said to have failed to ensure that good results at the micro-level are reflected in macro-level indicators of progress and development.

However, the efficiency of the organizations in performing according to expectations, depends to a large extent on the institutions of a particular country. The institutions set the rules of the game as they provide the legal, political, social and economic framework within which organizations operate. Organizational efficiency is therefore not only about the players (the organization and its members), but also about the rules of the game and their appropriateness. However, the causalities work both ways, institutions do affect the efficiency of organizations. But organizations, when they try to achieve their objectives also reveal the strengths and weaknesses of the institutions and can therefore have an impact on institutional change (North, 1993).

Institutional issues are difficult to avoid in any analysis of organizational performance. Especially as the historical legacy of many African countries has left them with implanted institutions more designed for control than development. North describes this institutional framework which has characterized a good deal of the economic history of the world in the following way:

> The possibilities which are available to political and economic entrepreneurs have a mixed content, but in general they tend to focus on activities which support redistribution rather than competition and which limit possibilities rather than widening them ... The organizations which develop within these institutional frames will become efficient, but more efficient in making society even more inefficient and to make the basic economic structure even more supportive of productive activities (North, 1993:25).

North makes the point that such a development path can become permanent since the transaction costs in the political and economic markets in these countries, in combination with the actors' subjective models, will prevent them from gradually choosing more efficient solutions.

Why then do many organizations in Africa find themselves in crisis? Is it a matter of a lack of resources, appropriate institutions, or is there something wrong with the prevailing attitudes to leadership and what an organization really is all about and what it is supposed to do? In this article I shall concentrate my attention on the organization, its current difficulties and the potential for change. In particular I shall look at management and leaders as critical issues for organizational effectiveness. From a perspective of organization theory we shall discuss management, leadership and the requirements for organizational change.[1]

What does a manager do?

In traditional management theory the manager is a person who employs people in order to have things done. His/her tasks consist of planning, organizing, appointing and promoting people, managing and controlling. The manager is a professional person who, independently of his environment is doing the things that need to be done for the organization to work.

Management theory has since progressed towards a more dynamic view of management. The manager is a member of a social system. When he or she is performing his/her tasks this is done within a social context where it is impossible to disregard habits and values. The external world in the form of governments and state systems is an important variable for a manger to consider when taking a decision. Good communication ability as well as an ability to work under conditions of uncertainty are crucial properties for a manager.

It is in this context that the concept *management by objectives* has emerged. This means that the work of the management of an organization shall be guided by clear and transparent objectives. Clear objectives, however, require a clear mission statement. One of the most important tasks of a manager is to institutionalize the organization, in

---

[1] A particularly important aspect of an organization's development is its institutionalization. An organization is an institution when the way it conducts its business is guided by culturally determined rules. The institution has developed a set of strategic values, which guides its action and is accepted by the members of the organization.

other words create an organization with a strong profile and character, which gives the members of the organization a feeling of ownership and commitment towards the organization and its mandate (Selznick, 1957).

On good grounds it is reasonable to assume that what a manager should do and what he/she actually does are two different things. The latter is something which classical management theory has hardly dealt with. Henry Mintzberg has in several important contributions to management theory tried to answer the question: "What is the manager actually doing?" His research has led to a questioning of many of the established truths of the classic management theory (Mintzberg, 1989).

First of all, managers are no systematic planners. Their work is instead characterized by a short perspective: a lot of variation, stop-go practices and a lack of reflection. Second, they do not plan and manage other people's work to the extent normally believed. Managers use much more time than one could expect directly interfering in operational activities. Third, a manager's information needs are rarely satisfied by sophisticated, often computerized management information systems. The manager prefers the telephone and meetings to get the information he or she needs to take a decision. Mintzberg's perhaps most important conclusion is that management is not a science. Most of the things that a manager does are based on intuition and experience and are hardly accessible for scientific analysis.

On the basis of his studies Mintzberg developed a typology of roles which a manager can play in an organization. In the box below we have summarized Mintzberg's typology. The roles can be divided into three major groups: interpersonal roles; information roles and decision making roles. Taken together they represent a picture of what management is all about.

Roles can be more or less pronounced, depending partly on the status and authority of the manager, partly on the demands the organization and its culture place on the manager. The distribution of roles is strongly determined by the history of the organization and the surrounding society and its structure, norms etc. Mintzberg's typology is based on the findings from his studies of organizations in the USA and Europe. Is the distribution of roles similar in other historical and economic settings?

The roles of the manager in an organization

The leader takes care of ceremonial activities which are associated with the exercise of management

The inspirer inspires members of the organization to carry out their duties in a good way. It is the inspirer who hires and fires, formulates the objectives of the organization, delivers rewards and punishments.

The co-ordinator builds a network inside and outside the organization. The contacts are mainly used to acquire, but also to distribute, information.

The monitor collects relevant information from various sources and creates a good climate for receiving information.

The distributor ensures that other members of the organization can access the information.

The spokesman represents the organization externally, particularly in environments that can be expected to exercise some influence on the organization.

The entrepreneur takes the initiative for changes which increase the efficiency and competitiveness of the organization.

The conflict manager manages conflicts in the organization so that they do not develop into a threat to the organization.

The resource manager distributes resources in such a way that their use gives the maximum contribution to the organization. This is one of the most important tasks of the manager.

The negotiator is responsible for negotiations with staff members, suppliers, customers etc. This is a major duty, irrespective of whether the manager is a managing director or a foreman.

Source: Mintzberg, 1989.

What does a manager do in Africa?

Initially let me make the point that, even though it is sometimes convenient to talk of an African manager, or for that matter a Swedish manager, such a concept is analytically misleading. It implies that there are some universal properties that are shared by every manager in Africa. This is not a very helpful point of departure for analysing managerial behaviour. The manager manages very much according to the "rules of the game" that exist in his particular environment. This means that management practices vary a lot from one end of Africa to the other. This does not exclude the possibility that, for example, managers of public organizations in various countries in Africa experience the same problems and restrictions in their management task.

Management in Africa is a much less researched area than in the US or in Europe. The knowledge we have is quite limited. This does not prevent most of us from having more or less well substantiated views on what a manager in Africa does when he or she exercises his/her management tasks. The popular picture of African management can perhaps be summarized in five major points:

- African organizations resemble feudal systems. The manager's responsibility concerns first of all his own social network and to a lesser extent the public which the organization is there to serve.

- In comparison with his European and American colleagues—who are involved in the long-term strategy and policy of the organization—the African manager is more occupied with operational issues, and questions which have to do with status and turf protection.

- The effectiveness of the African organization, and that of the manager, is disturbed by party politics and ideological considerations.

- Managers in the private sector are more efficient than managers of public organizations.

- African managers are conservative and unwilling to initiate changes.

To what extent does this picture tally with reality? Judging from the few empirical investigations that have been made of management on the African continent the answer must be—not very much. Regarding the first proposition the evidence seems to point both ways. Montgomery (1991) argues that managers of African public organizations rarely work with issues concerning the relationship with the public or act as spokesmen in Mintzberg's meaning. They are more oriented towards serving the social network of which they are a part. A study of public managers in Zimbabwe, on the other hand, presents some data which suggest that managers in Zimbabwe also showed an outward oriented behaviour (Gustafsson et al., 1991).

The second proposition finds more support in research. Managers in Africa do work more with the organization's internal, short-term operational issues, rather than more long-term strategic objectives. This may in turn be a reflection of the impact of the institutional framework existing in many countries. If it cannot offer enough security, i.e. guarantee conditions conducive to long-term planning, management behaviour will adjust to such a situation. The perspective of the manager will become short-term.

A well-established idea is that organizations in Africa are permeated by political games. There is really not much to support the notion that organizations in Africa would be particularly prone to politicking. Studies of European and American organizations clearly show that politics is quite a dominant feature of their organizational life. The idea that managers in Africa's private sector should be more efficient than their colleagues in the public sector is also a myth. We have found no studies that support this proposition, on the contrary, studies from Europe indicate that the type of ownership is not a decisive determinant of managerial efficiency.

Are managers of African organizations conservative and unwilling to undertake changes? Yes, when the conditions exist that reward such behaviour. Unclear and unreliable "rules of the game" and centralized decision making structures are conditions that tend to lead to a high propensity to avoid uncertainty and hence an unwillingness to take risks among members of an organization. When all major initiatives must be thoroughly discussed and accepted higher up in the hierarchy before a decision can be taken, and when the rules of the game are not stable, the cost for taking individual initiatives can be very high (and often prohibitive).

Are there common traits that would enable us to speak of a typical African management practice? Management practice varies according to the specific circumstances in each country. But there are certain institutional as well as economic factors that are common to many African countries. Lack of economic resources, lack of trained manpower, various institutional constraints are found in many countries. In such situations it is not too unrealistic to expect African managers to spend a lot of time on being resource distributors and conflict managers. Much less time is then spent on the functions of monitor, spokesman, entrepreneur and co-ordinator. Even less time is spent on what Selznick (1957) thinks is one of the most important tasks of a manager—that of institutionalizing the organization.

If this pattern is true, it suggests that the changes that organizations in Africa need, are perhaps the most difficult to accomplish. The manager must become more of a risk taker, more outward and "customer" oriented. This requires—which is the most difficult of all—the creation of an institutional environment and an organizational culture which are supportive of such behaviour.

What does leadership mean in Africa?

There is an important difference between management and leadership. The former is associated with the actual running of an organization. To be a good manager means that you run your organization in an efficient and effective way. A good manager should possess qualities that can, at least partially, be taught to others. The concept of leadership signifies the ability to lead others with the purpose of causing movement and change in an organization. The talents of the leader are not easily taught to others; they are part and parcel of the leader's personality. A central role is also played by values and norms when it comes to the leader's way of leading.

Are managers of African organizations good leaders? The question is difficult to answer. Our survey of the literature on African management literature would suggest that leadership is a scarcity. One basic problem is an institutional constraint: the nature of African political regimes.

> Leaders and followers are both ensnared by the politics of patronage, and society currently offers few countervailing forces. As long as leaders make arbitrary policy decisions not based on careful analysis and rule mainly through patrimonial ties rather than rational-legal norms, there will be little demand at the top for analytical capacity, technical skills, and good management in public administration (Brautigam, 1996:89).

The picture that pre-dominates in the literature is that of African managers more preoccupied with matters internal to the organization, such as resource distribution, personnel etc., than issues relating to policy matters and the long-term development objectives of the organization. Such strategic issues are closely linked to the organization's relationship to external stake holders which can mean taking considerable political risks. This is a system which provides a type of leadership most commonly found and contains a weak link between the personal career of the manager and the development of the organization. Much weaker than what is the case in, for example, many organizations in Europe. The manager builds his/her career by forming alliances with different members of the organization. This pattern is found in many organizations in Africa today.

Why should leadership have such difficulties in developing? Blunt and Jones (1992) take the view that the perceived particularism of African societies prevents strong leadership from developing:

> ... indigenous morality—and many African managers are deeply ethical, holding strong feelings of attachment and responsibility to their families and villages of origin—does not accord with bureaucratic impersonality and universalism (Blunt, et al., 1992–39).

It may very well be that ethics and bonds of loyalty to the family are important for many managers. However, this does not prevent leadership from occurring in many organizations outside the public sector. There are many examples from other areas than the public sector of strong leadership—politics, liberation movements, the business community, the church etc. The manager of a private firm, to take one example, can hardly afford an exclusive inward looking perspective on his/her business. An outward looking strategy is essential for survival. Thus, the explanation for the lack of leadership in public administrations should probably be sought elsewhere. Qualities of leadership have had difficulties in developing under the circumstances provided by post-colonial public administration systems. The public service has its roots in the administration systems that were introduced by the colonial powers. The administrative system's historical legacy is still strong, and has perhaps deepened through the development experience of most African societies after independence. Characteristic for these organizations is that they never were (or are) compatible with the surrounding social and cultural environment.

The most important consequence of this historical legacy is that the conditions for an effective leadership are difficult to realize within the existing organizational and institutional traditions. Even if the dichotomy universalism/particularism is more complicated than might appear from the quotation above, it nevertheless points to the differences that exist in societal conditions which can create immediate problems when African organizations are confronted with European and American values on what constitutes an effective organization.

Organizational development and change is simply not an issue of transferring one model—the western—to an African setting. A case in point is management training, a favourite of many donors when supporting capacity building in Africa. Such programmes cannot have as their point of departure that the basic functions of management—

control, planning and organization—can be transferred with little concern for the external environment in which managers work. Management systems cannot be transferred as blueprints from one environment to another. Another conclusion to be drawn is that a changed management role is not possible unless the organizational and institutional environment is basically changed. It does not make much sense to train managers who, when returning to their organizations, have no possibilities to practize their new skills and insights.

Organization as systems in Africa—some theoretical departures

Organization theory contains a range of different attempts to analyse and understand organizations. The interest in organizations grew from the end of the 19th century and the study of organizations took its point of departure in the contemporary industrialization process and conditions in the working life. The study of organizations can be described as having a technical orientation with the purpose of finding the "best" organization mode. Organizations were seen as a closed system. Interaction with the external environment was not part of the analysis.[2]

Gradually there was a shift in western thinking on organizations towards looking at the organization as an open system. There are a number of different approaches within this strand of thinking: the socio-technical, the situational approach, systems theory etc. Common to them all is that the organization is integrated with its environment and dependent on it for its functioning. Organizational work becomes an issue not only of designing efficient and cost-effective production processes, but also involving the relationship of the organization to other organizations and to the people that the organization is set up to serve.[3] The organization is analogue to a biological organism which picks its resources from its environment, processes them and offers the finished products back to the environment. The products can be goods or services.

Common to all the newer organization theories is that they describe and explain the organization as:

---

[2] Analyses which assume the organization as a closed unit often focus on the inner life of the organization: production processes, administrative system, staff incentive systems etc.

[3] This view is often summarily called "socio-technical systems theory" and was first formulated in studies of the British coal mining industry in the beginning of the 1950s.

- open, i.e. dependent on its external environment;
- objectives oriented, i.e. established to reach certain goals; and
- dynamic, i.e. undergoing constant change.

This explanation model puts the people in the organization in the focus of the analysis. People's attitudes and capacity/ability to learn are of key importance for the effectiveness of the organization. Organization development must therefore, as a consequence focus on the members of the organization, rather than bureaucratic forms and procedures.

Do organizations in Africa put people first? Some obviously do. But some also have a narrow, more bureaucratic view of the organization. Kiggundu describes them in the following way:

> Organizations in developing countries exhibit dysfunctional modes of conflict management, closer social and emotional interactions, inter group rivalry, little capacity for openness, trust and the rational expression of feelings, and well established hierarchical and social status barriers (Kiggundu, 1986:343).

In terms of organization theory they are dominated by classic approaches with the organization as a closed system. There is not much room left for the individual member to develop his/her capacity and abilities. The organization tends to be autocratic, relying on a strict framework of rules and regulations. This tradition is reflected in many management and staff training programmes in Africa. The curricula rarely leave any more significant space for, for example, workers' attitudes and opinions.

The more dynamic view on organization has had a rather slow start. There is a strong resistance towards changing the thinking on what organizations are all about. It is difficult to be more specific than this, since the African organization is not sufficiently well researched to enable us to give any more specific answers. Kiggundu (1986) offers, however, some possible explanations. Local circumstances have for different reasons not permitted any change. It has been difficult for local managers and other stake holders to switch to a more change inducing organizational work style. The conflict between the dominant social systems in Africa, on the one hand, and the properties of the open model, on the other, has been felt to be too strong. The necessary changes have therefore been slow in coming, simply because the conflict between the two cannot be easily solved.

Organizations in Africa—is it possible to generalize?

To organize is to co-ordinate. An organization structure is an organization's way of distributing and co-ordinating the work among its departments and individuals. Mintzberg has identified five main co-ordination methods: mutual adaptation, direct supervision, standardized work processes, standardized products and standardization of skills. All methods can coexist in various relations in one organization at the same time.

The structure of an organization is influenced by a combination of external and internal forces. Among the internal forces it is first of all technology and size that matter. The more sophisticated a technology is, the more important becomes co-ordination in the form of standardized work processes and skills. The more employees there are, the more co-ordination mechanisms are needed. The issue of co-ordination instruments and organization structures in Africa is a more or less unexplored territory.[4] Two simple examples can illustrate some typical African organization structures.

In a small African company with 5–10 employees, one would usually find a combination of direct supervision (the owner participates directly in the production), mutual adaptation (the workers communicate continuously with each other about what they are doing and what they intend to do) and, a standardized production process (the production process is divided into different segments such as welding, assembly and painting). Co-ordination can also take place through a standardization of performance (the workers are required to meet certain production targets). Co-ordination in the small company means in general great flexibility and possibilities to accommodate external as well as internal changes.

Public administration is different. The typical colonial administration built on a standardization of skills and work processes. The work of the colonial civil servant would then become both predictable and reliable, and demand a minimum of direct supervision. At the same time this co-ordination model contained a relatively low flexibility and a weak capacity to take on board changing circumstances.

The public administration we see in most African countries builds on the same basic principles. At the time of independence the African

---

[4] Many authors have claimed that research results are so clear and incontestable, that one can safely assume that they are universally valid. In other words: what is true in Canada and Germany is most likely also true in Malawi.

civil servant probably was less educated (generally speaking) compared to the average French or British colonial civil servant he/she replaced. That gap has since then been bridged and the weaknesses of African public administration today have much less to do with insufficient human capacities. The most pronounced weakness today is that the ideas and models underpinning colonial administration are still quite strong. As a consequence many African organizations have a rather low propensity to deal with demands from the external environment, a quality which would be useful given the turbulence of African politico-economic systems.

Organizations which work in stable environments have quite different structures from those that operate in environments that are characterized by insecurity and turbulence. In this connection it is helpful to distinguish between two kinds of organizations: the mechanical and the organic.

The mechanical organization is founded on a classic bureaucratic division of functions. Work tasks are clearly separated from each other. The decision making process is centralized and it is the duty of top management to ensure that the goals of the organization are being reached. Information flows from the top downwards. Employees at lower levels in the hierarchy conduct their tasks without any regard for the overall objectives of the organization. This is largely the rational-legal model proposed by Weber.

The organic organization is to a large extent the opposite of the mechanical organization. Here we find just as much horizontal communication as vertical. The employees are all familiar with the goals of the organization. Work tasks are not so heavily delimited and consequently joint problem-solving is common.

Is it possible to generalize organization structures in Africa? Are they mainly mechanical or organic, or a combination of both? Obviously the picture varies a lot. As it is not possible to generalize about European organizations and their structural characteristics, one should be careful about making too general descriptive statements about African organizations. The way you choose to set up your organization depends on a number of things—history, culture, external relations, levels of technology, size etc.—which clearly makes generalization difficult. Furthermore, given that the logic and rationale of an organization structure always have to be placed in their proper context, it not possible to pass any value judgements on the efficiency of African organizations. Some are very efficient, while some are clearly just a burden on the societies that maintain them.

We can illustrate our point by returning to our examples—the small business and the public organization. The small business has an organic structure. The reason is simple: no company survives in Africa without a high capacity to deal with change and uncertainty.

The African public organization, on the other hand, represents a more mechanical organization. Its historical roots and the African public service tradition are important factors explaining this situation. The irony is that the organization that needs a high capacity to adapt and manage external influences has a structure which makes this difficult.

The preconditions for organization development in Africa

Many aid agencies spend a lot of time and effort working with organization development, or as it is commonly called—institution building, management- and leadership training. This work is made difficult, as previously mentioned, by the fact that we do not know enough about African organizations and their leaders. Furthermore, the debate has suffered from a too strong focus on the public sector, which has come to represent the African organization. The private sector and its organization are much less known.

The experiences from organizational development work in Africa are not very encouraging. The continent probably offers one of the most difficult administrative environments imaginable. But the need for change is great. At the same time the resistance to change is just as great. This is a serious threat to all development efforts. The public sector in Africa has an important role to play, not only within public administration as such, but also in the actual production of goods and services.

How can this resistance to change encountered in many public organizations be explained? The underdevelopment of the private sector at the time of independence forced the state to make direct investments in agriculture, industry and infrastructure. No doubt this was a role which the state was seldom able to play very well. The inherited public service tradition, with its institutions, provided a culture and a structure which, together with the lack of competent managers, resulted in tremendously inefficient production. Most state-owned companies irrespective of sector could not survive without huge subsidies over the state budget. These subsidies were paid for by the export of raw materials from agriculture and the mineral sector. The result was a large, inefficient public sector with strong vested interests, which exercised a strong political influence.

Institutions which are mainly blocking productive activities have a remarkable tendency to remain in place for a long time. North (1993:152) makes the point that there are always organizations and interest groups that benefit from the restrictions of these institutions. Such organizations will try to influence political decision making in order to preserve the institutions and their own benefits. Such institutions often contain incentives which, for example, encourage authoritarianism, military dominance, religious fanaticism etc., but they rarely reward any distribution of economically useful knowledge. The dominant actors develop an ideology which not only tries to rationalize the current state of affairs, but also explains its weak performance. Institutional change in such a setting becomes a difficult affair, since it invariably involves attacking established and dominant group interests.

Since independence the role of the state has changed dramatically, but its public administration has kept its old structures more or less intact. The need for development and change is there. But is it possible to bridge these gaps and reconstruct what 30 years of post-colonial development has broken down? Can the traditions of today's domestic and foreign institutions be combined in order to provide a better administration of society? Is western based thinking about organizations really able to make a contribution to the rebuilding of Africa's current institutional and organizational weaknesses—and if so, to what extent?

In a research programme conducted by the World Bank—African Management in the 1990s and beyond (AM90)—this was a major issue. The programme started off from the assumption that the capacity crisis was more about institutional inability to use existing resources, rather than any particular lack of resources in the form of trained manpower, methods, systems and technology (Dia, 1996).

Let me briefly summarize the findings of this research, since it gives important insights into the causes of the existing situation, as well as some ideas about how to progress further. According to AM90 this institutional inability was primarily caused by the lack of links between institutions with their roots in the history and culture of the country, and institutions created according to western models.

Institutions set up according to foreign models often fail to evoke feelings of loyalty and ownership among people. They did not reflect the basic values and expectations of society, and they tended to possess little by way of legitimacy in the eyes of the people. With weak roots in society these institutions also lack the possibilities for a sustainable development. On a more general level, weaknesses in the legal framework add to the inefficiency of these institutions. Together this creates a climate where it becomes expensive to enforce contracts and procedures, and where sanctions are equally difficult to legitimize.

Domestic institutions, on the other hand, are much more rooted in local cultures and values, they are perceived as more trustworthy and performing a legitimate function in society. Hence they stand a much better chance of being able to enforce their decisions since people respect the institution and what it represents. People identify with these institutions, and become involved.

But domestic institutions do have their weaknesses. They are not functioning very well in certain areas (gender discrimination, for example, is a recurring phenomenon) and are not always developing according to the expectations of society. If they cannot manage to change with the times, they will soon lose their credibility and become relics with little dynamics. Without change from inside these institutions will soon discover that their ability to deal with an increasingly complex world will be limited, as will their possibility to maintain their position in society.

The strategic conclusion of AM90 is basically a combination of the best of two worlds. The current problem will not be solved by performing an institutional transplant—transferring systems and methods developed in another cultural setting. Equally inefficient is to rigidly remain with a traditional fundamentalism—the systems and principles of local society. What is needed is for the two systems to come closer to each other and find ways of coexisting. This presumes, however, that external institutions are willing to adapt to local circumstances, and that local institutions are willing to change and adapt to modern society. Only when domestic and foreign institutions meet and embrace the same objectives will there be a possibility to achieve a lasting development of viable institutions in Africa.

An important precondition for all organizational development work is that the organization itself recognizes the need for change. Further, there is a need for in-depth knowledge about the organization and its environment. What works and what does not work. Leonard argues that to a distressing extent such knowledge is rarely available.

> We certainly have no knowledge of what reforms might be used to improve the performance of Africa's public organizations. We can be reasonably certain that techniques imported from the West will fail unless they are revised quite fundamentally, yet we also know that some African organizations are performing much better than others. What we do not know is why (Leonard, 1987:229).

The resistance to change is deeply embedded in many mechanical organizations, irrespective of whether they are African or European. But we are doubtful to the proposition that organizations within the African public administration should not feel any need for change. It is probably the other way around. Most organizations, private and public, are facing strong pressures. Increasingly harder competition within the private sector and demands for a more efficient public sector are factors that force change. Many representatives of public sector organizations are themselves dissatisfied with their organization and want change. The problem seems to be a difficulty in articulating the needs in a more concrete way, coupled with a certain lack of experience of working with change processes.

Different attempts from donors and other western based actors have often failed because they have not understood the African environment and its impact on the thinking and practice of management and organizational life. The initiative has come from outside and the work has been understood as a matter for somebody else. Proposed plans for changes too often never leave the desk of the planner.

Add to this that those who work with organization development in Africa often seem to lack a rudimentary understanding of how work for change should be done. There is a lack of knowledge as to how to initiate such a process, carry it through and accomplish change. Organization development in Africa today is often a matter of changing structures—usually shrinking organizations—but more rarely a matter of changing people's attitudes to their work. The first is relatively easy to accomplish, while the latter is considerably more difficult. It requires a long-term perspective and patient work. Just changing the structure of an organization, without changing the people who work in it, usually does not lead anywhere. Neither is it very productive to work with various training programmes unless the

organization is changed so that it allows the members to practise their
new skills and insights. A holistic perspective of the organization is
therefore a basic precondition for any organizational change programme to be started.

This approach to organization building implies a somewhat different strategy approach than that proposed by Brautigam when discussing strategies for rebuilding state capacity. She argues that it is
important to get the basics right.

> Nothing in the twentieth century has proven Weber wrong on his basic
> framework. Rational-legal bureaucracies are still the best organizational
> form for state-promoted development. Building professionalism involves
> building meritocratic recruitment of a properly compensated civil service
> with a common esprit de corps. It also requires clear rules and proce-
> dures, with accountability achieved through review procedures that en-
> force the rules. Finally, bureaucrats need incentives to ensure congruence
> between their personal goals and their agency's goals (Brautigam, 1996:
> 100–101).

The problem with this line of argument is that most African public
administrations build on the principles of Weber, as did their colonial
models. What has happened is that these "rational-legal bureaucracies" have found it increasingly difficult to deliver their goods and
services. Brautigam essentially recommends a solution which is based
on an inward-looking classic organization theory. To argue that civil
servants need to be properly compensated and that there should be
clear rules and procedures etc., is missing the point. The point is that
organizations need to be rebuilt in such a way that they can accommodate and manage external pressures and still continue to effectively deliver their services. A strategy which mainly focuses on an
organization's internal systems will be seriously inadequate for taking
on these challenges.

Would it be an advantage for the African organization if the open-
system thinking became more accepted? Most probably this would be
the case. Within African public organizations there has always been a
tendency to focus all attention on maximizing the resources available
to the organization. There has been much less interest in looking at
what can be achieved in terms of quality with the resources that are
actually there. The open-system perspective, however, requires that
results and resources must be analysed as a totality.

The African environment is turbulent and both humans and organizations are very exposed to threats and disturbances of various

kinds. In order to survive the organization and its members must be flexible and ready to accept, and initiate, change. In order to do this the organization must be changed from within, primarily by mobilizing its members in the change process. Organizations with a high propensity for change are also organizations where learning is strong among the staff. Finally, it is likely that the open-system theory would create better preconditions for African organizations to develop on their own terms and find forms for their existence which are adapted to the reality of Africa.

Jerker Carlsson is Associate Professor in Economic History and Adjunct Professor at the Department of Peace- and Development Research at the University of Gothenburg. He is currently engaged by the Nordic Africa Institute to work with the research programme "Aid Effectiveness in Africa" and "EU Aid for Poverty Reduction".

References

Barnard, C., 1938, *The Functions of the Executive*. Cambridge, MA: Harvard University Press.

Blunt, P. and M.L. Jones, 1992, *Managing Organizations in Africa*. New York: de Gruyter.

Brautigam, D., 1996, "State Capacity and Effective Governance", in B. Ndulu and N. van de Walle (eds.), *Agenda for Africa's Economic Renewal*. New York: Transaction Publishers.

Carlsson, J., G. Somolekae & N. van de Walle (eds.), 1997, *Foreign Aid in Africa. Learning from country experiences*. Uppsala: The Nordic Africa Institute.

Dia, M., 1996, *Africa's Management in the 1990s and beyond. From Institutional "Transplant" to Institutional Reconciliation*. Washington DC: World Bank.

Drucker, P.F., 1977, *Management*. London: Pan.

Fayol, H., 1949, *General and Industrial Management*. London: Pitman.

Gustafsson, L., P. Blunt, P. Gisle & S. Sjölander, 1991, *The Future of Swedish Support to the Public Administration Sector in Zimbabwe*. Stockholm: Sida.

Kiggundu, M., 1986, "Limitations to the Application of Sociotechnical Systems in Developing Countries", *Journal of Behavioural Science*, Vol. 3, No. 22.

Leonard, D.K., 1987, "The Political Realities of African Management", *World Development*, 15:899–910.

March, J.G. and J.P. Olsen, 1984, "The New Institutionalism: Organizational Factors in Political Life", *American Political Science Review*, 78:734–39.

—1989, *Rediscovering Institutions: The Organizational Basis of Politics*. New York: Free Press.

Mintzberg, H., 1989, *Mintzberg on Management*. New York: Free Press.

Montgomery, J.D., 1991, "Probing Managerial Behaviour: Image and Reality in Southern Africa", *World Development*, 15(7), pp. 911–929.

North, D., 1993, *Institutionerna, tillväxten och välståndet*. Stockholm: SNS Förlag. Swedish translation of the author's book, *Institutional Change and Economic Performance*, published by Cambridge University Press in 1990.

Selznick, P., 1957, *Leadership in Administration*. New York: Harper and Row.

Taylor, F.W., 1911, *The Principles of Scientific Management*. New York: Harper and Row.

Gender, Organizational Cultures and Institutional Development

Prudence Woodford-Berger

The past two decades have witnessed increased awareness of the multi-dimensional character of poverty and suffering in the world, and thus also of ways of addressing these through international economic and development cooperation. Purely technological solutions have usually proved not to be sustainable for a variety of reasons, one of these being our poor understanding of the links between economic realities, political possibilities and the behaviour of individuals, groups and institutions in terms of choices available and decisions made at different social and administrative levels in a given societal or country context.

Since the 1980s, there has been a growing realization of the centrality of institutional frameworks and capacities for the enhancement of human resources in the pursuit of a development that is sustainable socially and politically as well as economically. Promotion of institutional development has prompted greater attention to the workings of both public sector and private sector organizations in the context of major changes in the divide between state and non-state responsibilities and roles with respect to the interests of various constituencies in particular national or other populations. Organization theory and organizational analysis and refinements of these as conceptual frameworks have been central in the identification of effective ways of promoting institutional development. These frameworks comprise particular ways of understanding the workings of distinct kinds or forms of institutions. They proceed from a perception of *organizations* as institutional settings that are responsible for the production of goods and/or services for designated categories of citizenry or other clientele. The fact that organizations are at the same time also workplaces and particular fields of social interaction means that analyzing them requires the application of methods and tools that incorporate social and political models as well as economic ones.

At present, there is still considerable ignorance of African institutional dynamics and of the ways in which organizations in Africa actually function, both inwardly as well as in terms of their links to social, cultural and political institutions in the surrounding societies. This chapter will discuss the necessity of augmenting traditional approaches to organizational analysis with gendered analytical perspectives and conceptual frameworks for optimal understanding of the way African organizations work and are interpreted by those within them, and by those dealing with them "from the outside", i.e. customers or the public.

Organizational structure, organizational culture

Traditional or classic approaches to analysing organizations reflect Weberian criteria for "rational" organization. Among other things, these approaches identify as key factors or variables, explicit—usually hierarchical—systems of specific, unequivocal roles and responsibilities, and promotion through supposedly objective merit systems in their analyses of organizational settings. Traditional approaches have focused leadership and organizational management, as well as the workings and development of industrial firms or other organizations according to a rationale of "rationality".

Sociological and anthropological studies of organizations as social systems have contributed to the development of organizational studies as a field of inquiry since the 1930s and 1940s (Wright, 1994). Key contributions include (1) perceptions of organizations as social systems, i.e. systems of social relations and social interaction between individuals and groups in a particular setting, and (2) the notion of *organizational "culture"*, conceiving organizations as consisting of systems of meaning as well as systems of rules and regulations.

The concept of culture as an essential feature of organizations (Geertz, 1973; Douglas, 1987) underlies the notion of organizational culture. This framework perceives organizations (particularly public-sector organizations)—and the wider institutions they are a part of—as social systems of roles, relations, symbols, values, ideologies and attitudes, and—more recently—of practices. This means that organizations' "effectiveness" and "efficiency" in terms of strategic decision making and actions (i.e. meeting the needs of clients) are the sum of social and political processes as well as of individual and/or group professional capacities with respect to goods and services produced.

The concept of culture is a complex one when it comes to organizations, and it is often used vaguely and with various definitions conflated into a single broad or general referent. On the one hand, "culture" refers to perceptions of meanings, values, ideas, symbols and attitudes that to some extent are shared among the staff or employees or workforce of a specific organization. On the other hand, organizational culture can be very unevenly distributed among a particular workforce, with the result that "culture" is then used to refer to what essentially are values, ideas, and attitudes imposed by management or outside interests on other parts of the workforce. While reasons for this may be to promote cohesion, like-mindedness and performance as a body in the production of goods and services, the effects of such imposition may actually mitigate against effectiveness.

The most useful conceptual frameworks currently for understanding how organizations work are those which distinguish between the *structural* elements of organizations on the one hand, and the *social and cultural* dimensions on the other, and which then attempt to address the interaction between the two. Structural elements include organizational make-up including staff positions and job descriptions, procedures, work activities and patterns, and regulatory mechanisms. Systems of social relationships, attitudes, beliefs and conviction are constituted through the women and men who work within them and who interact with one another as well as with persons outside the organization. Further, in this context, both structure and culture in organizational terms may, analytically speaking, be *formal* or *informal*, whereby formal dimensions refer to, stated policies and goals, explicit rules and regulations, and informal to systems of meaning and attitudes embodied in the social relations and processes of social interaction that make up the organization. Formal and informal structural and cultural dimensions involve both explicit and implicit valuations that are expressed in the form of practices and habits. Formal and informal dimensions of interaction and performance exist side by side in an organization, and interact with one another through the persons that make it up, and through various forms of action, e.g. assessments of competence with respect to specific work tasks or positions.

What is gender and why do we need gendered organizational analysis?

Gender—as distinct from *sex*, which refers to bodily or biological and physical markers, and divides the aggregate term "people" into women and men, or girls and boys—refers to cultural definitions of female and male, femininity and masculinity. Gender definitions include cultural perceptions of ways of working and ways of knowing, feeling, valuing, behaving and of relating to other persons of the same or the opposite sex. Gender relations are social relations, and as such they reflect learned behaviour through processes of socialization that are reinforced through systems of opportunity and the ascription of various roles and expectations to women and men respectively. Gender is *not* a variable sociologically in the same sense as class, but is rather a fundamental division of human categories defined in relation to perceptions and interpretations of sex that cross-cuts all other social and cultural distinctions.

Neither institutions nor particular organizational settings are gender-neutral. This is of course because specific organizations are connected to overall societal culture, attitudes and systems of meaning through their structures and symbols, and through the women and men who make them up. These persons have subjective identities and are bearers of gendered perceptions, personal experiences, specific interests and values, attitudes and behaviour which they bring with them to the organization. Thus, organizations are specific sites for the articulation of the surrounding society's social, economic and political structures, institutions, values and attitudes. As such, they are also in themselves arenas wherein particular kinds of socialization take place including reinforcement of gendered perceptions through the allocation of work tasks, through the relative positioning of women and men within the organization, through the distribution of authority and the legitimate use of power, and through symbolic representations of gendered social relations manifested in, e.g. language and metaphors, through regimented work practices, routines and processes.

Gendered perceptions and habits inform organizational performance and development as structures and as cultures, and with respect to both formal and informal dimensions. Organizations—as extensions of the wider institutional structures they are a part of, thus play a major role in the constitution of gendered social and political persons. In turn, those who work within them play—at least potentially—a major role in the (re-)constitution and continued functioning of the organization both internally and in relation to external interests, as well as in changes in these. Gender relations in organizations as an aspect of broader social and political relations contribute to the ways in which the organizations work, reconstitute themselves over time, and are able to realize their goals and visions.

By and large, the significance of sex identity and subsequently of inequality stemming from cultural interpretations of sex identity, i.e. gender, in organizational settings has been gravely neglected. This has resulted not only in male-centred perspectives of organization, but also in gender-blind and thus faulty and incomplete understandings of how organizations actually work—not only in terms of female-male interaction, but also with regard to cultural rationales and underlying assumptions involving both cross-sex and same-sex relations and hierarchies in specific institutional settings, and the ways gendered interaction affects organizational dynamics and production processes.

Undeclared or implicit assumptions concerning gendered perceptions and gender relations in organizations underlie the ways in which organizations have been studied and understood. A basic false assumption about organizations concerns their supposed gender-neutrality. Stemming from this are assumptions about the allocation to women and men of, e.g. work duties, management and leadership positions, salaries, employment benefits, overtime, access to skills upgrading etc., as well as about the needs and interests of different categories of male and female employees with respect to the organization. Assumptions are usually that the former *in principle* have nothing to do with sex, only with objective meriting systems, and that the latter means that, e.g. women as well as men can easily become union representatives, and be accepted negotiators on behalf of both male and female employees.

In actual fact, innumerable studies have shown that women and men may be assigned or considered qualified for very different work duties or benefits due to their different structural positions in the organization as in the society as a whole, and that they moreover may even be delegated duties and granted access to organizational resources in terms of what is considered to be "fitting" for their sex. Even organizations composed of nearly all women not uncommonly are controlled by men—women's branches or wings of political parties or other state or parastatal organizations are examples of

these—or have men in their top managerial and decision making echelons. Since various categories of women and men may have very different responsibilities, employment conditions, working environments, interests and opportunities for negotiation, they may also stand to win or lose in very different ways when organizations undergo processes of change or development. Subjective expectations and aspirations in situations of change are ultimately connected to how specific positions in the gendered organizational structures and cultures of opportunity are affected by the change. Because of this, organizations may also feature considerable amounts of tension and even conflict in terms of gender and other inequalities.

Perspectives on gender equality and women in organizations

Analytical perspectives that contribute to gendered organizational analyses have actually been in existence for a considerable time. Some early sociological and anthropological studies of women in organizations at workplaces in England used occupational approaches to explore the nature of women's work and the effects of physical changes in the working environment on women workers (Wright, 1994). By and large, there are two main organizational perspectives or bodies of studies that incorporate gender dimensions. One focuses primarily on women as a particular workforce. The other comprises feminist perspectives and analytical frameworks. While both perspectives address and to varying degrees challenge gender inequalities and imbalances of power and authority in organizations, the latter approaches specifically treat the interaction of organizational settings with wider societal dynamics and processes that involve the creation and re-creation of institutional structures and cultures including those concerning gender.

Where major societal conceptual frameworks define women as subordinate to men, and where considerable differences exist in the ways in which women and men are linked to the means and forces of production and reproduction, specific organizational settings will also exhibit differences in women's and men's opportunities. For women, sex as a biological attribute is often translated into intransigent roles and status in so-called modern, male-dominated work settings, despite superior professional capabilities, due to perceptions of women's work being connected to reproductive functions and care-giving in ways that men's work clearly is not (Cheater, 1991; Mills and Tancred, 1992).

Incorporating gendered analyses into mainstream organization theory and organizational analysis involves a systematic consideration of the significance of sex, of perceptions of femininities and masculinities. A key principle in gender analytic frameworks is the "unpacking" of organizations, i.e. identification of formal *and* informal structures within the organization rather than treating it as an indivisible unit. In terms of an organization's contact with its clientele, it is essential to discover the influence of gender perceptions on interactions between organization representatives and female and male members of the public as far as possible. Gendered organizational analysis also requires disaggregation by sex of the various categories of persons involved, in relation to the organizational structure, and in situating replies to, e.g. customer surveys or patient studies in terms of sex as well as in terms of other cultural and socio-economic distinctions.

Getting at the gendered organizational cultures involved is perhaps not readily accomplished by some of the standard mapping methodologies used in organizational analysis, such as self-administered questionnaires, assessing written job descriptions, etc. Rather, gendered organizational analysis requires observations and analysis of work practices as elements in a particular field of social relations and interaction. Identifying the factors that facilitate or constrain the access of women and men to various organizational resources, for example—both material resources such as salaries, eligibility for promotion and access to skills upgrading, and immaterial resources such as prestige and a high degree of independent planning of one's own work tasks requires awareness, insight, knowledge, skill and competence. For a variety of reasons, gender inequalities may not be clearly evident and/or may have the overt or tacit consent of many women as well as men. The implications of this for partners in development cooperation are apparent: a commitment and capacity to work with issues of gender equality in organizational development must be worked at in the context of a mutual learning process. Where, for example, neither partner in a twinning arrangement possesses adequate expertise in gender issues, this must be sought in the same way that expertise in other areas and for other substantive issues is sought out. Such expertise is nowadays to be found in nearly every country, as is witnessed in the country and regional reports compiled for the Fourth

UN World Conference on Women in Beijing 1995. The Beijing Declaration and plan for actions and measures to be taken are presented in the document *Platform for Action*, and were ratified by all 189 countries represented at the Conference

Prudence Woodford-Berger is a University Lecturer at the Department of Social Anthropology, Development Studies Unit, Stockholm University. She has published a number of articles based on research in West Africa. Ms. Woodford-Berger has also worked as a consultant to Sida and other organizations since 1978 and specializes in, among other things, issues concerning participatory development, gender equality and women's empowerment including introductory and sector-specific gender training courses. One of the sectoral areas in which she has led training in recent years has been that of public administration and democratic governance.

References

Acker, J. and D.R. van Houten, 1974, "Differential Recruitment and Control: The Sex Structuring of Organizations", *Administrative Science Quarterly*, Vol. 19, No. 2, pp. 152–163.

Alvesson, M. and Y.D. Billing, 1997, *Understanding Gender and Organizations*. London: Sage Publications.

Cheater, A., 1991, *Social Anthropology: An Alternative Introduction*. London: Routledge.

Chichava, Ana P., 1995, *Women's Move on Equal Opportunity in the Civil Service in Mozambique*. MSc (Econ) Thesis, University of Swansea.

Douglas, M., 1987, *How Institutions Think*. London: Routledge & Kegan Paul.

Geertz, C., 1973, *The Interpretation of Cultures*. New York: Basic Books.

Goetz, A.M. et al., 1995, "Getting Institutions Right for Women in Development", *IDS Bulletin*, Vol. 26, No. 3. Sussex: Institute of Development Studies (IDS).

Hearn, J. and P. Parkin, 1983, "Gender and Organizations: A Selective Review and a Critique of a Neglected Area", *Organization Studies*, Vol. 4, No. 3, pp. 219–242.

Kabeer, N. and R. Subrahmanian, 1996, *Institutions, Relations and Outcomes: Framework and Tools for Gender-Aware Planning*. Discussion Paper 357. Sussex: Institute of Development Studies (IDS).

Kanter, R.M., 1975, "Women and the Structure of Organization: Explorations in Theory and Behaviour", *Sociological Inquiry*, Vol. 45, pp. 34–74.

—1977, *Men and Women of the Corporation*. New York: Basic Books.

Mills, A. and P. Tancred (eds.), 1992, *Gendering Organizational Analysis*. London: Sage Publications.

Sweetman, C. (ed.), 1997, *Gender in Development Organizations*. Oxford: Oxfam (Focus on Gender Series).

Wright, S. (ed.), 1994, *Anthropology of Organizations*. London: Routledge.

On Developing Institutions in Africa

Anton Johnston

Introduction

"Institutional development" and "capacity building" are terms which have been used for many years and have formed the subject of hot discussion in both development theory and international cooperation. However, their content has varied considerably over the years. The theories lying behind the terms are presented below and their application within development cooperation is examined.

Knowledge, institutions and development

In the theories on economic development which became popular during the 1960s a simple economic growth model (a "production function") was used to explain production and growth, incorporating labour and capital as the relevant factors in the function. It soon became clear, however, that using the growth in labour and capital in the function only accounted for a small proportion of the economic growth actually taking place (Denison, 1967, 1985), and economists began to search for additional explanatory factors. New and more sensitive models were thus developed to integrate what is commonly called "human capital", whose importance was first popularized by Schultz (1961), in order to capture the dimensions of knowledge and scientific development in the production process.

The measurement of human capital turned out to be a difficult task. Prognoses into the future in the form of "manpower planning" on the basis of human capital projections have often been quite wrong and have led to erroneous investments being made, such as the faith mistakenly placed at one time in technical schooling at secondary school level (Psacharopoulos, 1985). It was nonetheless a step in the right direction that development models began to take into account the importance of technological progress and increased human competence. When human capital was introduced into production functions it became evident that this dimension of production would need to be taken into account in the development process, and the provision of "Technical Assistance" (i.e. expertise) to build capacity became central to development cooperation efforts.

However, explanations of development continued to be economistic, and the failure of "development states" in Africa and elsewhere in the late 1970s led to a strong anti-state reaction in many quarters, notably the Bretton Woods institutions. The slogan became "unfetter the market and roll back the state", which was promoted enthusiastically with development assistance throughout the 1980s and into the 1990s.

In the 1980s economists working within the neoclassical tradition began to identify additional dimensions of society which appeared to correlate with successful examples of economic growth. It was noted that countries in which social stability had reigned securely evidenced a higher rate of growth and technological progress than others. The explanation provided was that the societies in question were well equipped with "institutions" which set up a stable environment of rules and procedures to ensure the functioning of the market on a predictable basis. It was postulated that this institutional setting created the preconditions for economic development to take place (North, 1990).

North explained that all economic transactions carry with them a certain cost in time, effort and money. If the costs required to make the transaction are too high, or if the outcome or the reliability of the transaction is too uncertain, the transaction will simply not take place. The framework which reduces transaction costs and transaction risks comprises society's organizations, communications, legislation and legal system, i.e. institutions in the wide sense in which the term is used here. Countries with sustained economic growth have stable institutions which promote and protect economic activity (transactions) through the means of a just and transparent rule system. The "market" is one such institution, but the most important one is surely a developed, functional and legitimate state.

The discussions on what constitutes an institution and how it evolves have been extensive and lively. The concept was introduced into development theory in the 1960s by the modernization theorists, notably Talcott Parsons (see Moore et al., 1995). Organizations which contributed to attitude change in society along the spectrum from the traditional towards the modern were described as institutions. This inevitably loaded the term with a "modern sector" value system, which may have helped distract development practitioners from the institutions also inherent in traditional society.

The subsequent economic loading of the term by "institutional economists" is also unfortunate, as it distracts from the wider relevance and impact of other organizations at all levels of society, and from the significance of their norms and rule systems to social stability and development as a whole. This more "economicist" approach to institutions still pervades the thinking of development agencies. For example the World Bank, in its latest World Development Report (World Bank, 1997), takes a big step forward from its anti-state position of the previous two decades, but it still assumes that public sector institutions should exist principally in order to compensate "market failures" and to stimulate economic growth and rationality, and that these can be created and operated at will. To quote: "... this chapter outlines some institutional building blocks of an effective public sector and discusses promising options for putting them in place" (p. 79). To a large extent it still fails to come to grips with the cultural environment in which institutions—if they are genuine institutions— must be rooted, as well as with the role of social institutions beyond the field of macroeconomics, in particular as regards the political sphere.

Fortunately a counterweight is beginning to form, based on the path-breaking work of Putnam (1993), who examined the variations in societal development in different parts of Italy over several hundred years from the perspective of the evolution—or lack thereof—of social institutions which encouraged popular participation. The culture and institutions of democracy are beginning thereby to be widely understood as the basis for sustainable and successful social development, and thus economic development, in the future. The major problem raised by Putnam's work, however, is that it would seem to indicate that where societies have as it were "started wrong" from the beginning, this will place a dead hand on the successful evolution of that society for all time to come; i.e. a "negative" culture develops among the people of that society which sustains itself over centuries. This conclusion may help us understand Yugoslavia but it is hardly encouraging for development optimists.

In line with this latest research, in this chapter the term *institution* is used to mean an organization-based network of rules, laws, norms, administrative systems and social functions. Institution thus means something more than just "an organization" or even "a public organization", even though institutions are organization-based.

An institution is characterized perhaps most importantly by a strong and evident culture. Its values and traditions have evolved over a long period of time, and its culture is what holds together its members and unites their efforts. Institutions exist in the private (economic) sector, the civil society and the public sector, and in modern and traditional society. Civil society counts among its institutions the churches, NGOs, community-based organizations, professional associations, political parties—all of them an organized expression of norms and consensual values among substantial social groups. Together, the institutions of a society constitute the framework which protects its stability and promotes its cohesion.

In order for an institution to be legitimate, it is essential that it develops within the frame of society's values. It must be regarded as necessary and useful and it should generally be considered just and impartial. There is of course a substantial literature, starting with Marx and Gramsci, on the real sympathies of social institutions and in particular of the State, a literature which has much empirical evidence to back it up (Poulantzas, 1978). It cannot be denied that most institutions largely purvey the ideology of those who have power and influence in the society. But still, if they do so with manifest injustice or to the exclusion of important groups, they will be challenged and put under pressure to change—as, for example, is occurring with the Swedish judiciary in relation to its judgements on assaults on women and rape.

The state retains its legitimacy and its institutional character to the extent that it manages to organize substantial groups behind it and to neutralize its opponents, or rather, to integrate its opponents into the system so that they oppose it within the rules of the system and thus do not put into question the social stability which the majority of the population demands. A state and its legitimacy are also questioned if it does not manage to maintain economic stability, as economic instability puts the security of the majority at risk. The state, like all other institutions, walks constantly on a tightrope through a changeable social reality (Carnoy, 1987).

Thus, to be sustainable, institutions must be able to mediate and resolve conflict, and to adapt and change, which of course is facilitated if they arise within the context of a democratic social order and are managed according the precepts of good governance (Dia, 1993).

Durable institutions have of course arisen within the framework of a non-democratic order, to the extent of that particularistic order's legitimacy, and (qua Putnam, op.cit.) they may continue to influence society for centuries—see for instance the history of Catholicism or Islam. But they tend in the long run to fail in their role as stabilizers and to be changed by social upheaval rather than to adjust through a democratic process. The ramifications of this discussion are however beyond the scope of this paper.

In development assistance and development theory, the term institution has to a large extent come to be synonymous with state organization or state agency. This simplification (and creeping nationalization) of the term is unfortunate. Through terminological misuse one begins to ignore important aspects of the process of institution building: the necessary dimensions of culture and of legality, and the need for non-statal institutions to evolve. The risk arises that aid agencies, under the title of institution building, go about building up new public sector organizations with very little foundation in society, rather than supporting the development of institutions in the real sense.

In the theoretical debates it has in any case been concluded that both capacity building and institutional development are essential to a desirable development process, in both social and economic terms. Functional social institutions are accepted to be a *sine qua non* for economic growth and democracy.

The rise and fall of African institutions

A combination of uninhibited particularism, corruption, incapacity to resolve social conflict peacefully, external pressure and intervention, rapid technological outclassing, and economic incompetence has led since the late 1970s to declining legitimacy on the part of the African state and its institutions, in some countries encompassing even civil society institutions and the private sector. This has in its turn led to the marginalization of the state and in some cases its collapse.

Various structural adjustment attempts—which have usually been initiated by pressure from aid agencies—did not contribute to raising the prestige of the state. To begin with, the reform programmes aimed only at limiting the role of the state and reducing its budget expenditure. Their most enthusiastic advocates expressly promoted the market at the expense of the state.

This led to damaging impact on state capacity to deliver, and the state's legitimacy declined even further because the promised economic stabilization in many cases took a very long time to materialize. Instead, for over a decade African economies largely became characterized by high inflation, rising prices, wage depreciation, lost savings, bankrupt companies, sliding devaluation, falling exchange rates, and deteriorating services (Johnston and Wohlgemuth, 1995; Gibbon and Olukoshi, 1996)—the very opposite of stability. African states in effect looked on helplessly as their capacity and legitimacy bled away year after year.

This created a problem, however; who would actually implement the adjustment programme? The private sector and the civil society could hardly be expected to carry out the macroeconomic management that was needed. Neither could they implement the necessary transformation of the private sector or reconstruct the social sectors. The market continued to perform badly as its environment was still dysfunctional. Those who were expected to deal with the problem had been rationalized away. Civil servant salaries were no longer sufficient to live on, let alone to encourage the execution of complex reform programmes.

In addition, the programmes were often experienced as externally imposed by foreign interests. They were carried out in such a way that ongoing processes of democratization were undermined. Undesirable forces within the state were strengthened and enriched and the economic results were meagre—all because the programmes did not enjoy legitimacy and the state has not had the will or the capacity to execute them competently.

Against this background a debate has being going on between development theoreticians and practitioners (inter alia Hydén, 1992) as to what extent the African state (in the broadest sense) is at all rooted in African society. It is claimed that the rural population does not identify with the state, as it is alien to their cultural frame of reference, corrupt in its behaviour, fails to guarantee their security and does not influence their economic activities in positive ways.

Hydén's conclusion from this analysis follows closely on that of the neoclassical economists: the state is harmful and its role should be reduced. He has thus inter alia advocated the founding of so-called autonomous funds under a committee of wise men from civil society and the private sector, parallel to the state, as an alternative channel for aid (Dag Hammarskjöld Foundation, 1995). Why such funds should enjoy greater legitimacy or be free of corruption remains to be explained.

It is however incorrect to claim that the state is alien to Africa, or that the only large formal organization on the continent has been the extended family. There is quite sufficient evidence that organized state structures existed in most parts of Africa hundreds of years before its social structure was laid waste by slavery and colonialism. These states, under hereditary monarchies, were characterized by complex institutions such as age-based military conscription, taxation, advisory structures, an education system, a judicial system, markets and so on.

Nor have the people and the state been alien to each other in all circumstances since then. Of course the imposition of colonial governance did nothing to bring the people and the state together, and the perception that the state is today in the hands of foreign interests is not likely to diminish that distance. However, the independent states enjoyed a period of very high legitimacy, and Africa's history rather gives an impression that people have relied altogether too much on the state and its authority than that it should be alien to them. It has been shown that many peasant families in their planning for the future actually orient at least one (usually male) child towards public service to ensure not only a constant salary income but also a foot in the door. This means investing heavily in the chosen child's formal education while the other children get less or have to do without. This hardly constitutes an indicator of people perceiving the state to be irrelevant. In short, where the state delivers on its promises it has the people's support; if not, of course it loses people's confidence. "Rolling back the state" has proceeded altogether too far and is threatening stability and growth. In today's situation the problem is becoming whether, as problems multiply and the economy stagnates, post-independence states will lose the last of their legitimacy and collapse altogether.

Africa thus requires the reconstruction of its public sector and its other institutions. In order for the state to be reconstituted and to recover its credibility, such a reconstruction programme will however have to be firmly anchored among the broad population.

Contradictions naturally do remain between modern and traditional forms and institutions of governance and between state and people. This has led to a number of discussions on how to integrate the traditional and the modern into one African-style state (Dia, 1993).

Modifications to the "West European" model are certainly possible and possibly desirable, but it looks as if in its essence this model will continue to be the model for African governments in the future.

Institutional development under reigning circumstances will not be easy or problem-free. Probably public sector organizations will fail to win renewed confidence until such time as the economy starts recovering, the state finds a sounder political footing, and life begins to look a little brighter. The ongoing democratic experiment (since 1990 almost all African countries have held elections for multi-party parliamentary government) may help in this regard. Democracy has certainly shown itself to be the best system we know for controlling bureaucracies and engaging people in their own governance. The present experiment is however rather too associated (once again) with outside pressures on governments and countries to toe the line, which casts a certain shadow of suspicion over the exercise. If elected governments fail to act democratically, use the state as an instrument for favouring particular groups and punishing others, and fail to deliver on their promises, there is always a risk that parliamentary democracy will lose its legitimacy also.

Despite these problems, the process of indigenous institution building is sure to continue, as this is the way that societies seek to stabilize themselves. My conclusion is also that it is possible for external agencies to provide support to the reconstruction of Africa's institutions—not, however, from a dirigiste position, where the external agency decides what is best and tries to force it through, but instead from a supportive position of understanding and respect for the recipient institution's culture and efforts. Certainly organizations that do not correspond to society's concerns can be built, but their possibilities of "institutionalizing" themselves will be extremely small.

Conditions for institutional development

The first important condition for institution building is that the institution is addressed as a complete entity. On the micro-level this means that no programme should be planned without the whole organization being analysed and involved, both as an integrated organism *per se* and as a part of its environment.

In the case of the public sector, this implies that institution building cannot take place without taking the "superinstitution" of the state into account. An aid agency can contribute to *organizational* development by providing internal support to a state agency, but *institutional* development is not possible until the sector as a whole is permeated with the same basic changes in values and praxis.

The same conditions apply for the private sector and the civil society. An aid agency can support *organizational* development within part of a sector, but change is required outside of the particular organization in question before any real *institutional* development or revitalization can take place. The market or political parties do not arise because a firm or an NGO has been given organizational development support.

In the case of a weakened or marginalized public sector, which is rather characterized by institutional collapse, measures need to be taken which in the first instance orient themselves towards the effectivization and reconstruction of the state's key institutions, i.e. those organizations which are responsible for the rule system, legislation, planning, and distribution of resources.

Experiences from numerous programmes indicate that development efforts are doomed to fail if they do not make progress on all these fronts, if possible simultaneously. An organization can be rebuilt and effectivized to some degree without taking its surroundings into account. However, it will not be long before the programme runs into problems with staffing rules, management instruments, the salary system, the state budget, laws and regulations (or the lack of them), as well as with other organizations and groups which are the clients for the organization's products and services.

Institutional development programmes thus affect the public sector's appearance and behaviour across the board and so the goals of the programme must be acceptable not only to the aid agency but— much more importantly—to the partner country also. It is difficult to start, and even more difficult to execute, a development programme whose goals do not correspond to the values in the sector and in a large proportion of the society. The partner must want and own the programme for it to be a success.

Different approaches to institution building in the public sector

To simplify somewhat, support to building an institution can be provided in three ways:

–   technical assistance, i.e. individual experts work within the target organization and by example and training transfer the knowledge and skills needed for the institution to progress;

–   setting up a training institute in which people from target institutions are provided with basic and advanced training; and

–   cooperation between the target institution and a homologous, but more advanced, institution in another country, so-called institutional cooperation or twinning.

Technical assistance has shown itself to be ineffective as regards attaining sustainable results in the long-term. A Nordic evaluation (DANIDA et al., 1988) of the effectiveness of technical assistance within 55 projects in three African countries showed that the short-term objectives had been attained in almost all the projects, but that sustainability of the results was conspicuous by its absence. The 1997 World Development Report also acknowledges the ineffectiveness of TA for institutional development: " ... [The] focus on institutions is very different from the traditional approach of technical assistance ... The emphasis here is on the incentive framework guiding *behavior* ..." (World Bank, 1997:79).

Nor has the training institute approach worked particularly well (Dyrssen and Johnston, 1991). Besides all the problems to do with the individual public servant's will and ability to apply the acquired skills and knowledge when he or she returns to the workplace, a number of difficulties arise through the failings of the institute itself.

From these experiences we draw the conclusion that capacity building must take place within a different environment and organizational form, i.e. at the workplace. The task is in fact to train the entire organization, and it appears that such a goal is easier to attain within the context of institutional cooperation.

To summarize, for institutional development to be successful, the following conditions need to apply:

–   the institution as a whole is involved (organizational base, functions, laws, rules and bearer systems);

–   essential portions of the state and society are in accordance with the programme and feel they own it; and

–   mutual comprehension pertains between target institution, aid agency and assigned experts, who together define how the programme of support should be shaped in order to succeed.

Institutional cooperation

Once the goals have been set, activities are initiated within the host (or "target") organization. The measures to be taken need to be relevant both for internal organizational development and for the development of the rule system, legislation and administrative functions. The best place to look for the knowledge and experience required to assist in this is in a twin organization.

If the support is being provided to a state institution, the aid agency engages a twin state organization to play the part of adviser to the target institution. The "twins" collaborate through personnel exchange, training, equipment support, long-term experts and short-term consultancy inputs. The cooperation needs to be guaranteed for a sufficiently long time-period, as institutional development is a lengthy and often difficult process. However, it can be useful to set a fairly definite termination date and develop the work plan on the basis of this fixed time period, as this permits the parties to dimension the support to be provided in an effective way.

Institutional twinning has a number of positive features. The target institution acquires a broad range of relevant knowledge and resources from an agency with similar responsibilities and internal organization. A forum for the exchange of professional skills and institutional praxis is created. The collegial relationship which develops between the partners facilitates the reform process, which becomes more legitimate than it would have been if the process had been launched by a private company. (Similarly, in supporting the development of private firms an aid agency can obtain better results by financing "company twinning" than by setting a state bureaucracy to work). The twins after all have the same tasks, use similar instruments and meet comparable demands from their respective governments, clients and societies (SCB, 1994).

In order to be successful, however, both twins must be prepared to undertake a common learning process, as technology, culture and attitudes cannot simply be transferred from one context to the other.

The self-evident target institutions to be addressed first within the public sector are those agencies which are responsible for the indicated state systems and functions:

- the ministry of finance (taxation, budgeting and accounting);
- the public service ministry (personnel and salary systems);

- the ministry of local government (local government and local administration);
- the ministry of planning (planning system); and
- the ministry of justice (systems of legislation and justice).

Once these organizations are on their way to functioning well, similar support can be given to organizations like the central bank, the audit office, the statistics bureau and the like.

Within the frame of its public administration development support Sweden has set a large number of such twinning programmes into operation. The audit offices of four countries in Southern Africa have been twinned with Sweden's audit office, while Sweden's statistics bureau cooperates with its twin in six African countries. Cooperation within one and the same sector in the same geographic region opens especially favourable conditions for institutional development, as South-South cooperation can also be developed within the twinning framework.

In the case of Namibia, for example, exchanges take place between Namibia's, Sweden's and Zimbabwe's statistics offices. Zimbabwe has contributed to strengthening Namibia's statistical capacity, particularly in field surveys, while Zimbabwe has benefited from improvements to its national accounts (see also Winai et al., 1997).

In Mozambique a city twinning programme is being carried out between Gothenburg and Beira. Although the cooperation is focused primarily on developing Beira's financial systems, support has also been provided to the city's cadastral system. From the twinning programme cooperation has also arisen within the areas of culture and care for street children.

Also in Mozambique, cooperation is proceeding between the Ministry of State Administration and a Brazilian foundation with similar tasks in the state of São Paulo. The programme has produced the first proper personnel administration and salary systems in Mozambique. In parallel the ministry has increased its capacity to carry out its other tasks as regards reorganizing the state apparatus and developing local government. Sweden also provides support to the Ministry of Finance through its National Audit Office, with the aim of developing the systems of budgeting, accounting and auditing, which in its turn has brought about closer cooperation between the Ministries of Finance and State Administration.

Problems with institutional cooperation

Although it has been argued above that institutional twinning is the most effective method for institutional development, problems can arise even here.

To begin with, it is not worth the trouble to mobilize a twin institution into a relatively limited organizational development project. It is also the case that the "more developed" institution can be insufficiently equipped to help its twin with very specialized questions. In the context of a full twinning relationship the twin may be forced to seek expertise beyond its own walls.

Indeed, an immediate limitation on institutional cooperation is the lack of resources. Even if all countries with a "developed" network of institutions were prepared to participate in exchange programmes, the supply of twins would be insufficient as the number of twins in need of help is larger than those able and willing to provide it. It is to some extent an historical accident that Swedish state institutions are legally able to operate as twins on an institutional basis (see RRV, 1990). Most other countries whose public sector can be regarded as "developed" do not allow full twinning. This means that individual experts from these state agencies can be supplied as technical assistance through third parties (usually a firm), but that the institutional cooperation mode is not possible.

Some Swedish state agencies have not shown any particular interest in such cooperation either. Some of them in fact regard their societal mandate in Sweden as excluding them from entering into partnerships abroad and taking on responsibility for developing parts of a foreign government.

As the number of twins is so limited, helpful twins risk becoming swamped by cooperation partners and stretching their resources too thin. This can result in the institutional twinning relationship becoming less effective than a commercial consultancy would have been.

One cannot assume either that agencies from "developed" countries will automatically enter into partnerships in the right way. In the first place it is necessary that they build up their own project administration internally which is both effective and flexible, otherwise the cooperation can fail technically. Secondly, there is a large risk that the "developed" twin, secure in its own moral and cultural superiority, will expect a passive and grateful recipient and trample in with its knowledge held high. In such a case it would be better not to offer any support at all. Fortunately the Swedish authorities do not carry with them connotations of any colonial or otherwise despotic past which could put an open relationship into question.

Twinning arrangements are expensive, as through their goals and by their nature they cover a wide area of operation over a protracted period of time. They also demand continuous extra investments in the donor country. However, they are not subject to the same level of risk that they end up with a shortfall of resources, cultural conflicts, methodological quarrels and general organizational disorder as is the case with many "individual expert" projects. The results are thus probably worth the expense in the long run. Nonetheless, the high costs always carry with them the consequence that they consume resources that could have been used elsewhere.

The follow-up process is also problematic in this type of programme. The aid agency may well find that it is difficult to exercise authoritative check-ups within a twinning arrangement, as one of the twins involved is a state organization from the same country with equal status within their common government.

Twinning relationships are instituted in a context where difficult goals are expected to be attained in an uncertain environment over a lengthy time period. Twinning relationships are by their nature not commercial, but rather built up on the basis of mutual respect and confidence between the three organizations involved, i.e. the aid agency, the target institution and the "home" agency. Under these circumstances it is harder to apply a value-for-money perspective and more difficult to identify and prevent "arrangements among friends" from taking place. It is equally difficult for the aid agency to terminate the arrangement once the agreed time-period for cooperation has come to an end. On the other hand, it is the atmosphere of mutual trust and respect which is one of the particular strengths of the twinning relationship. The aid agency must thus manage to walk the tightrope of promoting amicable relations while simultaneously seeing to it that the programme keeps itself on track as regards expenditure, effectiveness and goal attainment—a difficult task!

When is institutional development finished?

This question, although of great concern to aid agencies and governments, is in fact incorrectly put. An organization and the surrounding functions and systems which together make it an institution are never

ever really "complete", as they are composed of changeable systems, relationships and people in a constantly changing world. On a more practical plane everybody knows that an organization can look fully competent and productive and seem to be properly inserted into its social functions, but that a sudden change in its economic situation, its leadership or its legal status can lead to its rapid collapse. The question is nonetheless relevant, in the sense that it is important for the organization in question and for the aid agency to be able to identify when support is no longer necessary.

Nowadays, with aid agencies to an increasing extent demanding a well-founded planning process through which concrete goals and measurable results are established, the issue has come increasingly into focus.

Winai and Andersson (1993, 1997) have carried out extensive investigations into the issue on behalf of Sida. In order to establish the necessary criteria for evaluating an organization's capacity, they have proposed a descriptive model built up in four sequential and developmental steps. (The model is presented thoroughly in Winai and Andersson's contribution to this book, in the next chapter). In brief, the question they were asked to answer was, how can one measure what level of development an organization has reached? To answer it, the authors concluded that a range of different factors need to be examined in order to arrive at a well-founded answer.

An initial issue is of course whether the organization has access to the minimal level of resources it needs to function properly, in terms of finance, personnel, skills and competence, and equipment. On the side of personnel, issues such as the degree to which the posts in the organization are filled, the level of education of staff, and the staff turnover rate give interesting insights into an organization's stability and competence.

Another simple indicator is the salary level and structure. Are salaries at least to some degree competitive, and are they high enough for the employees and their families to live on? In some countries economic mismanagement and structural adjustment has led to civil servants' salaries being depreciated to such an extent that they are unable even to carry out their tasks on a full-time basis, but are forced instead to "moonlight" to make ends meet. Salary differentials may be so small that skilled workers find no incentive to work hard; or, as is more often the case, the differentials are so high that a large proportion of the staff harbours grievances about the injustice of the situation. Until such problems are resolved it is very difficult to demand that an organization function efficiently.

Additionally, the level of financing of an organization's running costs is of decisive importance. For example, if a government cannot afford to carry an organization at a given level it is hardly worthwhile building it up to that level, however necessary it might appear to be to have an organization of that capacity.

A more complex factor to measure is change in an organization's internal culture and values. It could be a good idea to make a baseline study, somewhat along the lines of Hofstede's (1980) research, of an institution's cultural profile in order to be able to identify what kind of changes—if any—have taken place on this front. It is probably no exaggeration to say that changes on this variable could be among the most important of all for a development project to bring about, e.g. an institutional attitude change from authoritarian to democratic, or from control to facilitation.

An important indicator is the production of the organization. At least three dimensions need to be measured: the quantity (whether it produces what it should), the quality (whether what was produced is useful, relevant, timely and accurate), and the accessibility (whether the products in question are made available to the users easily and punctually).

Criteria for diagnosis:

Time frame
Focus
Planning
Mode of change
Management
Structure
Perspective
Motivation
Development
Communication
Leadership

High-performing

Proactive

Respon-
sive

Reactive

On somewhat similar lines to Winai and Andersson, Nelson and Burns (cited in Andersson and Winai, 1997) have also proposed a four-step model for evaluating an organization, though theirs is not linear and incremental in the same way. The four stages they propose are "the reactive", "the responsive", "the proactive" and "the high-performing" (see diagram). They apply twelve keyword concepts as benchmarks against which to evaluate an organization and to place it in one of the four categories.

A common problem with stage models is that evaluations often indicate that different parts of the organization function at different levels or stages, i.e. it is not easy to assign the organization in question a single unambiguous "score". However, it is often the case that it is just as interesting to identify differences in performance within the organization, as this provides a good guide as to the areas which need to be concentrated on.

In their study of Botswana's Ministry of Local Government, Lands and Housing and its local offices, Jones et al. (1995) attempted to measure a number of these diagnostic criteria, inter alia the ministry's management, leadership, structure, planning, motivation and internal communication. The method applied was attitude research among the ministry's managers. It provided an interesting insight into how managers interpreted the reality around them and the problems in their workplace, and revealed a good deal about the organization's internal values and culture. The organization showed itself to be inward-looking and absorbed in its own internal procedures, indeed hardly interested in attaining its external goals. However, more problematically, the replies to many questions were so divided that it was hard to form a more general impression of the ministry's condition—other than that there were a lot of internal differences.

As the goal is not merely that of organizational development, but also institution building, the work done by any organization needs to be evaluated in relation to its impact on its surroundings and on its society, its value for its direct clients, its treatment in the press and so on. What counts in the long run is after all the institution's effect on society's development and norms, i.e. the "development effects" of the programme.

There remains a lot to be done before we have easily applicable methods for measuring institutional development ready to hand. Nonetheless the methods discussed above indicate possible avenues of approach, in particular as regards the kind of questions that need to be asked.

Summary

It is generally accepted that most of the development cooperation going under the name of institutional development has had very limited success. The following issues need to be emphasized:

– As regards the concepts of institution and institution building this chapter advocates the use of a broader approach and a wider analysis than that of mere organizational development; though this does not mean that much of the work to be done on building institutions will not consist of organizational development activities.

– Institutional development requires a thorough base-line analysis and continuous follow-up, in particular of the political situation. Institutional development has very little chance of succeeding without strong political support in the country in question, as the work to be done by definition involves the development of laws, rules and procedures with consequences far beyond the target agency.

– Previous experiences of institution building have shown that the individual-expert and the training-institute approach have been relatively ineffective. An alternative which has shown itself to be rather more effective is that of institutional twinning, although even this has its limitations and failings, and the possibilities of applying it are restricted.

– If an agency is to involve itself at all in institutional development, it must reckon with the process requiring lots of time, considerable flexibility, space for regular policy dialogue, and above all enough resources.

– Moore et al. (1995) propose that aid agencies should create provisional "organizations for institution building" when no suitable twin institution is available. This chapter argues that cooperation between homologous organizations is preferable, inter alia because experience has shown that the best results have been obtained through collegiality and mutual understanding between people who work with the same issues towards common goals.

– Although institution building demands flexibility it is still no less important to set up clear goals and (at the least provisional) time limits. Attempts to measure the extent and sustainability of institutional development work must be carried out as professionally and comparably as possible.

–   Against the background of what has thus far been argued, it is more than evident that a programme for the development of a single institution should be supported by as few aid agencies as possible, and preferably one only.

–   Greater efforts need to be made to support and organize an independent network of professional bodies (of accountants, lawyers, personnel managers etc.) around public sector organizations. This is an important dimension of institutional development which thus far has largely been neglected.

Anton Johnston holds a doctor's degree in international education from Stockholm University and is a practitioner of development cooperation with a background in law, political science, linguistics, economics and adult education. He is currently employed in Sida's Division for Democratic Governance. He has previously worked in Southern Africa, for the longest periods in Mozambique and Namibia, and has been one of Sida's policy formulators, in particular as regards public administration development.

References

Andersson G., and P. Winai, 1997, *Diagnosis of Organizations in Development Cooperation*. Report to Sida, Stockholm, February 1997.

Carnoy, M., 1987, *The State and Political Theory*. New Jersey: Princeton University Press.

DANIDA, FINNIDA, NORAD, Sida, 1988. A Nordic Evaluation of the Effectiveness of Technical Assistance Personnel. Joint Evaluation Report. Stockholm: Sida.

Dag Hammarskjöld Foundation, 1995, *Autonomous Development Funds in Africa. Report from an expert consultation in Kampala, Uganda, 4–6 April, 1995.* Uppsala.

Denison, E.F., 1967, "Sources of Post-War Growth in Nine Western Countries", *American Economic Review*, Vol. 57.

—1985, *Trends in American Economic Growth, 1929–1982*. Washington: The Brookings Institution.

Dia, M., 1993, *A Governance Approach to Civil Service Reform in Sub-Saharan Africa*. World Bank Technical Paper No. 225. Washington: World Bank.

Dyrssen, H. and A. Johnston, 1991, "Cooperation in the Development of Public Sector Management Skills: The Sida Experience", *Journal of Management Development*, Vol. 10, No. 6. Oxford: Pergamon Press.

Gibbon P. and A.O. Olukoshi, 1996, *Structural Adjustment and Socio-Economic Change in Sub-Saharan Africa*. Research Report No. 102. Uppsala: The Nordic Africa Institute.

Hofstede, G., 1980, *Culture's Consequences: International Differences in Work-Related Values*. London: Sage Publications.

Hydén, G. and M. Bratton (ed.), 1992, *Governance and Politics in Africa*. Boulder: Lynne Rienner.

Johnston, A. and L. Wohlgemuth, 1995, "Civil Service Reforms in Developing Countries", *21st Century Policy Review*, Vol. 2, No. 3, Winter 1995. Maryland: IDO.

Jones, M., P. Blunt and K. Sharma, 1995, *Managerial Behaviour, Organizational Functioning and Performance in an African Public Service Organization*. Report to Sida, Stockholm.

Moore, M., S. Stewart and A. Hudock, 1995, *Institution Building as a Development Assistance Method*. Sida Evaluation Report 1, 1995. Stockholm.

North, C. Douglass, 1990, *Institutions, Institutional Change and Economic Performance*. Cambridge: Cambridge University Press.

Poulantzas, N., 1978, *State Power and Socialism*. London: Routledge.

Psacharopoulos, G. and M. Woodhall, 1985, *Education for Development: An Analysis of Investment Choices*. Oxford: Oxford University Press (for the World Bank).

Putnam, R.D. et al., 1993, *Making Democracy Work. Civic Traditions in Modern Italy*. Princeton University Press.

RRV, 1990, "Statlig Tjänsteexport". PM 1990:12. Stockholm: Riksrevisionsverket.

SCB, 1994, *Guidelines for Institutional Cooperation: Based on Experiences in the Statistical Field*. ICO Report No. 18 Stockholm.: Statistiska Centralbyrån.

Schultz, T.W., 1961, "Education and Economic Growth", in N.B. Henry (ed.), *Social Forces Influencing American Education*. Chicago: University of Chicago Press.

Winai, P. and G. Andersson, 1993, *Diagnos av institutionell utveckling* (Diagnosis of Institutional Development). Report to Sida, Stockholm, December 1993.

Winai, P., I. Colbro and C. Schumann, 1997, *Namibia Central Statistics Office: Assessment of Its Institutional Capacity*. Report to Sida, Stockholm, August 1997.

World Bank, 1997, *The State in a Changing World*. World Development Report 1997. Oxford: Oxford University Press.

World Bank, 1992, *Governance and Development*. Washington: World Bank.

Measuring and Diagnosing Institutional Development

Göran Andersson and Peter Winai

Why should institutional development be measured?

Institutional development is a concept often used in the development assistance discourse. The necessity to strengthen and improve institutions in developing countries has become a generally accepted axiom for development. At present a greater part of development support resources are allocated to institutional development as compared to a decade ago. The long lasting economic and political crisis in Africa and the collapse of the Soviet Union have probably contributed to a shift of the development support in this direction.

The concept institution is defined differently depending on context, but there seems to be a consensus that "organization" is included. In the following we use the concept as being synonymous with organization, and institutional development as synonymous with organizational development. We make this simplification for practical reasons although we are aware that the two concepts are not always identical. In other parts of this anthology the concept institutional development is discussed more extensively.

There are two main factors behind the development of the staircase model.

The first is connected with the difficulties of the development cooperation agencies in objectively assessing the results of a project aiming at the development of an organization. Which criteria should be used to assess the level of development achieved? How could organizational development be measured? Is the development level that has been reached sufficient and sustainable—i.e. will the organization maintain and develop without further assistance?

The second factor is associated with the shift from budgetary control to result-oriented management of governmental activities. This shift has sharpened the demands on the development agencies to present results, i.e. to describe with fair objectivity what has actually been achieved by the assistance. Institutional and organizational development are areas where methods to describe results of development assistance have been exceptionally difficult to find.

Naturally, the purpose of result-based management is to improve effectiveness in operations. Thus, the availability of methods to describe results is a condition for the improvement of management and monitoring of development assistance efforts.

Institutional development in developing countries

In the elaboration of methods to describe the development level of organizations in developing countries, there are two apparent problems: Firstly, in what respects is the situation different from that in a developed country? Secondly, which factors is it relevant to measure?

When it comes to organizational development the situation in a typical developing country differs from that in a developed country in one important way: in the developing country it is often a matter of building completely new organizations or developing organizations which struggle with great difficulties to deliver any output at all. Normally there is a lack of physical, financial and human resources and of competence to manage activities. Furthermore, an undeveloped infrastructure hampers all effective work.

In the developed country, the situation is generally different. Normally the organization manages to produce. Problems appear at other levels, although these may be just as serious relatively speaking.

Thus in a developing country a relevant model to describe the progress of an organization must start from scratch or at least at a very early stage.

What is it that reflects the stage of development that an organization has reached? The model identifies two main dimensions of measurement. One dimension relates to the *output* of the organization. Is anything produced at all and if so, in what quantity and of what quality? Has the output been produced with a reasonable input of resources? Is the output relevant to the customers and have the desired effects or outcomes been achieved?

The second dimension relates to what is accomplished within the organization in terms of *changes*: in types of output produced, in production methods, in administration and management. Changes in these respects reflect the development ability and capacity of the organization.[1]

The staircase model

A staircase model to diagnose the development level of an organization first discussed in an anthology published by Sida in 1991.[2] The model was then further developed and tested by the authors on commission from Sida[3] and guidelines for its application were presented in 1997.[4]

The staircase model provides a frame for descriptive analysis. It consists of four stages of development. It should be used to describe, not to explain organizational development. However, the model also carries a normative element: it is an assumption that it is necessary for an organization to reach one stage before the next. Reality is of course more complicated. The organization may have reached a high degree of development in one respect, while in other respects it is still struggling with basic problems.

The four development stages identified in the model are:

Stage 1. There is an organization, but with low and unpredictable output

At stage 1, an organization has been established, but output is unpredictable and of low quality. Output is defined as the products or services produced by the organization for use *outside* the organization. Output is measured in quantitative and qualitative terms.

Stage 2. The organization is able to deliver expected output with reasonable reliability and quality

Production is carried out within the installed capacity and with available resources. However, the organization lacks the capability to re-

---

[1] In addition to these two dimensions a third one can be identified: the value of output in the client system. An important condition for increased client value is active interaction with the client; thus it can be looked upon as a separate dimension. On the other hand, the client value represents quality of the output; in that respect it can be included in the output dimension.

[2] Andersson, G., 1991, "Några reflektioner om organisationsutveckling i u-land", in I.B. Mothander (ed.), *Erfarenheter av organisationsutveckling i u-land*. Stockholm: Sida.

[3] Three case studies of institutional development have been published by Sida in 1994, 1995 and 1996.

[4] Andersson, G. and Winai, P., 1997, *Diagnosis of Organizations in Development Cooperation. Guidelines for Application of the Staircase Model*. Stockholm: Department for Democracy and Social Development, Sida.

spond to new demands if external conditions are changed or if key staff leaves the organization.

Stage 3. *The organization carries out changes on its own*

When the organization has reached stage 3, it meets the performance standards set for delivering output. It is also capable of making changes on its own, and actually executes such changes: in products, production methods and administrative/management systems.

Thus this stage of the model is based on the assumption that the ability to develop is manifested in implemented changes and on-going development activities.

Stage 4. *The organization works actively with its clients or customers*

The organization which has climbed to stage 4, works actively to increase the value of its products or services in the client/customer system. It knows the clients, has an on-going dialogue with them and allocates resources to facilitate utilization of its output.

Figure 1. *The staircase model for organizational diagnosis*

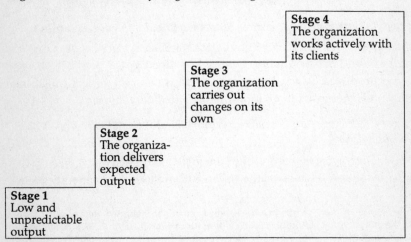

Thus, as stated above, output and ability to change are the two basic dimensions used to describe the development stages of an organization. To facilitate diagnosis, the measuring of these two dimensions has to be complemented by different measurements in relation to other aspects such as productivity, staff turn-over, service level, resource allocation and resource consumption.

Dependence

In development co-operation it is also necessary to find out how output and change have been brought about. To what extent is the organization dependent on external financial and technical assistance?

This question can be answered by assessing the dependence on external funding and competence in current operations and development of the organization. The figure below illustrates four typical situations that need to be assessed.

Figure 2. *Financial and competence dependence in current operations and development activities*

	Financial	**Competence**
	A	**C**
Current Operations	To what extent is the organization dependent on external financial support to sustain operations?	To what extent is the organization dependent on external technical assistance to carry out operations?
	B	**D**
Development Activities	To what extent is the organization dependent on external financial support for development and change?	To what extent is the organization dependent on external technical assistance for development and change?

Financial dependence implies that the organization uses external financial support to carry out its *operations* (A) *and development activities* (B). The dependency may be measured as the relation between external financial support and its own financing. *Dependence on external technical assistance to carry out operations* (C) is manifested in the classical gap-filling type of support. *Dependence on technical assistance for development and change* (D) is manifested in the extent to which expatriate personnel on long and/or short term assignments are instrumental in identifying problems, articulating visions, preparing projects, implementing project activities, monitoring and reporting progress and evaluating results.

The model does not explain the causes behind a certain level of development. Therefore it is not a sufficient tool for designing a development programme for an organization. It is however instrumental in describing a factual situation, which can be used as a basis for problem analysis as well as identification and design of development measures.

The fact that an organization uses external expertise is in itself no sign of critical dependence of importance for its ability to produce, change and develop. Independence or self-reliance in terms of competence may be defined as follows:

– the organization has the ability to define its competence needs which cannot be met internally (e.g. for a particular specialist), identify where the missing competence can be found and how it can be acquired and use it within the organization; and

– the organization has the ability to identify, formulate and solve problems and maintain this capability.

Looking at the organization in terms of input-output

The model is based on a common picture of an organization as an open system: the system receives *input* in terms of different resources and also in terms of items to be processed. The system then delivers an *output* to be consumed/ used by its clients in order to have certain desired outcomes or effects.[5] For the system to survive in a long-term perspective, i.e. to continue to receive inputs, it has to produce outputs that are relevant, of acceptable quantity and quality and cost to the client. The output must generate outcomes which are valued by the clients. How the organization is actually producing the output is not of primary interest to the clients as long as it meets their requirements. Figure 3 captures the system and relationships with which the model is concerned.

The production *process*, at least initially, is looked upon as a black box, i.e. the production process as such is not the main issue. What is in focus is the output produced, its quantity and quality. In order to survive and develop the organization must be able to change. In order to observe change one must look into the black box. Ability to change is manifested inside the organization but also in change of type of outputs produced. Changes of inputs also require that the black box be opened. Such changes appear, for example, as quality changes regarding personnel competence. Technical and financial inputs provided by donors reflect the external dependence of the organization.

The concepts the model focuses on are indicated with bold letters in Figure 3. To facilitate analysis and diagnosis different kinds of *ratios*

---

[5] Thus, the model observes *both* the client perspective and the societal effect perspective.

may be utilized. One type of ratio is *efficiency*, which is generally expressed as the relation between output and input. *Cost-effectiveness* measurements capture the relation between costs to produce output and the outcomes. *Effectiveness* as illustrated in the figure above, is defined as the relation between the value of outcomes and the value that was intended and expressed as an objective.

Figure 3. *The organization as an input-output system*

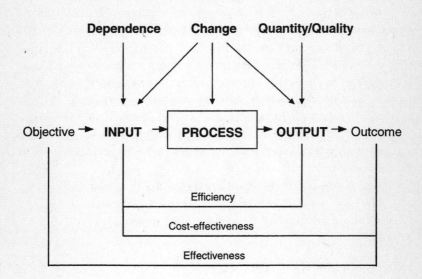

Focus of measurements

Generally we find it appropriate to focus on performance measurements in the first stages. Here it may be difficult to identify problems related to the relevance of performance. Measurements will largely be of a quantitative nature. Further up in the staircase it will be increasingly important to concentrate on qualitative aspects of change and re-orientation.

The possibilities to measure output and change depend on a number of circumstances.

One of the most important preconditions for the model is that it concentrates on the development of *organizations*, as opposed to individual development projects. A project, according to its definition, has an end, whereas the basic idea of institutional development is the opposite: to create sustainable organizations.

The next question that arises is whether the *whole organization or part* of it should be subject to measurement. This choice has to be made from case to case. The difficulty in defining performance in a measurable way will increase the more one wishes to include in the analysis, i.e. the higher the aggregation level. Furthermore, important strengths and weaknesses in the capacity to change may disappear from view when measuring larger areas.

In order to draw conclusions regarding changes it is necessary to make *comparisons over a period of time*. Availability of information regarding both the present and the past then becomes crucial. The organization itself may possess data on the present situation—which can be obtained with a certain amount of effort—but historical information may be more or less impossible to obtain. In certain cases the observations may have to be limited to a general description of the situation. If this is the case the diagnosis cannot be supported by previous measurements which capture the dynamics of the organization.

An undesired effect which arises when measurements are made in a social context must be mentioned: the act of measuring affects what is being measured. It is not possible to ask a question about, e.g. results, without influencing those questioned in some way.

Model development through case studies

Three case studies have been carried out in order to test and develop the model: one on the Statistical Bureau in Tanzania, one on the Telecom Company in Namibia and one on a the Province Administration in South Africa.[6]

These organizations represent very different kinds of performance and production methods. The first two are however similar in one respect: both statistical and telecom performance is fairly easy to specify—which is why they were chosen as the first pilot cases—the possibilities to obtain production data were considered to be good. The third case—the Province Administration—is altogether different. The

---

[6] During recent years the Staircase model has also been applied in other studies and assessments of institutional capacity, e.g. the Bank of Namibia (1995), the National Statistics Office in Namibia (1997), and the Bank of Zambia (1997).

production largely consists of output with low specificity:[7] many of the products are difficult to specify and quantify, such as policies and ad hoc initiatives to bring about change in, e.g. schools or hospitals in the Province.

Critical questions

The model indicates the main areas for data collection. These are:

– Output; quantity and quality;
– Changes in output and production methods;
– Changes in management; and
– Attention to client value.

In each of the case studies detailed sets of questions were prepared to obtain data in the above areas. Data were collected through interviews and through document studies. The case studies have been of help in the development of the model, and allow us to be more precise as to which values of the variables to expect in different stages of the staircase.

Figure 4. *Expected values of critical variables at the different stages of the model "Signs" refer to concrete manifestations in the organization*

Variable	Stage 1	Stage 2	Stage 3	Stage 4
Attention to client value	No sign	No sign	Emerging signs	Signs
Change of –management –production	No sign	Emerging signs	Signs	Signs
Output –quality –quantity	Low Unpredictable	Low– Medium Predictable	Medium– High Predictable	Medium–High Predictable
Competence and resources	External in-put crucial	Adequate for regular production, inadequate for change	Adequate for regular production and change	Adequate for regular pro-duction and change

---

[7] The concept of specificity is further explained in Andersson and Winai, 1997, ibid., p. 19ff.

Table 4 summarizes the staircase model and its stages in terms of the expected values of the crucial dimensions measured. Each stage is characterized by a certain combination of requirements and at each subsequent stage new requirements are added.

The expected values of the different variables at the various stages constitute the normative element of the model. By setting these norms a yardstick is obtained. Such a yardstick is necessary to enable the observer to record the development of an organization over a period of time.

Diagnosis of the cases

The case studies illustrate that subjective interpretations of data cannot be avoided when diagnosing the development level of an organization. An important reason for this is deficiency in the quality of data obtainable. Interpretation would be easier if time series data were available in all question areas. The necessity for subjective interpretations also becomes greater the further up the staircase we proceed, as more and more variables have to be aggregated to a common assessment and quality becomes increasingly important in the changing of the organization.

In the case of the Bureau of Statistics we concluded that the organization was on its way to stage 2. This diagnosis was based on the fact that it was able to deliver regular statistics with reasonable predictability. However, quality was low. Furthermore there was evidence of changes in products as well as production methods and administrative systems. All these changes, however, were supported by technical assistance. The dependence on external competence was great. The organization was also dependent on financial assistance to maintain production at the level of capacity for which it was built. There were no signs of an active involvement with the clients to increase the value of the output.

In the case of Telecom Company we found the organization to be closer to stage 4 than stage 3. The reason was that telecom services were produced with a fairly high predictability, although quality and productivity were still far below standards in the developed countries. Changes had been carried out and took place in all performance areas, in certain cases with technical assistance, in other cases by their own efforts. In relation to the volume of change the development support was small and decreasing. Our assessment was that Telecom had become independent of external competence in the sense that the organization was able to define competence needs on its own, acquire that competence and use it. The organization was very profitable and was able not only to finance current operations but also investments with its own capital or loans on the market. Telecom was able to show several instances of active dialogue with the customers.

In the case of the Province Administration our diagnosis was that the organization had reached stage 2 in the staircase. There were no real examples of measures taken by the two departments studied to enhance the value of their outputs for their primary clients. No instances of change of administrative and managerial systems were observed but there was intense work going on to build up the new structures and adapt to the framework set by higher levels. The outputs produced presented a mixed picture. The organization supplied its primary clients with outputs which facilitated production of health care and education and which could be assessed as predictable. However, outputs in terms of change initiatives (changes of direction of services and changes in support systems) could hardly be characterized as predictable. The departments were self-reliant in terms of financial resources. The operations of the departments and the delivery system were funded at a level which allowed for regular production to continue. The resources for change were however inadequate. Technical support through international and local consultants, was provided from outside and the competence to plan and implement change was inadequate.

Applicability and usefulness in practice

The basic idea behind the staircase model is to provide a tool which can be used in designing and evaluating organizational development projects. The case studies which have been carried out in order to test and develop the model indicate it has the potential to be a useful tool. Further use of the model will hopefully contribute to its refinement. Only through practical application will it be possible to improve its usefulness.

There are a number of issues that should be kept in mind when applying the model.

How to improve relevance of the model?

The model is descriptive and provides a normative framework for placing an organization at a certain level of development. For donors and recipients it is highly relevant to have access to a tool that helps to define the situation at the start and also helps to determine what should be achieved, e.g. the project should help to take the organization from stage 1 to stage 2 or to stage 3. Although it is possible to limit the use of the model to only describe a baseline situation, the relevance increases if the model is applied repeatedly during a project. In considering the use of the model it is therefore important to determine how it should be fitted into a project's decision making and reporting processes.

How to improve precision?

The model has not yet been used as a regular tool in planning, monitoring and evaluation of organizational development projects and its usefulness remains to be proven in practice. The usefulness will largely be determined by the precision of the diagnoses that are made. If they are impaired by too large margins of error they will be of little help.

The limitation to four steps makes the model easy to manage and reduces complexity, which is often an advantage in the follow-up dialogue, especially when many projects are assessed. In other situations however, it may be a weakness that the steps are too few. Although placed at the same stage, organizations may still have many different characteristics. Development assistance is typically extended to organizations at stage 1 and 2 and there may be a need to divide these stages further in order to better distinguish between different levels.

A strength of the model is that it attempts to *measure verifiable phenomena* by recording quantity and quality of actual performance, manifestations of actual change and activities to increase client value. In this respect it measures objective realities which then form the basis for interpretation. It does not make any attempt to explain why things look the way they do. A weakness then, is that the interpretation of data leading to the diagnosis is not guided by explanatory information. The need for explanatory information when interpreting data should be further looked into.

The problem of interpretation increases at the higher stages of the staircase. More observations have to be interpreted. In the case studies the quality of changes, for example, has not been assessed. The criterion "carries out changes on its own" implies that the changes are of an acceptable quality. Assessments of the quality of change require in-depth studies. On the other hand it can be argued that such assessments are not required as the quality of changes will manifest itself in output and productivity measures at a later point in time. This argument also underlines the importance of follow-up studies.

How to improve application in practice?

Questions regarding the practical application of the model may be divided into two categories. One is connected with the access to data, and the other with the psychological preparedness to be observed—and assessed.

The question of *access to data* is crucial when using the model. Data are not always available in the format required by the model. In the case studies, the information sought regarding the basic variables was relatively easily available. However, in many cases it may be necessary to conduct special studies in order to retrieve relevant information, and also to invest in special measures to make relevant information retrievable for future use. Our observation is that the lower the development level of an organization, the more likely it is that basic information, e.g. regarding performance, is not available. It is also likely that performance has not even been defined.

Associated with the question of access to data is the need for specialist competence to search for and assess information. If specialists are needed, e.g. in the fields of statistics or telecommunications in the cases in question, the practical application of the model appears somewhat restricted. Our principal approach is that it should be possible to carry out the exercise without specialists in the team, but that some *pre-understanding* of the field is helpful. Also, it has to be taken into account that involvement of new people, e.g. specialists who may not be used to evaluation or similar tasks, and are not acquainted with the model, would require training.

Naturally there has to be a *psychological preparedness* in the organization concerned, to be measured and assessed. In our studies this has not been an obstacle. However, it should be kept in mind that it is not self-evident that the organization is prepared to give out information not directly connected with a development co-operation project. As mentioned above, the object of the model is not the project but the organization as a whole, and these two entities do not necessarily match. Certain information may be considered sensitive for political or commercial reasons.

Areas of development

The staircase model must be seen as a framework which can be further developed in terms of both the concept and measurement techniques. The following are some areas for model development, linked to each stage of the staircase:

The concept of organization

The first stage of the model states that there should be at least an organizational embryo, implying that there is an actor, a management and common objectives of some kind. But an organization may be more or less dependent on other organizations. A governmental agency may be part of a ministry, share its budget and staff. If the organization is greatly dependent on bodies at higher levels, e.g. when recruiting personnel, the organizational development is affected accordingly. A question here is: *To what extent does the management actually control its organization?*

The concept of output quality

The model itself does not define the meaning of quality in output and production. It uses the quality definitions available in the specific situation. However, it has become more and more obvious in developing countries too, that "quality" must also include common societal and social values, e.g. consumer safety and environmental care. So a question to be answered is: *To what extent does the organization fulfil demands for contribution to sustainable development?*

The concept of internal change

Change in itself is not necessarily good. The crucial issue when establishing whether the organization has reached stage 3 is who it is that is orchestrating change. The question here parallels the one regarding organizational autonomy above: *To what extent does the management actually govern its own change?*

A way to establish the quality of the change process is repeated studies of the organization. Development will show whether the changes have been for better or worse. In other words: *Have the changes carried out contributed to long-term development?*

Another issue of internal development concerns the degree of commitment amongst staff. Motivation to participate is important. But there is a great difference between on one hand being "motivated" by a good salary and on the other understanding the mission of the organization and sharing the values on which that mission is based. The organization with members committed to its mission has reached a higher degree of maturity. Thus a crucial question is: *To what extent do the individuals share the mission?*

In management and organization development we often make a sharp distinction between "the inside and the outside". In reality there is no such sharp distinction. Production costs have to be at the same level as those of competing organizations. Values inside the organization have to be in harmony with the development of values in the society as a whole, for example, does the organization work for improvements in racial and gender equity? Or more generally: *Do inside changes reflect the striving for democratic development in society?*

The concept of client value

It can be argued that client value is not a dimension of its own. Output quality reflects the value clients give the output, in its subjective or functional component. However, stage 4 of the model focuses on the ways the organization actually deals with its clients, for its output to be useful. Thus the model at this stage emphasizes the external interaction with clients and its reflection in terms of internal attention to demands. So the "staircase studies" which have been carried out have been confined to measurements inside the organization or its interface and not in the recipient client system. Client studies would contribute to the picture of organization development, but they also require resources. A question which could be elaborated on is: *How is the organization and its output perceived by the client?*

The model in itself does not in any way exclude elaboration on the above questions. It is perfectly possible to shed light on both internal and external conditions within its framework. However, development of checklists and measurement tools for different applications would definitely be an important, and welcome, contribution to the model.

Göran Andersson has a Master of Business Administration degree from Uppsala University. He has worked as a teacher at the Department of Business Administration, Uppsala University, at the Swedish Agency for Administrative Development and the Swedish Central Organization for Salaried Employees (TCO, *Tjänstemännens Centralorganisation*), and at the Sida Office in Tanzania. Since 1984 he has been a consultant within development assistance and one of the owners of SIPU International (Swedish Institute for Public Administration).

Peter Winai, Ph.D., is associate professor at the School of Business, Stockholm University and Managing Director of GOAB Intermanage, working with institutional development in Sweden and internationally. Previous experience includes work at the UNDP Office, Lesotho, the Swedish Agency for Administrative Development, the Port of Stockholm and Sevenco Consultants, dealing mainly with leadership questions.

Capacity Building in Africa—The Role of Multilateral Financial Institutions (MFIs)

Henock Kifle

Introduction

The importance of capacity building for sustained economic development and transformation in Africa is now almost universally recognized. Indeed, capacity building has alternatively been identified as the "missing *link*" in Africa's development, or as the "key" to Africa's accelerated development. There can be little argument with the emphasis that is nowadays placed on this issue. National development capacities—broadly understood as a nation's collective capacity to chart and implement *its societal development project*—is undoubtedly a *sine quo non* for development. Without such capacity, "development" is bound to be unsustainable.

The record of development in Africa, and in particular the record of the last two decades, however, points to rather limited achievements in creating the essential capacity for development. Few countries have succeeded in building up their developmental capacity—as manifested in the build-up of the requisite human resources and skills and in the emergence of strong public and private sector institutions and organizations—so that it is sufficient to enable them to chart and manage their development autonomously. The challenge of capacity building in Africa thus remains.

This paper addresses some of the salient aspects of this challenge. In the next section, an overview of the challenge is presented from a historical perspective, with a view to drawing out a number of important lessons from the experience of the past. In the third section, an attempt is made to identify some of the strategic areas of interventions that are required to arrest the deterioration of capacity in the public sector and to build and strengthen it. In the fourth section, some of the key areas that multilateral financial institutions (MFIs) could consider for support to capacity building initiatives are delineated. The experience of the African Development Bank is used as a backdrop for the discussion, and the importance and the desirability of co-ordination and concerted action among MFIs and, more broadly, among the donor community, is emphasized.

Capacity building in historical perspectives

At the time of their independence from colonial rule, most African countries had limited indigenous capacity for development. While colonialism did leave behind in some countries the rudiments of a functioning bureaucracy and a public administration system, most of the key positions in government were, however, manned by expatriates. Moreover, few countries had at the time the cadre of trained and educated personnel required for the efficient management of the government or the economy. Indeed, in some countries, the number of college graduates at the time of independence was said to number only a handful.

In the initial decades following independence, most African countries began to invest heavily in their social sectors, and in particular in education and health. As a result, impressive achievements were made in increasing the levels of school enrolment, the adult literacy rate, as well as in increasing life expectancy, and reducing child mortality.[1] And in time, many countries did start producing significant numbers of secondary school and college graduates. Some progress had thus started to be made towards increasing the general capacity of the population for development. Significant inroads were also made towards building up the capacity of governments to manage their nation's development.

Capacity building is, however, a long-term process, requiring favourable conditions to prevail in both the political and economic realms. The economic crisis that a large number of countries began to face in the mid-1970s—following the onset of the first oil crisis—and the veritable global economic crisis that followed the second oil crisis of 1979/80—not only undermined the progress made, but also served to reveal the limited gains that had been attained. The problem was

---

[1] Life expectancy which was estimated to be 40 for the countries of sub-Saharan Africa in 1960 was estimated to have increased to 52 in 1992; the adult literacy rate increased from 26 percent to 51 in 1992; and under-five child mortality is estimated to have declined from 284 per 1,000 live births to 183. See UNDP, *Human Development Report*, various issues.

further exacerbated by the political instability experienced by a large number of countries.

The adverse effects on national capacity for development that the prolonged economic and political difficulties that most African countries faced in these last two decades could be summarized as follows: a weakening of *public administration systems in general and civil service systems in particular*; a decline in the *quality of systems of education* at all levels; and, in particular, at the tertiary levels; declining *investments in the social sector*, particularly in the education and health sectors—in some countries this has resulted in a reversal of some of the gains that had been achieved in earlier periods;[2] the out-migration of significant segments of the educated elite resulting in a considerable "brain *drain*" for many countries; and a weakening of the *institutions of civil society* as a result of the prolonged economic and political crisis.

Partly in response to domestic crises, and partly in response to far-reaching changes that have occurred on the global scene, many African countries have, in the last decade, embarked on a process of fundamental economic and political reform. Many countries have sought to liberalize their economies and create a more conducive environment for private sector-led growth. And on the political plane, the reforms of the last decade have resulted in the establishment of democratic systems in some countries, and in the liberalization of political systems in many more.

While the economic and political reforms undertaken by the countries of the region are beginning to have positive impacts in terms of creating greater economic and political stability and generating positive economic growth rates, the capacity of governments and nations to push through sustained economic changes, nonetheless, continues to be weak. The need for targeted interventions in this area thus remains. In this endeavour, it is essential that capacity building interventions take into account the fundamental re-alignments that have taken place—and continue to take place—in the relations between government, civil society, and the private sector. There is thus a need to ensure that interventions to build capacity are directed to current and future needs, and not to those of the past.

---

[2] For the countries of sub-Saharan Africa, the enrolment ratio for all levels (i.e., for ages 6–23) appears to have declined from 39 percent in 1980 to 35 per cent in 1990. See UNDP, *Human Development Report*, 1994, p. 137.

Strategic areas for intervention

In considering strategic areas for intervention, not only should the contemporary reality be taken into account, it is also essential that a few key guiding principles be adhered to, in order to avoid the pitfalls and the mistakes of the past. At the outset, the importance of political and economic stability for sustained progress in capacity building needs to be stressed. While capacity building is a pre-requisite for development, it is also clear that political stability and economic development in turn support capacity building. Stability at the institutional and organizational level is also essential for capacity building in the long-term. While the institutions of government have to grow and change over time, this needs to take place within a fairly stable framework, if *learning by doing* is to be achieved and institutional memory preserved. Indeed, this is one of the fundamental reasons for developing a civil service that is autonomous, as such autonomy is required to provide it some degree of protection from political vicissitudes.

Similarly, it needs to be emphasized that interventions should ultimately aim at creating *capacity for creating capacity*. This is essential if both capacity building and the development process are to be self-sustaining. This principal can be illustrated as follows. Providing assistance for the external training of government officials responsible for economic affairs, for example, will undoubtedly contribute to the enhancement of a government's capacity for managing its economy in the short term. Long-term capacity will, however, be created only if a nation develops its capacity *to produce* the types of manpower it requires.

Capacity building efforts in the government/public sector must necessarily take into account the fundamental functions that governments—*as governments* —must discharge, as well as the new roles that the government and the public sector are expected to play in promoting economic development. However, while the classic public administration function of governments must necessarily be strengthened, the newer types of capacity that are now required to enable governments to perform their current economic functions need also to be developed. Within this new context, the following two key areas, namely, *capacity building for public administration and capacity building for effective economic management*, could be considered for particular emphasis.

Capacity building for public administration

A fundamental function of government must necessarily be the administration of the territory that it controls, and the people that inhabit it. The provision of effective public security, the adequate functioning of the judiciary system and the efficient functioning of the other branches of government are fundamental pre-requisites for a nation's welfare. They are also essential for sustained economic development and transformation in the long-term. Recent studies have, for example, demonstrated the importance of such *public goods* for sustained development and the structural transformation of economies in the long-term.

Capacity building for effective economic management

In many African countries, the role that the government is expected to play in the economy is rapidly changing, with the state no longer expected to play the dominant role it had in the past. Yet the state must still discharge effectively certain economic functions even within a private sector-led economic framework, if rapid rates of economic growth are to be achieved. This requires that certain government capacities, particularly those *for strategic planning and sound macroeconomic management* are strengthened.

All countries are today affected to one degree or another by the far-reaching and rapid changes that are taking place in the global economy. Countries thus have to devise effective national strategies to take advantage of the opportunities offered by globalization, and, as importantly, to minimize their possible adverse effects. African countries are, by all accounts, the most vulnerable to the adverse impact of globalization; yet, they are also the least prepared to cope with it. Accordingly, the capacity of governments for such strategic planning should be developed and strengthened. This will require that the capacity of key institutions such as the office of the Prime Minister/President, ministries responsible for national planning and development, national "think tanks" universities, and policy analysis units be developed.

It is now generally recognized that creating and maintaining appropriate conditions for economic growth and development require, inter alia, that governments maintain a stable macroeconomic environment. It also requires that governments provide essential public goods and services, such as public schooling and physical infrastructure, in an efficient manner. As the institutions of government in most countries in Africa lack such key capabilities, attempts will need to be made to strengthen and build up the core *economic institutions of government*. These would include government organizations such as: the Central Bank—for sound monetary policies; the Ministry of Finance—for prudent management of the fiscal resources of government; and the other line ministries such as those responsible for providing or regulating key economic services, such as infrastructural services.

As part of the build-up up of these capacities, it is clear that government personnel will need to be *trained*, and new *organizational and administrative systems* put in place. As many countries may not have the domestic capacity to train government personnel or to devise and implement new organizational and administrative systems, there will, in the short-run, be the need to use external expertise and facilities for these purposes. In the longer-term, however, sustained capacity building will require the strengthening of national and sub-regional *educational, training, and management* institutions to provide the requisite service. An innovation that is specific to the public sector, and which some countries may wish to experiment with, is the establishment of *civil service colleges* that cater specifically for the needs of the government/public sector.[3]

Multilateral financial institutions and capacity building in Africa

Multilateral financial institutions (MFIs) in general, and the African Development Bank (ADB) in particular, have historically been important players in capacity building efforts in Africa, and continue to be so today. The support that MFIs have provided can perhaps best be grouped into the following: support for *general capacity building* initiatives, as manifested in loans and grants for investments in the social sector, and, in particular, for investments in education; support to *specific institutional development* projects, often in the context of economy-wide or sector-specific adjustment loans; *project or programme-related training* undertaken by the MFIs themselves, including high-level policy seminars and training at enhancing development management;

---

[3] Some countries in Francophone Africa, such as Côte d'Ivoire and Senegal, have experimented with such colleges. A systematic evaluation of their experience in public administration capacity building could possibly yield useful results.

and *joint capacity building efforts* such as the African Capacity Building Foundation (ACBF), and the African Economic Research Consortium (AERC).

Although the impact of multilateral (and bilateral) assistance to capacity building is generally felt to be inadequate, the considerable efforts that have been made, and the considerable resources that have been made available, in support of such capacity building need to be acknowledged. In the case of the African Development Bank, for example, the resources that have been made available to regional member countries in support of investments in education and health have been quite large. During the five-year period 1989–93 (i.e. until the end of the sixth replenishment of the African Development Fund), a total of $1.75 billion was made available to regional members in support of health and education projects. This constituted 11.6 per cent of the total loans and grants made available by the Bank Group during this period.

Similarly, as part of its policy-based loans the Bank has supported various institutional strengthening and reform undertakings. Although the bulk of these loans have been used to provide balance of payments support, proceeds from the loans have also been used for activities related to capacity building. In some countries, for example, support has been provided for strengthening and reforming judicial systems; and in still others, policy-based loans have sought to bring about major reforms of the civil service. Proceeds from such loans have also provided resources for the training of government personnel.

In addition to such capacity building efforts, the Bank has sought to enhance capacity in regional member countries through the training activities of its African Development Institute (ADI). The Institute has provided project and programme training with the goal of improving the efficiency and development impact of Bank-financed projects. It has also sought to enhance the capacity for development management through the policy and development seminars it has conducted on various development issues for high-ranking government officials.[4]

---

[4] The World Bank's Economic Development Institute, as well as the IMF's Institute have provided, on a much larger scale, similar training for government officials, and, in the case of EDI, for some non-government personnel as well.

Despite these considerable efforts of the African Development Bank and the other multilateral financial institutions, there is general agreement that much remains to be done to strengthen the developmental capacity of African countries. This will, in general, call for more focused efforts in the future, as well as new interventions in certain key areas.

Priority areas for MFI interventions in the future

In the effort to give sharper focus to capacity building efforts in the future, and ensuring that capacity building does indeed become self-sustaining, the MFIs may wish to consider the adoption of two basic principles to guide their interventions in the future. First, MFIs should target their interventions to *capacity building in the economic arena*, as too large an agenda could result in the dilution of efforts. In this regard, a case can indeed be made that bilateral organizations and NGOs would have a greater comparative advantage in assisting countries to develop their capacity in other areas—such as capacity building in public administration and in civil society. Second, as a number of studies have pointed out, MFIs (and the donor community in general) should accept that capacity building must ultimately be *the responsibility of the countries themselves*. For if such efforts are to succeed, countries must demonstrate a commitment to their own capacity building by putting in place a coherent long-term strategy and by implementing it. Within this broad framework, MFIs may consider supporting the following capacity building efforts.

Priority to investments in the social sectors

As in the recent past, MFIs should continue to support the efforts of governments to build up their human resource base by providing resources for investments in the educational and health areas. In the case of the African Development Bank Group, this has indeed been a priority in the past, and will remain so for the future—particularly for the African Development Fund. Investments in the social sector continue to be essential for building up the general capacity of countries for development. In this regard, it should be recalled that many studies have shown that the returns to investments in primary and secondary education continue to be high.

Support for building up the core economic capabilities of governments

There is a need to build up the core economic capacities of governments, if governments are to provide the essential environment and support for sustained economic growth. Although, this is an area of capacity building that is most suited to MFIs, past efforts have generally been ad hoc and sector specific. Much would thus be gained by adopting a more *comprehensive and co-ordinated* approach.

Revitalizing African universities and institutions of higher learning

As argued above, sustained long-term capacity building will require that countries develop *their capacity to create capacity*. This will require the re-constitution and building up of African universities and higher institutions of learning. Clearly, MFIs can play a large role in this undertaking. In this renewed effort, however, new policies to enable these institutions to become more self-sustaining and less dependent on government support must be sought.

Strengthening of regional/sub-regional training institutions

In addition to helping countries revitalize their institutions of higher learning, a major effort should also be made to strengthen regional and sub-regional training institutions, particularly in the area of management training. Given the high costs of such training in the advanced countries, a case can indeed be made for strengthening a few high quality sub-regional training institutions.

Broader international co-operation for capacity building

The international donor community has in the past co-operated in a number of region-wide capacity building efforts. These include the African Capacity Building Foundation (ACBF), the African Economic Research Consortium (AERC), and the Council for the Development of Social Research in Africa (CODESRIA).[5] As a result of the success that these organizations have achieved in capacity building, these organizations are increasingly viewed as important African capacity

---

[5] Other co-operative undertakings are the UNEDIL Programme for Strengthening Management Institutions in Africa (UNDP, EDI, and ILO), and the Agricultural Management Training Programme for Africa—AMTA—(IFAD, ADB, and EDI).

building institutions in their respective areas. These programmes are thus a testimony to the success that can be achieved in international co-operative efforts at capacity building. The MFIs should therefore consider strengthening and expanding these programmes, as well as launching similar undertakings, with the involvement of both multi-lateral and bilateral donor agencies. Co-ordination of such efforts can perhaps be achieved within the new capacity building initiative that has been launched by a number of African governments in co-opera-tion with the World Bank.

Conclusions

It has been argued in this paper that although the importance of capacity building for sustained development is now almost univer-sally recognized, the record of achievement of African countries in this regard remains far from satisfactory. And while the limited gains are historically accounted for by the limited legacy of colonial rule, the political and economic difficulties that have beset a large number of countries in Africa in the last two decades also account for the current state of affairs. Thus, given the low level of development of capacity in the region, the need for targeted interventions in this area remains a high priority.

It has also been stressed in the paper that current efforts at capac-ity building for development must necessarily take into account the considerable political and economic changes that have taken place in the region in the last decade, as well as the recent evolution in devel-opment thinking. In addition, such efforts should be informed by im-portant lessons from the past. A few in particular stand out: success in capacity building requires *political and economic stability*, as well as organizational institutional stability; there is a need to develop *capac-ity for capacity building*, if capacity building is to be sustainable in the long run; and *national leadership and commitment* are essential for sus-tained progress.

The paper has argued that support for capacity building by the multilateral financial institutions (MFIs) should largely be restricted to the economic arena, as too large an agenda could dilute their efforts and impact. Within this framework, it has been suggested that capac-ity building should focus on four strategic areas, namely: continued support for investments in the social sectors; support for building up the core economic capacities of governments; revitalizing African universities and institutions of higher learning; and strengthening of regional/sub-regional training institutions. In all the capacity building efforts that MFIs may engage in, it is evident that close co-operation and co-ordination among the international donor community would be productive. Indeed, in those few cases where the donor community has acted in such a manner, important achievements have been recorded.

Henock Kifle is the Director of the African Development Institute of the African Development Bank (ADB). During the period 1969–76, he served in various capacities in the Ethiopian Government, including that of Permanent Secretary of the Ministry of Agriculture. Since then he has worked extensively on African development issues for the ADB and other international development organizations.

References

African Capacity Building Foundation, 1996, *1995 Annual Report*. Harare: ACBF.

African Development Bank, 1993, *Governance and Development in Africa: Issues, and the Role of the African Development Bank and Other Multilateral Financial Institutions*. Abidjan: ADB.

African Development Bank, 1996, *Compendium of Statistics*. Abidjan: ADB.

CAC International, 1996, "Final Report: Summative and Prospective Evaluation of the UNEDIL Programme 19857–1995".

Deng, L. et al., 1991, *Democratization and Structural Adjustment in Africa in the 1990s*. Madison: African Studies Program, University of Wisconsin.

Deepak Lal and H. Myint, 1996, *The Political Economy of Poverty, Equity and Growth*. Oxford: Clarendon Press.

Dia, Mamadou, 1996, *Africa's Management in the 1990s and beyond: Reconciling Indigenous and Transplanted Institutions*. Washington, DC: World Bank.

Economic Commission for Africa, 1996, *A Framework Agenda for Building and Utilising Critical Capacities in Africa*. Addis Ababa: ECA.

Jaycox, E.V.K., 1993, "Capacity Building: The Missing Link in African Development". Transcript of Address to the African-American Institute Conference, 1993.

United Nations Development Programme, *Human Development Report*. New York: Oxford University Press, various issues.

World Bank, 1989, *Sub-Saharan Africa: From Crisis to Sustainable Growth*. Washington, DC: World Bank.

World Bank, 1995, *A Continent in Transition: Sub-Saharan Africa in the mid-1990s.* Washington, DC: World Bank.

World Bank, 1996, *Partnership for Capacity Building in Africa.* Washington, DC: World Bank.

Building Sustainable Capacity and Institutions in Africa

Apollinaire Ndorukwigira

Introduction

In recent years, the world economy has accelerated its globalization and all countries now face the challenging task of adjusting to the new environment in order to benefit from the opportunities thus created. Africa is among the least prepared continents to face these new developments. Despite recent improvement in growth performance by a large number of African countries, the majority of states are still characterized by weak capacity to formulate development policies and ineffective bureaucracies to implement strategic priorities and development programmes.

The recognition of the critical role of the state in fostering economic growth and in alleviating poverty has brought to the fore the question of the capacity of the state to formulate policy and implement development programs. African governments have embarked on economic reforms by adopting policies aimed at creating a macroeconomic environment conducive to increased private investments and sustainable growth. In the process, they have benefited considerably from technical advice provided by donors. However, in the majority of cases, accompanying measures to the reform programs were taken to ensure efficient implementation of those programs but they did not sufficiently take into account the need to build indigenous capacity to sustain the reforms. Most of the instruments used to support the reforms were drawn from the recipes of technical co-operation which gave primacy to short-term results instead of focusing on institution building.

Capacity building entails both skills enhancement and institution strengthening, and was hailed as the missing link in the development strategies supported by donors in Africa over the last 30 years. While there is an emerging consensus that capacity building is central to the development nexus, the question is how to ensure sustainability of

capacity-building interventions in order to avoid the pitfalls of technical cooperation experiences in Africa.

The goal of capacity and institution building is to create efficient and responsive institutions and sustainability could be considered as one outcome of an effective intervention. The critical question is not whether donor-supported projects are sustainable but whether the capacity created through a project is sustainable.

This paper attempts to discuss the issue of sustainability of interventions aimed at enhancing human and institutional capacity in the area of policy analysis and economic management. The lessons learned from the experience of the African Capacity Building Foundation (ACBF) in strengthening capacity in economic management could also be applied to other sectors where there is a need for institution strengthening and capacity enhancement.

Factors affecting sustainability[1]

For capacity building projects to survive and prosper beyond the initial funding stages, there must be a modicum of political and economic stability, low risk of violent social conflict, an atmosphere of support for the capacity building effort from political and economic elites as well as interest groups. The following elements of the enabling environment for capacity building should be viewed as interacting and mutually reinforcing.

– *Stability and predictability.* Political stability implies that power and governing authority in a given national setting is neither exercised nor challenged through resort to violence or other means that provoke social upheavals. Economic stability means that national production and consumption are not subject to large fluctuations from year to year.

– *Local ownership.* Ownership entails, first, the commitment of national authorities. There must be a demonstration of willingness to utilize the capacities. The second critical aspect of ownership involves the support of civil society in recipient countries. It is critical that politically influential elites are favourable to capacity building ideas, but also that it is not unpopular with the population at large.

---

[1] This section bases itself on the paper *ACBF, The Sustainability of ACBF Funded Projects* of December 1994.

- *Good governance*. This entails the presence of five critical qualities: accountability of government officials, transparency in procedures and decision making, predictability of government actions and behaviour, openness in the provision of reliable flows of information, the rule of law permitting economic agents to operate without risking arbitrary action of the state.

- *Supportive of local conditions*. The civil service environment must not provide rewards to employees on the basis of patronage and personal connections, nor be an environment in which compensation is inadequate, or in which there are no institutional protections from political interference.

- *Local sources of funding*. In the long-run a key to sustaining capacity building projects will be the availability of local sources of funding.

- *Donor attitudes*. There must be a commitment of donors to lessen their provision of expatriate assistance at low or zero cost to African authorities. The ready availability of technical assistance has had a major impact on the thinking of local authorities, in perpetuating their comfort through avoiding the political or financial costs involved with committing themselves to the development of local capacity.

Circumstances will never be ideal with respect to these criteria. It is therefore important to make an in-depth assessment of the enabling environment, before entering into a project design phase. The point of departure for such an assessment should be the realisation that sustainability requires a governance framework which will establish a minimum of cohesion and stability in the organizational structure of government, consistent with the society's vision of its social and economic development goals. Any assessment of the conditions for sustainability could then focus on three basic conditions: the institutional framework, the capacity of the civil service and the budget process. Below we shall discus each of these in more detail.

Restructuring the institutional framework

An enabling environment for capacity building would demand a strong commitment on the part of the government to undertake a far-reaching *review of existing institutional frameworks* in order to establish a deep-rooted system of accountability of government institutions responsible for the management of the development process.

This commitment could be demonstrated by the political leadership in launching a broad-based consultation including the government bureaucracy, the private sector and the civil society. From this consultative process, a broad vision on the role of the state should emerge. This vision should in turn be translated into specific policy guidelines that will clarify the mandates and functions of public institutions responsible for policy formulation and co-ordination as well as for the delivery of services to the public.

Depending on the country's institutional environment and capacity, the task of restructuring the institutional framework could be assigned to an elite corps of senior officials drawn from key economic agencies and influential members of the private sector and the civil society. This approach could be applied more successfully in a country with an established tradition of centralized governance which ensures peace, enforcement of laws, and the guarantee of social mobility for its citizenry. If the task of restructuring the government machinery is to be successful, the designated body leading the reform exercise must enjoy access to and the support of the political leadership. It must also have credibility vis-à-vis the public and donors. The credibility from the public could be gained through a process of consultation with key stakeholders and by having the required autonomy to implement the programs approved by the political leadership.

Institution development is a slow process. As a result, like any other long-term investment, it will require a stable and predictable institutional framework in order to flourish. The clarification of the institutional framework will facilitate the process of determining the profile of human resources required for supporting policy formulation and policy management as well as programme implementation and evaluation.

Capacity building interventions should be selective. However, where there is explicit demand for supporting a process of institutional reform or rehabilitation, assistance should be provided. Since 1992, ACBF has extended support to capacity building programs in more than 16 sub-Saharan African countries. The foundation pursued a demand-driven strategy, and although an established record of commitment to economic reform was often taken into account, it was not the determining factor in lending support to the recipient country.

Countries which benefited from ACBF assistance were at various stages of economic reform and management capacity. Some of these countries had relatively more efficient bureaucracies (Senegal, Côte d'Ivoire and Ghana), whereas others had weak administrative capacity given that they were emerging from long periods of civil strife or economic decay.

In all those countries, the nature of ACBF's intervention was tailored to the country's environment. In some countries, priority was given to the enhancement of policy formulation capacity within the public sector, whereas other capacity-building programmes focused on strengthening the management capacity of institutions responsible for policy co-ordination and management.

It is still too early to assess the impact of projects aimed at enhancing policy formulation capacity on the overall policy environment of recipient countries. But there is growing evidence that governments and other professional associations are seeking advice from local policy institutes on a wide range of policy issues, including macroeconomic and sectoral reform policies. This represents a change in the decision making culture of those governments, and such culture enhances ownership and commitment to home-grown development strategies which are pre-requisites for an effective co-ordination of development assistance by government. The sustainability of the policy formulation and co-ordination capacity created with donor assistance depends on the ability of the recipient government to retain skilled policy analysts and development managers.

Revitalizing the civil service

Reforming the civil service in Africa will require bold decisions on the part of the political leadership. A more focused role of the state and a review of effective ways of delivering social services and maintaining infrastructure will have a direct effect on the size of the state bureaucracy. This more focused role of the state must be the result of a continuous appraisal of the institutional environment which allows government to strategize its reform priorities based on clearly identified constraints and opportunities as well as focal points for implementing its agenda for institutional change.

Building effective public institutions relies on the availability of a corps of motivated, competent and dedicated civil servants. Over the last decade, donors and governments undertook to empower local experts in the management of development projects as a means of improving the effectiveness of technical co-operation. This represented a step in the right direction for building indigenous capacity.

ACBF-supported programs were preferably located in existing institutions. However, broad operational autonomy was granted to the project implementation units by the recipient institutions to ensure that resources allocated to the projects were not diverted to other purposes. Senior officials heading the government structure benefiting from the intervention were intimately associated in the supervision of the project management unit. They were involved in setting project priorities and drawing up annual work programs as well as in the review of the performance of the units concerned.

ACBF's involvement in project management is minimal. However, the foundation requires that the project present satisfactory administrative and financial procedures, including clear procurement and sound auditing procedures. This contributes to strengthening project management capacity and enhances the accountability of the recipient. This approach has the advantage of reducing the administrative burdens imposed on the recipients and may create conditions for a smooth take-over of the project activities by the recipient. One major hurdle to sustainability of projects remains the limited capacity of the public administration to offer attractive salaries to the policy analysts and development managers. Only Zambia has undertaken to offer competitive salaries to staff assigned to the project. This situation is less serious in countries such as Botswana and Namibia where the civil service offers competitive salaries.

If African governments are to be successful in leading the development agenda of their countries and in creating the necessary capacity to manage development programs, then they must commit themselves to far-reaching civil service reform. The deepening of civil service reform enables the establishment of competitive salaries and flexible employment schemes which will allow the funding of specific skills through contractual arrangements. Government must plan a gradual take-over by the recurrent budget of the funding of those specialized services supplied by the bureaucracy or out-sourced to other local institutions. The need to increase the competitiveness of the public sector incentive system cannot be overemphasized. For senior officials who are responsible for the management of development programs and regulating the economy, it is critical that the state provide an environment that will foster professional excellence and reduce corruption. Despite the disappointing results of civil service reforms in the past, donors should be prepared to support reforms where there is a demonstrated commitment to serious civil service reform initiatives.

Budget reform as a focal point for institutional development

In Africa, development programs have been largely ineffective, and even apparently successful adjustment programs failed to restore the robust economic growth necessary to reduce poverty. Despite considerable donor assistance in improving policy frameworks, the fact remains that Africa does not have the management capacity necessary for sustaining the policy orientations brought about by the reform programs. An entry point to strengthening management capacity is the reform of the budget process.

Donors' assistance to bold administrative reforms, including support to salary rationalisation efforts should be time-bound and linked to the performance of budget reforms aimed at creating more transparency in the budget process. The macroeconomic framework, planning and investment programming should be integrated in the budget process. The transparency of the budget process is a key element in the effort to restore fiscal discipline and fight corruption. Efforts to ensure donor co-ordination of development aid will remain largely inefficient as long as they are not grounded in a budget reform program. Past efforts to reform the budget process were fragmented and limited in scope. They focused on streamlining administrative and accounting procedures without connecting them to the reform of the planning, investment and debt management process.

Public expenditure reviews were not used as an instrument to assess the effectiveness of government programs, and no subsequent dialogue was initiated with implementing agencies in order to improve management practices and investment decisions. Co-ordination between civil service reform and the budget process could contribute to strengthening the management capacity of government agencies and to providing a more rigorous basis for down-sizing public administrations. A successful budget reform effort, combined with an effective civil service reform, will create conditions for sustainability of donor-funded programs by ensuring their take-over by the government recurrent expenditures budget, including competitive salaries paid to specialized personnel working in development projects.

Summary and conclusions

This paper has attempted to show that building sustainable capacity must start with a clear understanding of the institutional environment. It appears also that the task of conducting an institutional environment assessment must follow a participatory process in which top-level officials as well as other stakeholders are fully involved. The outcome of this institutional appraisal provides a framework for institutional reforms which clarify the role of government and the functions and responsibilities of public institutions involved in economic management and policy co-ordination.

In order to create a virtuous cycle of strengthening institutional capacity and creating a policy environment conducive to growth, it would be necessary to tackle the problems of civil service and budget reforms. The responsibility of leading these challenging reforms lies in the hands of African governments themselves. The leadership must demonstrate that the framework for institutional change is indeed a domestic response to clearly identified development challenges rather than an undertaking resulting from conditionalities imposed by donors. Capacity and institution development is a long-term process. Donors should be prepared to commit themselves to supporting well thought through institutional reform programs which will put the responsibility for their implementation in the hands of African governments.

Why could Africa succeed today in this challenging undertaking of building sustainable institutions when past efforts have failed ? With few exceptions, the majority of African countries gained independence in the context of the cold war. Despite the very good intentions of nationalist leaders to improve the welfare of their people, they did not have the administrative capacity to assess the soundness of their economic policies and development programs. Until late 1980s, bilateral as well as multilateral donors did not place a high premium on policy environment as a criterion for providing development aid. Strategic considerations were the dominant factor in the allocation of aid.

Despite the dismal record of economic growth and the deterioration of the standards of living of the majority of the population in many African countries, an educated elite forming a new pressure group through the civil society and a small middle class have emerged. The civil society is made up of trade unions, teachers' and student associations, religious groups as well as trade and manufacturing associations. These internal developments together with the end of the cold war have changed the political environment within African countries , and their leaders can no longer enjoy a free ride in the way they manage their countries.

Against this backdrop, a new brand of leaders committed to the development of their countries has emerged which has created unprecedented opportunities for tackling some of the challenging policy reforms under the leadership of Africans themselves. This opportunity should not be missed as deserving reformers should be supported through provision of technical and financial assistance in order to create a sustainable enabling environment for economic growth and poverty reduction.

Apollinaire Ndorukwigira, Ph.D., is Principal Programme Officer at the African Capacity Building Foundation (ACBF) in Harare, Zimbabwe. He joined ACBF in 1992 and has been involved in the design of projects aimed at strengthening policy analysis and management capacity in Africa.

References

Berg, Elliot J., 1993, *Rethinking Technical Co-operation*.New York: UNDP/DAI publications.

Burnside, Craig and David Dollar, 1997, "Aid Spurs Growth in a Sound Policy Environment", *Finance and Development*, December 1997. Washington DC: World Bank.

Land, Anthony, 1995, *Management Audit and Self-Assessment in the Public Sector: Lessons from a Capacity Development Exercise in Zambia*. ECDPM Working Paper 95–3, Maastricht.

van de Walle, Nicholas, 1997, *Improving Aid: Preliminary Policy Conclusions of a Collaborative Project on Aid Effectiveness in Africa*. Washington DC: Oversees Development Council.

World Bank, 1997, *World Development Report*, June 1997. Washington DC: World Bank.

Experiences of Financial Management Development in Eastern and Southern Africa

Åke Sahlin and Peter Murphy

This article is based on experiences of public sector financial management development work in Eastern and Southern Africa. The experiences and lessons learnt presented below are based on work in a number of countries in the region as well as current co-operation with the region's accountants general aimed at documenting and exchanging experiences in the field of government accounting. However, we believe that our experiences represent conclusions that reflect the basic conditions for financial management that prevail in most of the countries in question.

In theory, financial management is a tool for promoting and controlling the efficient implementation of government policies and priorities utilizing scarce resources. In practice, a number of common approaches, methods and tools can be identified which together comprise the framework for financial management. The application of these is limited by political, organizational and technical factors as well as by the availability of human resources with sufficient skills and experiences.

The institutions directly concerned with aspects of government financial management are the central bank (monetary policy, balance of payments, control of inflation, regulation of financial institutions), the planning function at a ministry of planning, a president's office or a prime minister's office (economic growth, macro economic planning, sectoral planning) and the ministry of finance (fiscal policy, expenditure, taxation, government financing, off budget expenditure, parastatals).

The interface between the political system and the public administration

The use of financial management as an instrument for policy implementation can be assessed from various angles. Financial management is one important component of the interface between the political system and the public administration and is therefore a fundamental issue which holds the key to success in many cases and situations.

Sound management and utilisation of resources in accordance with government policies and priorities require that these are:

– clearly formulated;

– supported by the executive and the administration;

– understood at the level of implementation; and

– that the complimentary inputs exist which will enable implementation.

In practice there are a number of major problems which, taken together with the absence of an effective parliamentary opposition, inhibit effective policy making, co-ordination and decision making. These include:

– vested interests at all levels which result in serious conflicts between personal/party and public interests, and

– weak political leadership with an ill defined political ideology or direction resulting in inadequate definition and cohesion, inadequate leadership direction, poor management and implementation capacity.

These problems result in fragmentation of the government's decision making bodies (cabinet, PS's groups etc.) at all levels which negatively effects activities requiring a high degree of co-ordination. In the financial field this has meant weak planning, budgeting, budget execution and financial control year after year resulting in budgets which are substantially overcommitted or underfunded. These overcommitments arise from:

– many years of making investments (often unproductive) and expanding services without ensuring adequate recurrent financing;

– inadequate efforts to secure necessary revenue collection and over-reliance on donor funding;

– mismanagement and low productivity;

– inadequate or ineffective co-ordination of external support; and

– in some cases massive and uncontrolled corruption and fraud.

In some cases it appears that it is only external pressure from bodies such as the IMF, the World Bank and from the donor community which can impose any discipline or co-ordination on the system. However, paradoxically, where discipline is supplied externally then the political situation can destabilize as resistance mounts from the groups whose vested interests are threatened. Obviously these are powerful arguments for democracy with an effective opposition.

Democracy, financial management and institution building

Many of the Eastern and Southern African countries have recently held multi-party elections for the first time since independence. Pressurized by various donors and in some cases domestic public opinion, transition to a western style political system has taken place quickly and sometimes without sufficient concern about the implications of such change for the *institutional system* which is in place in implementing policies and priorities formulated at the political level.

At the level of the parliament, multi-party democracy requires that a mechanism exists which allows for negotiations between the political forces in parliament to secure the necessary support for new policies or a re-allocation between major programmes. Given the complexity of government operations and the many "technical" issues that are involved, for example in the budget process from the issuing of a call circular to the final approval of the budget by parliament, an organizational body is required where a professional in-depth analysis and discussion can take place and where various solutions can be negotiated. We believe that it is essential to have a functioning budget committee in place at an early stage. In principle, this also applies to countries where elections have given one party a strong majority for the first term.

Current practice on the expenditure side continues to support approval of detailed input oriented rather than output oriented budgets. This practice serves to inhibit effective discussions about the budget, performance analysis by the central institutions and sound budget execution by budget managers. In effect:

– parliament approves salary and other payments without any clear idea of what then money will be spent on;

– the central institutions have no real basis for assessment of budgetary performance; and

- managers have no specific measurable goals that they are required to achieve.

A third important, often overlooked, organizational issue is the need for a strong so called *linking pin* between the political structure and the administrative system. In a multi-party environment the actual co-ordination of political issues, policies and government activities normally takes place within the prime minister's office on the basis of cabinet decisions. The financial implications of such issues and decisions are subsequently dealt with by the ministry of finance. How well this works depends to a great extent on the quality of the interaction between the prime-minister's office and the ministry of finance.

Once again it can be stated that the transition to multi-party democracy requires adaptation in both the role and functions of entities within the existing structure. During one party rule, it seems as if there was a tendency to let more of the political co-ordination take place at the level of the ministry of finance while the prime minister's office had more of a subordinate role. The minister of finance and his permanent secretary dealt directly with the cabinet and other line-ministries.

The development of a more appropriate structure requires that the prime-minister's office is given not only a clear mandate but also that relevant competence is made available for the office to be able to act with the necessary authority.

The role of a ministry of finance in the public administration

Given the above, the main role for a ministry of finance today is to serve as the unit within the political and administrative structure that promotes the idea that all government activities and decisions are made on a *rational basis*. This means not only that the decision or activity should be cost efficient but also that it should contribute to the accomplishment or fulfilment of overall government visions and objectives concerning the country's social, industrial and economic development.

The rationale for the latter is that an economy or a public administration always runs the risk that sectoral interests through line-ministries emphasize their own objectives and programmes, something which might not always be in the best interest of the overall economy since financial and administrative implications of different decisions might counteract each other. To be able to carry out this function, a ministry of finance must be furnished with competence as well as sufficient political backing. In this context the relationship and interaction between the ministry and the prime-minister's office becomes important as a means of solving conflicts of interest as well as dealing with financial and administrative consequences of political decisions.

Political backing for the ministry of finance is of great importance for all aspects of financial management. This is most obvious in the development and execution of the government budget, the resource allocation process. Political backing for discussions between the Ministry of Finance and the line ministries on allocations, revenue raising and financing should be secured from the very beginning of the planning cycle by the prime minister's office. A joint document to cabinet should be produces for the cabinet outlining the options within the framework of macro economic limits and sectoral goals. This must then be discussed, agreed upon and approved.

The more detailed budget guidelines should then be constructed by the ministry of finance on the basis of this memorandum and the discussions. This would give detailed direction and guidance on policies, priorities etc., and hopefully resolve all but the most difficult or sensitive issues. Rolling plan and forward budgeting processes have been introduced (by planning functions) in some developing countries in an attempt to do this, but currently these appear to be more of a technical than political exercise and have only marginal influence on the outcome of the budget process.

It is vital that the prime minister or cabinet secretary support the ministry of finance within the agreed options outlined in the budget policy memorandum. This should result in the responsible ministers resolving conflicts within the overall guidelines. Again this does not always appear to happen. It is the ministry of finance which is left to make priorities and arbitrary cuts. In fact the resource allocation process at this stage can easily degenerate into a war between ministers and their staff as to who is to get what. Quite often battles are over a few specific items or projects which are of particular interest to one ministry but which may be inconsistent with the overall budget framework or of a low priority.

Much less attention is given to the real problems associated with restructuring or the need to improve efficiency and effectiveness or revenue generation arising from the changing needs and economic situations. In other words at the end of the day the resource allocation process represents little more than an unrealistic plan involving largely a continuation of existing programmes at a level which cannot be financed and in which no one is seriously committed to achieving any special outcomes.

Similarly once the budget has passed into law all parties should be committed to its content (in theory at least they have no choice in the matter) during execution. Real consensus at cabinet and PS level might ensure this. However since consensus is often limited, commitment is lacking and the budget is unrealistic the result has been non-compliance and substantial overspending. This outcome is reinforced if the spending agencies are subsequently allowed to overspend at will.

All this results from inadequate political commitment and interest in developing an implementable plan of action consistent with the needs of the community and the available resources

An additional task of importance for a ministry of finance is to predict the development of government revenues in order to plan for future increase (or decrease) in government spending. Many African countries are faced with a situation where important sources of income are beyond their immediate control; remittances from migrant workers, development aid, customs duties etc. Therefore, a ministry of finance also has to enforce a policy where a high level of flexibility is maintained in the more costly programmes.

To summarize, a well functioning public sector financial management system requires that the ministry of finance concurrently performs the roles of:

– managing the government's finances, controlling spending and maintaining flexibility to be able to adjust these to changes in levels of revenues;

– promoting rationality in government decision making at sectoral level in relation to overall political goals and ambitions; and

– functioning as co-ordinator and assisting in solving conflicts of interest within the cabinet or line-ministries.

Carrying out the above tasks does not necessarily mean that the ministry of finance itself has to be expanded into a "super-ministry". Such a development could in itself lead to sub-optimisation where the ministry starts looking at it own specific interests rather than looking at the totality of government operations. However, additional competence is often required, for example the budget department should have expertise representing the sectors it is dealing with within its ranks. Obviously, some of the traditional administrative tasks such as tax administration and regulation of the financial sector should be maintained as items on the agenda for a ministry of finance.

Accountability

The issue of accountability in the government sector is closely related to the transition which is taking place in many African societies towards multi-party democracy. At the political level people have often in the past not been held accountable for the simple reason that audited financial reports and statements were not produced at all or after years of delay. The absence of an organized political opposition and the necessary institutional mechanisms contributed to a situation where the other side of the coin, the quality and availability of public services were not discussed or at least not measured against the cost of producing them. Furthermore, holding officials accountable requires that there is within the structure an institution which has the mandate and the instruments necessary to react in cases of misappropriation or mismanagement and which is willing to actually do so.

There are many other dimensions to the issue of accountability than simply the political aspect. Within the public administration, or any other organization, people at lower levels should be held accountable for delegated tasks or current programmes for which they are given the responsibility. The organizational culture in African public administration with a highly centralized decision making process has not promoted the idea of delegating authority with its resultant taking of responsibility. Poor information systems with unreliable or no available data on physical progress and resource consumption have also obstructed the introduction of what could be perceived as more appropriate management techniques. Finally, the absence of systems for feedback from users of public services has prevented public administration officials from being forced into a dialogue which would demand they take responsibility for their actions.

Financial management as a tool for decision making at sector or programme level

The efficient use of scarce resources to provide public services in accordance with political priorities and ambitions mainly depends on how the manager at the programme level perceives his role and to what extent he uses information from the financial management system and other similar sources in the decision making process. By choosing between various methods or resources for the production of a certain service, the programme manager has the opportunity to improve efficiency and learn from previous periods and situations.

The financial management system is in this process a powerful tool which, if properly designed, can provide useful information for the programme manager. For this to happen, certain conditions must be fulfilled. The manager must perceive himself or herself as a manager who participates in a recurrent production process where he or she has the mandate and is expected to create a learning situation which gradually leads to improved performance. According to our experience, further discussed in Jerker Carlsson's chapter of this book, the African management and organizational culture does not encourage that kind of leadership. For example, the introduction of programme budgeting requires not only training in budget techniques but also more basic management training which promotes the idea that being a manager is more than just being placed at a higher level in the organization. Therefore, it is easy to underestimate the time required for the introduction of management tools such as new budgeting techniques.

Building up demand for management information

An issue closely related to the above discussion is how a demand for management information can be built up. With the introduction of modern data processing capacity, programme managers at line-ministry level are offered a range of reports and data compilation options. A problem in this respect is the tendency for information to be supply driven. Central ministries such as a ministry of finance tend to be exposed to data processing systems and receive assistance to develop them much earlier than line-ministries which may even maintain manual systems. Therefore, it is likely that units such as a treasury or a budget office take the lead in systems development and move much faster than the rest of the public administration.

For a financial management system to contribute to increased efficiency, the programme manager must also understand that a financial management system could provide more information than only *accounting data*. The development and effective utilisation of a *management information system* require that the environment within which the manager operates is strengthened in terms of systems and procedures, but more importantly that the idea of active, improvement oriented management is promoted. We have seen cases where the functional systems offer multiple data processing and report generating facilities than nobody would ever dream of requesting because the management culture within the organization does not promote risk taking or change.

A lesson learnt from the above is that a development process must always balance central ministry systems development with organization and management development efforts among the users of financial information. Otherwise, the financial system ends up providing accurate and up-to-date accounting information for external use which in itself might have a value but does not necessarily contribute to increased efficiency in the production of public services.

Developing a development capacity

Promoting sound financial management, for example in the context of aid financed development projects, encompasses not only the strengthening of existing systems and procedures, introduction of new tools or staff training. A crucial issue when designing a development project is also to decide to what extent the project should aim at establishing or strengthening a capacity within the administration for continued development work.

One extreme would obviously be to say that it is sufficient to establish a capacity within the ministry to maintain systems and procedures that are being introduced. Such an approach would entail training of staff on how to manage the system as well as how to deal with commonly encountered weaknesses and bottlenecks.

A totally different view on institution building and financial management systems strengthening is to consider it as a *continuous approach* where the essential aspect of the development process is to *create or further develop the ministry's ability to gradually adapt its systems and procedures* to changing conditions and an increasingly technically complex environment. The main issue is of course to what extent the established development capacity is sustainable.

Given the nature of the operations within a ministry of finance and in particular a treasury, one would argue that systems development should be carried out as an internal task. Unfortunately, history has shown the difficulties of governments and public administrations to keep skilled manpower on their pay-roll. The competition from the private sector with its often better conditions of employment is in many cases too stiff and the public administration ends up in a vicious circle where it trains staff who soon leave their positions for greener pastures elsewhere. This is for example the case among computer programmers in many countries in the region. The obvious risk in this situation is that the development process continues to be dependent on foreign expertise.

An approach to this problem which has been applied with certain success in the recent past in some countries is to engage local consultants at an early stage in the development process. The aim is to bring the ministry of finance and local consultants closer to each other but also, and maybe more important, to strengthen the consultants' skills in relevant areas by making them part of the exercise.

The advantages of this approach are several. Firstly, the ministry is often less restricted in offering remunerations to a consultant than in the case of an employee where existing salary structures and regulations have to be applied, positions have to be established and so forth. Secondly, local consultants are offered an opportunity to benefit from a development exercise and to become familiar with government systems and procedures. Thirdly, the public administration is made aware of and put in touch with a resource which it might be able to afford in the future when the development project has come to an end and external financial resources have been exhausted.

The main disadvantage of the approach is the lesser degree of control that the administration has over consultants as compared to regular staff and problems of unavailability that might occur. The issue of availability could be solved through framework agreements with selected consultants who are guaranteed a certain amount of work. In return they commit themselves to being available at short notice.

Recommendations for the design of future financial management development projects

Our experiences of financial management systems development can be summarized in the following observations and recommendations which should be considered when future projects are conceived and negotiated.

The institutional framework

Successful financial management development work requires that a clear policy framework exists against which effectiveness and efficiency in government operations can be measured.

The institutional framework for implementation of policies and programmes has to change and be adjusted to the new political situation and democratic systems existing in many African countries.

Financial management systems development is an on-going process. To maintain a reasonable level of momentum in the process once external support has come to an end, support from local expertise has to be secured, preferably through participation at an early stage in the development process.

Components in a financial management programme

For financial management development to succeed, the programme has to strike a balance between development of systems, organizations, management and human resources. Modern information technology offers a series of tempting development opportunities which assumes a management approach and organizational culture which does not prevail in African public administration. The potential for organizational change defines the scope for development of financial management systems and other management information systems.

It is essential to implement financial management development as a phased activity. During the early part of the programme, an internal systems development capacity or even unit should be established and equipped to function as the pivot of the development process. Concurrently, organizational and managerial tasks and issues relating to the development process should be dealt with and necessary staff development activities be conducted.

Government financial management concerns not only the core ministries and the political level of government. The line-ministries are normally the producers of public services and potential beneficiaries of a modern financial management information system. The latter assumes that they are made part of the development process and that they understand the potential for active management which modern information technology offers.

Human resources development and personnel administration are essential aspects of a financial management development programme.

Changes in roles and responsibility including delegation of authority require not only training and motivation but also that these changes are formally recognized by a ministry of public service or a similar body. The establishment and strengthening of a professional cadre of financial managers is facilitated by a delegation of the authority to appoint members of the accounting cadre to the ministry of finance/treasury.

Management support

Given the high degree of centralization in many African organizations, successful development work requires the commitment and participation of senior management. Since financial management concerns a key aspect of government operations, no sustained development takes place unless the highest responsible officials within the organization participates and are perceived as assuming full responsibility for the change process and its outcome.

Senior management involvement seems to have a "trickle down" effect both by mobilizing human resources and putting activities in focus. The latter "information dissemination" aspect is of particular importance in a culture where information is not easily accessible at lower levels in the organization.

Åke Sahlin is Managing Director of ISO Swedish Management Group. Previously, as a senior consultant within the company Sahlin co-ordinated the company's financial management projects in Lesotho and Tanzania. Sahlin has also carried out a large number of short-term assignments in the framework of development co-operation, mainly in English-speaking Africa and in south-east Asia. For several years he was a programme co-ordinator at the ILO in Geneva.

Peter Murphy is a senior consultant at ISO Swedish Management Group and a member of the *Chartered Institute of Public Finance*. Murphy has during the last 15 years worked with financial management projects in Eastern and Southern Africa. He has been the team leader for developments projects at the Ministry of Finance in Lesotho and Tanzania respectively. He also assisted in the formation of a body for co-operation between the Accountant Generals of the region. In addition to financial management projects Murphy has devoted much attention to organization development and management issues in recent years.

Personnel Administration and Personnel Development

Christer Wallroth

Background

During the past few years the long-term effects of official development assistance have been widely debated. Many projects have been
wrongly designed in relation to specific countries' cultural environments and traditions. Solutions originally designed to apply in quite
different contexts have been used in developing countries as well.

Another reason why the results have not been sustained is the
weakness of institutions and other organizations in developing countries as regards organization and management. These institutions
have lacked the strength and ability to pursue, maintain and further
develop what has been attained with the help of development assistance. One conclusion drawn from this is that it is necessary to
develop institutions and organizations in such a way that their capacity is reinforced.

Many institutional development projects in Africa have, however,
been initiated against the background of what I have described above.
I have been involved in a range of projects with such a focus and have
had the opportunity to test out different working methods throughout
the years thereby acquiring a fairly broad experience of applied
theory.

Personnel administration—some definitions

The meaning of personnel administration has changed over the years
and concurrently with the development of the perception of human
resources. Granberg gives two definitions of the concept.[1]

---

[1] Granberg, Otto, 1989, *Personaladministration och Organisationsutveckling.* Natur och
Kultur: Stockholm.

According to the first definition personnel administration is all the contributions made to plan, carry out and follow up personnel matters. Personnel administration includes the following areas: personnel policy, personnel mobility, personnel development, salary administration, occupational safety, social activities for personnel and personnel administrative planning.

The emphasis is thus on different components of the personnel administration's area from a functional point of view.

The other definition emanates from another perspective: "personnel administration is all the contributions concerned with human capital which are carried out for the company to achieve its goals and to develop".

The Manager's Handbook[2] is a good example of this shift in perspective: the notion personnel administration no longer exists. The personnel's importance is very strongly underlined and issues regarding communication and development of people are central themes in the book. The book mirrors an important change in approach and underlines the responsibility every manager has for his/her personnel and their development. Previously it was primarily the personnel department that had this responsibility.

The above shows that the issue of development of personnel administration can be approached from two sides: either with the aim of improving and developing the personnel function within an organization, or with the aim of developing the whole organization's ability to utilize its personnel resources in order to obtain the overall objectives of the company.

Personnel administration was initially regarded as a purely salary/fiscal function, and companies' line managers were not very involved in this function's work and activities. Later, personnel administration was developed into a specialist function working with recruitment, selection, training and education, systems for salaries, etc. The line managers involvement was still limited. The latest stage of development means that each manager has a clear and expressed personnel responsibility and that personnel administration has more of a supportive role towards the line. These days, questions concerning personnel policy and development are important parts of company strategy.

---

[2] Ernst & Young, 1994, *The Manager's Handbook*. Warner Books: London.

Personnel policy and personnel development—some experiences

The perception of personnel policy outlined above is integrated in various development projects. Projects can deal with issues such as:

– development of personnel administration and managers in a country's public administration;

– development of personnel administration and managers in national telecommunications companies, one of several components in enterprise development projects. Such projects also include development of service, business lines and techniques; and

– development of organization and operations at training institutes.

The aim of the projects has been to bring about a lasting development of the organization within for example the areas of management patterns, the level of the personnel's competencies, personnel planning, communication and decision making, as well as that of managers' competencies (as managers).

The projects have been ongoing for quite some time, often for several years. Most frequently, a consultant employed for a long-term assignment has been working within the client organization, with a range of short-term experts at his/her side.

Often, the management of the organization has carried out study tours in neighbouring countries or in Sweden to learn how similar problems are tackled in other countries and organizations.

One of the most important lessons learned is that development work as regards personnel administration is strongly influenced by the organizational culture within an organization. The attitude towards change is also important.

There is also considerable experience pointing at the fact that a range of problems regarding organizational development in companies and public administrations in Africa have the same causes as similar problems in other parts of the world. Co-operation and communication problems may for example originate in the structure of the organization, or in changing job content and altered technology, and this requires development of the competence of the staff. On the other hand, the organizational culture in Africa although differing from country to country is generally unlike the one found in the Swedish public administration and companies. The most crucial distinguishing features of the African organizational culture can be described as follows:

Decision making is often very centralized. The manager (who almost always is a man) is expected to have the best knowledge about each issue and is therefore regarded as the most appropriate decision-maker. Systematic delegation is rare. Instead, questions and decisions are moved upward in the hierarchy, i.e. colleagues hand over sensitive or difficult tasks to the manager who is then supposed to solve them. Responsibility for tasks is rarely distributed according to goals, responsibilities or authorities. When the manager is away no decisions can be taken, since no one else has that authority. The handling of various issues is often done by written communication—the file system.

Team work is not common, partly due to the deeply rooted idea that a colleague's opinions are not supposed to differ from those of the manager. The availability of information is often limited since information gives power.

The educational level is overall low, but a small group has a good education, often a university degree, sometimes from abroad. Appointment to posts is often done on the grounds of formal education. At promotions, years in service are highly valued along with formal qualifications. The level of salary is in some countries so low it is impossible to live on it.

There are often informal structures within a public administration, structures based on kinship and tribe. These structures are of crucial importance and may sometimes influence the appointment of staff. Good relations of that kind can also give access to valuable information and possibilities to influence decisions.

Frequently, public administration receives directives from the political establishment regarding a certain action. All other tasks are then immediately put aside. Similar situations also occur as the result of an order from the closest manager. Planning consequently often becomes very short-sighted and the work is about solving one acute problem after the other.

The African organizational culture makes very high demands on the top managers. They have to be extremely knowledgeable and be constantly present to take decisions, distribute tasks and work load, etc. We have seen examples of a strong, competent, "dictatorial" manager acting with great efficiency within an organization. However, in most cases the boss is not a superman or superwoman making the shortcomings of the administration very apparent. In all these situations, the need for development and change is great.

The challenges confronting African organizations, as described above, are indeed considerable. Efficient, service minded organizations with a high capacity for change are the ultimate objective. But changing an organizational culture is never an easy task.

Lessons learnt

My experience from working with organizational development has taught me that what is most important is not to make analyses and to elaborate proposals regarding what has to be done. Instead it is necessary to create a situation which is conducive to change. Attention must therefore be given instead to the change process as such.

The greatest difference in working as a consultant in Sweden and within an organization in a developing country lies within the client relationship itself. To change organizations as an external consultant implies a contribution of ideas and knowledge in close co-operation with the organization's management, as well as influencing attitudes and values that may be deeply rooted. In Sweden, the organization's management is often both customer and client. The customer may have different motives, but behind the assignment is often a desire to bring about some kind of development. In the African case it is mostly a donor taking the initiative to employ a consultant and who presents various proposals to the organization's management. The assignment is paid for with official development assistance. This distinction is essential since the relationship between client and consultant is of great importance to the change process and its results.

The first and most important lesson learnt is that it is not possible to initiate change in an organization unless its management is committed to the task. An assignment may mean building up a personnel information system. Technically, it can be possible to install the system without significant involvement on the part of the management and the staff. But to be of real value, the organization must make use of the information the system produces, and this requires changes regarding the way in which people work, as well as a strong involvement on the part of the management.

Some practical examples

Two examples based on my experience as an organization consultant follow below.

The first example relates to a management development programme in a country in Southern Africa aimed at developing the competence of all managers, down to departmental level, within the public administration. The project started with two workshops, organized with the entire group of permanent secretaries. One important feature was to involve participants in an inventory of the development problems within the administration. The group was itself able to identify a large number of relevant and desirable changes. We could thus establish that a group of key actors within the public administration had good insight into the administration's situation and a fairly clear opinion regarding the existing needs for change.

This case illustrates some basic lessons. It is important to start at the top, with the top managers, when it comes to developing a programme of this kind. The programme focused on practical action and we therefore ensured co-operation on the part of the managers by inviting them to participate at an early stage in the problem analysis. This worked very well with them becoming very involved.

However, a problem proved to be the group's difficulty in prioritizing. A priority implies an acknowledgement that some proposals are less important than others. This was a conflictual situation which the group could not deal with, since everyone was on the same hierarchical level. Several of the questions were also of such a kind that the participants referred them upwards in the hierarchy, i.e. to the ministerial level. In addition, some of the problems discussed were also very difficult to limit in scope, and in some cases it was genuinely difficult to identify underlying causes.

The greatest problem is not to identify all types of necessary changes, but to really succeed in carrying out some of them. Many donors demand changes in the public administration. To accomplish everything that is expected or demanded of it is beyond the limits of what an administration can achieve and the situation can create a feeling of resignation within it.

In this country there was earlier a special ministry for personnel issues. Parallel to the ministry, there was also a Public Service Commission whose task was to handle all new appointments. This dual system led to very protracted procedures. This was combined with the fact that those who carried out recruitment had little real knowledge about the various posts' professional conditions and requirements. The system was installed by the British colonial administration and can be found in similar forms in many African countries.

The aim was to counteract nepotism and corruption through letting an independent commission decide on selection and recruitment. The modern British administration still operates within the framework of this system—adjusted, however, to a modern management way of thinking and a new approach to management systems for organizational development. The Public Service Commission in the UK today deals primarily with policy issues and the real decision making takes place at the ministries.

Many administrations divide personnel into special cadres. There is for example a special economic personnel cadre within the public administration. Recruitment, employment and career advancement take place within the same cadre and not at the place where the specific person works. Consequently the responsibility for personnel issues is shared between several authorities and possibilities for actions within one's own organization are limited. The particular manager has in this way only limited possibilities to take action vis-à-vis his own personnel. The result is often that the manager does not feel any real responsibility for the employees.

The public administration is thus organized according to functions and in such a manner that division of responsibilities and comprehensive overview are rendered difficult. Many have insight into existing problems and have opinions about what should be done in order to bring about change, but few have the mandate to implement change.

The administration is a heritage from the colonial era and there is often an exaggerated respect for regulatory systems. Some officials use the old-fashioned systems as an excuse to avoid change. Others fail to realize that these rules and regulations actually can be changed. There are persons whose professional pride lies in their knowledge of the existing regulatory framework. Change is therefore considered a threat to their professional identity. Furthermore the group which is aware of the need for change is very small. This small group is also overwhelmed with work and is often away on business trips. The time available for these people to really become involved and act for change is severely restricted.

One other reason for this group's heavy workload is all the foreign (donor) delegations which demand considerable time. In a small country like the one discussed above, the international delegations and their projects are in fact competing for attention. Within the public administration this usually led to the proper authorities being involved with a specific problem while the relevant delegation was in the country, only to abandon it after their departure.

The public administration development project must have a long time perspective. It is about changes which take time to implement, partly because the administration is not organized in a way to carry out changes through its own efforts, and partly because many changes affect so many different parts of the administration. This work, which started with seminars for the permanent secretaries, led to several changes.

One of the outcomes was that a managers' development programme was implemented by the Personnel Ministry in co-operation with training institutes and the university. No fewer than 500 managers participated in a training and development programme. As a final step each ministry established a personnel development function. It was also decided that each ministry in principle was to take responsibility for its own personnel development.

Another outcome was that the Personnel Ministry developed a computerized personnel information system. Through this, the ministry obtained a good overview over the personnel structure within the administration regarding age, salary and occupational structure. This is an important prerequisite for a well functioning personnel administration and seems to be successful.

In contrast, it proved to be difficult to spread the system further to the rest of the public administration and to make it a tool for the managers at the various ministries so that they could work actively with personnel issues. It also proved to be problematic to build up functioning routines for up-dating and development of the system.

This small example shows that the development and installing of a computerized system requires considerable work with support systems and training of users for it to be fully beneficial.

A third development programme started within the ministry of finance, aiming at developing the financial management systems within the public administration.

Finally, a Public Service Improvement Programme was developed, which in principle included the entire public administration's organization and activities. This is the logical result of the fact that many problems must be attacked in one single context. The difficulty is that the task of effecting change becomes so demanding and comprehensive that it therefore threatens to paralyse the whole project.

The second example is taken from the telecommunications area. As regards the area of telecommunications, globalization, along with the rapid and all penetrating technical development, have drastically altered conditions for the African telecommunications administrations. They have all been forced to start a comprehensive restructuring programme to create service minded, competitive and business oriented activities. The adjustment is radical and affects the majority of employees. The difference between dealing with subscribers (before) and serving customers (now) is very great and requires a change in attitudes and a more decentralized and customer oriented organization.

Swedish Telecom initiated a similar change process at a time when it had a developed, well functioning methodology, high technological competence and a well developed organization. Despite this the change process has taken more than ten years. African telecommunications authorities/administrations are in a much weaker position and have to carry out the changes much faster. If they do not succeed there is a great risk that these organizations will be driven out of the market through competition. One of the major difficulties in this context has been to bring about a functioning decentralization in a culture marked by centralism and lack of competent managers.

One special case of relative success is Namibia, whose telecom company was previously part of the South African public administration. Traditionally all managers were white and were also the only ones having the required technical competencies. After independence was won, affirmative action as regards recruitment became regulated by law. Thus demands to rapidly create space for black people at management levels were great. An ambitious trainee-programme for a specially recruited group was initiated. The training was alternated with practical work and each participant had his or her own experienced manager as supervisor. The result of the programme was most satisfactory.

Conclusion

Development of personnel administration is an important part of institution building. Many African organizations are not using their personnel to their full potential. To succeed, the development work within this area must be carried out consistently and with long-term ambitions. Many of the changes, however, require simultaneous changes in the current organizational culture. Consequently many projects within this field must have developing the whole organization as their goal.

One general problem is how a consultant can contribute to change in an administrational culture which is reluctant to change. To do this it is necessary to develop a work methodology based on strong and active participation from all those involved.

The specialist functions within the personnel administration are often very undeveloped. Basic information regarding the number of staff and their assignments is often missing. Routines for recruitment, personnel planning and wage management need to be improved. If personnel administration is to develop, one of the first requirements is that the basic functions work efficiently. The number of employees must be known and the routines for payments of salaries improved so that the employees receive their appropriate salaries at the right time. These are obvious and basic requirements. If they are not fulfilled a part of the development work must target them.

A particular problem in many African public administrations is the fact that responsibility for personnel administration is fragmented. It is impossible to find overall responsibility for personnel administration contained within any one organizational unit. Here lies a great need for development. Improvement demands organizational changes which will create a situation where each manager has total responsibility for all staff members, as well as changes of the roles within and among public organizations working with personnel development.

Finally, we would like to underline one of the fundamental problems within many African administrations, namely the fact that the level of salaries is so low that the monthly salary only lasts a few days. Consequently a basic condition for rendering personnel administration and development more efficient is missing. It is obvious that when salaries are not sufficient to live on, there will be problems both with motivation and attendance at work.

Christer Wallroth is Chairman of the Board at ISO Swedish Management Group, a firm of consultants working with organizational and institutional development in many countries. He is a Doctor of Business Administration and has several years experience working as a consultant in these areas.

Administering and Leading a University

Lennart Wohlgemuth

As in so many other areas, the shortage of resources in Africa increasingly requires that universities be run efficiently. The question of treatment of staff, money and premises is growing in importance and is becoming more difficult to handle. The issue of management is thus becoming the focus of attention.

A multitude of organizations conduct investigations and make recommendations in this area. They include local and regional research groups (*Eastern and Southern African Universities Research Programme*, ESAURP and *Association of African Universities*, AAU), international organizations (the World Bank, UNESCO, *International Institute for Educational Planning*, IIEP) and bilateral donors headed by the Ford and Rockefeller Foundations. In Sweden a special report on the subject was drawn up by what was formerly SAREC and Sida. An international working group was set up under the name of *Association for the Development of African Education: Working Group on Higher Education*. It consists of members of donor organizations and people from the leadership of different African universities. The educational material the IIEP produced for its courses in university management is particularly interesting.

Thus a great deal has been written on the question of university management, of both a theoretical and an empirical nature, but all of this has hardly affected what is really happening.

What then are the problems?

The situation at African universities today

Universities in Africa have a very short history. Development has, however, been rapid: from six universities in 1960 (excluding South Africa) to 97 today. The number of university graduates rose from about 20,000 in 1960 to 70,000 by 1983. Today more than 500,000 are studying at the universities. The quality of the education varied dur-

ing the first 20 years, but was for the most part acceptable. The problems faced were more concerned with the place of the university in general social developments than with managing resources from day to day.

The economic crisis that gained a secure hold in most African countries during the 1980s drastically changed these conditions. Today there is general agreement that the situation of most African universities is particularly difficult. The way in which the crisis is manifested is described in detail in several reports.

It is founded on a shortage of resources, which in turn has led to both a crisis of quality and one of management. The dissatisfaction of the students has led to conflicts between the university and the political leadership. Thus the issue of universities' position in society and their autonomy has come to a head.

There are exceptions (Botswana, Mauritius and South Africa), but in this article we will focus on the countries with difficulties. The problems will be further discussed below.

First, universities have allowed, and in fact were often forced, to increase the number of students admitted without any relation to either the needs of the labour market or the resources of the university.

In most countries, secondary school has expanded very rapidly and thereby the demand for tertiary education has increased. The ambition to educate students for the needs of society was replaced by an ambition to offer higher education as a right to all who acquired the necessary qualifications. At the same time, the opportunities to find employment in the public sector have been reduced and in several countries unemployment is rising among academics. University degrees are, however, still regarded as a desirable ticket to a well-paid job and the growing middle class is counting on having access to higher education for their children.

The combined pressures have led many governments to ordering the university to increase admissions far above the available capacity. At the same time, new universities are being established, often privately run (Kenya, Mozambique, Uganda, Zimbabwe, etc.).

Second, the lack of financial resources at most universities has led to what is a virtually untenable situation: a lack of textbooks, libraries and educational material, run-down premises and laboratories, overfull student residences and generally poor material conditions for

students, poor pay and insufficient material conditions for the lecturers and staff.

The predominant reason for the lack of resources is the economic
crisis. Most countries have succeeded in allocating a relatively constant portion of their national expenditure to the educational sector
and within that budget higher education has taken a relatively large
share. The real value has, however, been undermined year by year.
This has entailed a substantial reduction in the universities' finances,
while the value of foreign support to higher education has remained
constant at best.

Most serious is the effect on the salaries of university lecturers
and other well-educated staff. In many instances, pay does not cover
survival needs. Those who can move overseas—to Europe and the US,
where it is estimated that 100,000 well-educated Africans live, or increasingly to South Africa and its neighbours. Among those who do
not move away, many move to the domestic private sector. Those
who remain must eke out their salaries by taking on all kinds of other
jobs.

The cost crisis is reinforced because most universities have been
built according to the campus model in which society is responsible
for all services and all costs for lecturers and students, from housing
and meals, to clinics, clubs and sports facilities. This naturally increases the number of employees per student at a time when the
number of lecturers per student is twice as high as in most industrialized countries.

Third, the quality of education has been greatly reduced during the
past decade. The lack of resources in combination with the increased
intake of students has meant that the funds to cover running costs and
for research per student have been reduced to a minimum. Working
conditions at African universities are thus becoming increasingly difficult. Both the quality of the teaching as well as the conditions for research have seriously declined.

The investment in quantity in the educational system has led to
serious deficiencies in quality. Students are accepted who have poorer
prospects of success in higher education. All this leads to many students dropping out and a decline in the efficiency of undergraduate
studies.

The lack of resources also involves a deterioration in the opportunities for more egalitarian recruitment to universities, which pri-

marily affects the rural population and women. This is partly connected to a corresponding deterioration in the quality and localization
of secondary schools, and partly due to lack of adequate residential
facilities for them. In terms of subjects, the natural sciences and technology are worst affected, as it is particularly costly to run meaningful
education in these departments.

Research is another important area that has deteriorated during
the university crisis and it is undermined because of the lack of time
and resources. Potential researchers devote themselves to tasks that
only in exceptional cases contribute to the development of an academic environment. Often there is not even time to offer supervision
of term papers. The number of new researchers is decreasing.
Research institutions are affected by this inferior academic environment and the poor quality of the education and are the first institutions to be closed down when the lack of resources becomes over-
whelming. (The University of Lusaka has closed four of its five research institutes.)

Fourth, the relevance of university education is increasingly called into
question by both the state and the public. The quality is often so poor
that new graduates' knowledge is inadequate in the workplace.

Fifth, relations between state and university in many African countries
have deteriorated, which has meant that the question of university autonomy has once again arisen. The reasons for this relate to the above-
mentioned factors. The lack of resources together with the reduction
in quality create dissatisfaction among students and lecturers. This in
turn disturbs politicians, who regard the university environment as a
breeding ground for criticism and political opposition. While the university demands autonomy to find solutions to its problems independently of the state, the state regards the solution as lying in an increased involvement in the day-to-day running of the university. At
the same time as the state increases its involvement, its opportunities
to act are reduced, since there is no money to pay for the required reforms.

Several universities in Africa have, despite their formal status, a
relatively high degree of academic autonomy, i.e. the right to select
teachers and students, the right to determine the content of the
courses and the standard of the examinations. More rarely they have
the right to determine conditions of employment and the allocations

of resources in general. Lecturers' salaries are usually subject to the same provisos as those of state employees as a whole and the budget for running the university may be minimal. With a higher degree of self-government, the role of the state becomes supervisory and instead clear accountability is demanded of the university.

Administration of the university

Management, or administration of such a complex organization as a university is difficult even under ideal conditions. The literature from all around the globe is full of such examples. In the situation that pertains at most universities in Africa today, the task is virtually impossible. At the same time, every measure that aims at better utilizing the very restricted resources which the university has at its disposal can have very satisfactory results. Consequently, it is logical that good administration of the university has come into focus.

In the World Bank study *Higher Education. The Lessons of Experience* it is said that improved management is one of the most promising short-term strategies to ease the financial pressure on universities. By evaluating and reorganizing administration as a whole, training administrative personnel, fostering initiative and rewarding efficiency, the university can generate gains that increase its freedom of action.

In a study of two universities in East Africa in 1990 (with a follow-up study in 1995) I drew the conclusion that at least the most vulnerable universities must first be given sufficient funds to work with, before beginning to discuss reforms. The available resources are quite simply too inadequate to be utilized for anything meaningful.

Nevertheless, there are no universal solutions in this area. Each university is unique and the preconditions vary from country to country. The IIEP approaches this problem in its comprehensive educational material by presenting ways in which different universities around the world solve a specific question, point by point. As a result, many different solutions are offered and each university can choose the one that suits it best.

Organization of the university

A study of the organizational structure of a university should be approached from two perspectives. The first of these is the federal nature of the traditional university organization. The organizational structure—central administration, the faculties and the departments—is both centralized and de-centralized at the same time. This gives rise to different management systems which sometimes co-exist and sometimes conflict with each other. The second perspective is the relationship with the state. The university as any other public sector organization is dependent on the state in terms of finance. It is also guided by the state's policy on higher education and research. The degree of self-determination enjoyed by a university may therefore vary from one country to another. Regulations may be unclear, but even if they are clear, the state may choose to become involved to varying extents. It is, however, important that the regulations are clear and well-known to all the parties and that the parties keep to the rules.

In Africa, very few universities have any higher degree of self-government. As a rule, the university is directly subordinate to the state, usually the ministry of education. In Francophone Africa, the management of the universities is often rather authoritarian, while in English-speaking countries, the universities have inherited a system that is more based on dialogue between the management and the employees. In far too many cases the existing administrative structures work against internal and external co-ordination of the university. Management is authoritarian, is too rigidly controlled by the state and is hamstrung by a decision making structure that is too complex.

Here there is a great deal of reorganization to be done: clearer decision making functions, better information systems and increased decentralization are needed. Among the most important changes is a reasonable incentive structure, that ensures that it is more profitable to follow the rules within the existing system in co-operation with all colleagues.

A management reform thus first entails doing a review of the organization as a whole and the way decisions are taken. Then the various functions must be reviewed. Below we shall pay particular attention to financial administration, staff administration, management of the premises and research. Several more areas could be discussed, for instance, relations to the labour market.

The financial administration

State and university make different demands on financial administration and these demands are not always compatible. The state requires a distribution of resources and a system of accounts that make it possible to check whether value for money is received and that there is no waste. The university, on the other hand, needs a system that involves stability, reliability, a fair distribution and simplicity. But reduced accessibility to funds, which in addition are apportioned in small amounts and often too late, makes particularly great demands on the system.

The basis for an improved financial administration is good financial planning and budgeting. What, however, does one do if available funds only cover a fraction of what is budgeted for as essential? According to a study by Robert Blaire, relations between state and university are chaotic in this area, to put it mildly. The way in which the state cuts the budgets of the university at the same time as it does not permit the university to reduce the number of employees and even prescribes an increase in the number of students, entails a disaster for the university.

There is, nevertheless, even in this difficult situation, room for improved cost control and more efficient use of funds. African universities still have relatively high administrative costs. This is partly a result of the lack of guidelines for the number of students per teacher, space standards per student, teaching hours, etc., and partly due to deficient knowledge of budgeting, accounting and control. In addition, there is a dearth of modern computer equipment.

With better methods of budgeting and accounting, the question of financing (or underfinancing) becomes clearer. It becomes easier to differentiate certain costs that do not directly involve the core sections of the education and research and to seek financing for them from different quarters. In a growing number of countries, demands are being made that the students themselves pay for certain costs and in some these demands have already been met. Measures in this direction have—at least in the short term—consequences in the form of strikes and protests and consequent barring of students.

Assistance from various donors is an important source of financing for the universities. This is, however, a very uncertain resource that is often beyond the control of the university's planning and administration. The direction and extent of support is determined by the donor, goes directly to the chosen faculty often with various conditions attached, e.g. that the university must contribute from its very limited resources to that particular donor-supported project.

In addition, it takes a great deal of time for the administration of the university to follow up all the various routines agreed on and the accounting demands of each donor. It is also very time-consuming to receive the many negotiation and evaluation delegations. A great deal of the external support arrives in kind. Lecturers are recruited and sent out by donor organizations. Educational and research grants are administered by the donor country. In addition, donors often build up special structures for the administration of project support to the universities that receive assistance.

Financing from sources other than from finance ministries is becoming increasingly important in the crisis situation of today. It is not unusual for universities to make their own contributions to their finances by means of various business transactions. They can sell services in the form of consultancies or education as well as run agricultural production and other kinds of businesses. Makerere University in Uganda, for instance, covers 30 per cent of its budget through sales of, above all, evening courses.

In addition, alternative financing forms, such as different types of study loans, should be offered. The administration of different types of systems for study loans is a major question as such, and is well documented in, among other places, a number of studies done by IIEP.

Personnel administration

A basic precondition for an efficient university administration is efficient staff. Salary costs are always a heavy item in the budget, particularly when there are limited funds. In some cases they may encompass 90 per cent of the total costs. The issue of staff working conditions is a central question for all administration.

Personnel administration is concerned with how one plans, recruits and retains good staff. It includes quality control, staff development and negotiation about contract conditions with individual people and professional organizations and trade unions. How these questions can be solved is largely dependent on the autonomy of the university. In Africa, the salary level and promotion sequence are often set by the government department responsible. In some cases the department may even determine the number of posts and incorporate them in the public sector as a whole, subject to the same conditions as other civil servants. The universities in Francophone West Africa as a rule belong to this category while the majority of the others have relatively large autonomy when it comes to staff administration.

Studies show that most universities in Africa lack clear and comprehensive regulations for personnel administration. Most do, however, have staff training plans indicating how a newly qualified lecturer can advance to senior lecturer by taking a Master's degree and a Ph.D. What is lacking is a strategy for an improved personnel administration, and above all, ideas about how to retain accomplished staff. The brain drain is perhaps Africa's greatest problem at present and must be tackled immediately if the university is to have any future. We are once again back to questions of salaries, as well as to the educational and research environment at the various faculties.

Some of the universities, for example, in Nigeria, Kenya and Uganda have opened evening classes on a cost-recovery basis. Part of the extra revenue is distributed to the staff, thereby improving their working conditions somewhat. The expansion of the private sector in some countries has also allowed the academic staff of the public universities to work as part-time instructors providing extra income. However, this has called for extra monitoring and control of the proper utilization of staff time. The IIEP has developed a monitoring mechanism for the utilization of academic staff time.

Administering and leading research

Research is a particularly vulnerable area when there is a lack of resources. Many universities in Africa allocate very few of their own funds to research today and the research that is undertaken is financed mainly by donors. Contact with the labour market is minimal and the very basis for research, i.e. the Ph.D. courses and a good research environment, are at risk.

Total dependence on donor financing entails that the universities themselves hardly have anything to say about priorities or support to their other work. Donors usually design assistance in the university sector as co-operation between faculties or groups of researchers in the donor and recipient countries. A university can have hundreds of such agreements, known as *twinning arrangements*. Each input is usually well-financed and the university is often able to finance all the work of a faculty from just that directed support.

Many universities in English-speaking Africa, have a special committee, called a *Research and Grants Committee* to decide on priorities in research policies, and distribution and control of funds to researchers. The individual faculty prepares its own submissions, but decisions are taken by this committee. It worked reasonably well as long as there was money to distribute. Nowadays, there is a lack of local funds in many places and donors do not wish to take a detour via this committee. This, central control over research, in principle belongs to the past.

In this area as well, a great deal has been written about how administration could be improved. IIEP's educational material describes in detail how an efficient administration can be built up so that it can formulate a research policy, design a functioning management structure, work out procedures for research and improve the research environment. As long as the university administrations, including the faculty managements, lack their own funds and are forced to accept the detailed instructions given by the donors, there is little space for such administrative reforms. A ray of hope is the somewhat changed attitudes of certain donors led by the IDRC and Sweden's Sida/SAREC. They realize that it is important to work on the basis of a holistic perspective, i.e. that one must develop research environments instead of individual projects.

Administration of premises

It is only during the past decade that the question of premises and equipment has been given a more prominent role in management discussions. The cost of premises and equipment is substantial for a university and maintenance is a heavy item in the budget in times of crisis. Thus it becomes particularly important to make rational use of the available space. Here a great deal can also be done. Admission policies, available infrastructure and equipment, ability to plan and rethink when it comes to working out course programmes all have great significance when making maximum use of existing resources.

Almost without exception, African universities suffer from a lack of premises and as a result crowding. The buildings are run down. At the university in Dar es Salaam the situation was so bad a few years ago—the drainage system, for instance, was not working and the buildings were very dilapidated—that the students could no longer stand it and went on strike.

It is perhaps in this area that solutions from other countries are easiest to copy. Questions to keep in mind are, for instance, the following:

– Which premises are actually the responsibility of the university? Traditionally, most universities in Africa are still responsible for board and lodging for both students and lecturers. Everything that can be done to transfer responsibility to the students and the lecturers themselves makes things easier for the university. A reform in this area must, however, take account of the fact that there are students who are poor and/or come from far away.

– How intensely can premises be used? This concerns how many hours per day/week/year that education is permitted (a university's hours of opening may vary from 900 to 4,000 hours per year) and how the premises are utilized. Proper inventories are required by staff responsible for the premises with the authority to take decisions within their area. Those responsible must learn to use the premises better and to link the syllabus to a plan for use of the premises. In addition, more resources for maintenance are required. A sensitive issue is whether decisions concerning premises should be taken centrally at the same time as attempts are made in other areas to decentralize responsibility to the faculties.

Strategic planning and management

Keeping in mind the above problems, the Association for the Development of African Education (ADEA, the former DAE, Donors to African Education), in its meetings of the Working Group on Higher Education (WGHE), has reached consensus on the following points in respect of proper administration and leadership of a university:

1. Universities must seize the initiative in confronting the current crisis: they are best placed to provide creative leadership.

2. They should update their mission statements to reflect changes in the outside environment.

3. They should be encouraged to develop strategic institutional plans to implement their mission statements.

4. Strategic planning should be a participatory process involving the university administration, academic staff, students, the government and other stakeholders.

5. The completed strategic plan should be used as a frame of reference to guide funding negotiations with the government and donor community.

Several universities (Tanzania, Zambia, South Africa (University of Natal) and Mozambique, for example) have prepared strategic plans although their implementation has not always met with success.

Conclusions

In the above, different areas have been discussed where the question of management and its efficiency is acute, taking into account the difficult crisis situation in Africa today and its effect on the universities. A great deal can be improved, even with the scarce resources that are available. Considering the conditions, it is impressive that so many universities manage to keep going and that the standard of education is as high as it is, despite everything. In a few cases, particularly inventive entrepreneurs in the administration have shown that they can do a great deal by trying out new ideas, supported (directly or indirectly) by their governments. Despite the initial difficulties in many countries, there is hope of improvement in the future. But in order to really be able to utilize all the management ideas that have been discussed above, the universities require increased resources.

Lennart Wohlgemuth has been the director of the Nordic Africa Institute since 1993. Prior to this he worked for many years for Sida, most recently as Assistant Director General and Head of the Sector Department. Between 1981 and 1987 he headed Sida's educational division, and since 1989 he has been a board member of the International Institute for Educational Planning (IIEP).

References

AAU, 1991, *Association of African Universities: Study on Cost Effectiveness and Efficiency in African Universities; A Synthesis Report*. Accra.

Ade Ajayi, J.F. et al., 1996, *The African Experience with Higher Education*. The Association of African Universities: Accra.

Blair, R., 1993, *Staff Loss and Retention at Selected African Universities*. Harare.

Coombe, T., *A Consultation on Higher Education in Africa. A Report to the Ford Foundation and the Rockefeller Foundation*. London, 1991 and Harare, 1993.

ESAURP, 1987, *University Capacity in Eastern and Southern African Countries*. Dar es Salaam.

Fine, J.D., 1991, *Graduate Training in Economics and Reform of African Higher Education*. Nairobi.

King, K. and Buckert, L. ,1995, *Learning from Experience: Policy and Practice in Aid to Higher Education*. The Hague.

Sanyal, B., 1995, *Innovations in University Management*. Paris: IIEP.

Sanyal, B. and Martin, M., 1997, *Management of higher education with special reference to financial management in African institutions*. Paris: IIEP.

Sida/SAREC, 1992, *Att äga, utveckla och förvalta kunskap. Bistånd till universitet i u-länder* (To own, develop and administer knowledge. Assistance to universities in developing countries). Stockholm: Sida/SAREC.

WGHE, 1995, "Donors to African Education, Working Group on Higher Education", Notes from a meeting in Maseru, Lesotho, January, 24–25, 1995. Washington, DC: AFTHR, World Bank.

Wohlgemuth, L., 1990, *University Minimum Requirements—the Cases of Mozambique and Tanzania*. Stockholm.

Wohlgemuth, L., 1995, *University Eduardo Mondlane, Mozambique—Basic Needs for Efficient Running*. Uppsala.

World Bank, 1994, *Higher Education. The Lessons of Experience*. Washington DC: World Bank.

Basic Education—Management of an Extremely Complex System

Ingemar Gustafsson

The institutional base of formal systems of education

Every education system has an institutional base. It consists of a set of commonly shared values considered as valid knowledge, an organizational structure and competent staff. These three characteristics of education systems are for the most part taken as given.

The institutional aspects are less obvious perhaps than the pedagogical and the financial ones. We tend to forget that the formal education system is a large-scale and complex organization. Very often, the Ministry of Education is the single largest employer in the country and handles the largest share of the national budget.

The creation of state systems of mass education comes with modernization. In Europe and the United States this occurs during the latter half of the 19th century. In the Soviet Union and in Japan it takes place at the beginning of this century. It is also at this point that education systems become part of the core activities of the state. This is also the framework for the expansion of formal education in the independent African states, which began in the late 1950s.

Institutional aspects of education in Africa

The education systems of newly independent African countries were seen by the leaders to serve two main purposes.

One was to spearhead modernization. The other was to help to transmit values of national unity, such as respect for the new national symbols; the head of state, the flag and the use of the national language. For the great majority of students and parents, formal education was seen as a route to better paid jobs outside subsistence agriculture. They valued such knowledge and skills that they thought would help them to achieve this objective.

This was the institutional framework in the sense of what counted as valid knowledge. The organizational structures which had been founded on the organizations built up by the churches were now taken over by the state. In many countries, the teachers became state employees.

The need to review what counts as valid knowledge

The environment within which such value questions are formed is in a state of change which is driven both by external and by internal factors. The external factors have to do with globalization.

Globalization means among other things that information and values are spreading faster and more easily than ever before. New technologies have emerged which facilitate access to data bases in all parts of the world but which also open up new possibilities for transfer of knowledge.

Globalization in the economic sense also means that all countries increasingly find themselves part of intense world-wide economic competition. Investments in education as a means to improve productivity are considered crucial by most governments today.

Internally, most African countries have moved away from a centrally planned economic system and consolidation of the nation state towards pluralism, market economy and democratization of the political system.

These developments imply that uniform value systems around which education systems can be organized, are being questioned. They may also imply a changing role of the state and of civil society, as regards influence over and responsibility for education.

Planning of education can no longer be seen as a technical and linear process which follows discrete steps of problem analysis, policy formulation, implementation and evaluation within a stable policy framework. Rather, all these steps take place concurrently within a context of change and instability. Policy making and planning should instead be seen as a gradual process of negotiation and consensus building between many different actors.

With growing dependency on external funds for the financing of mass education, the funding agencies have increasingly become part of this institutional framework.

This process which is going on in many countries also has implications for the organization of education. A number of the issues will be touched upon here.

Education systems as complex organizations

A Ministry of Education has many tasks. It should organize the school year, deliver textbooks to the schools, prepare an annual budget, collect and analyse data, organize teacher training, develop the curriculum etc. All these tasks and functions are there to support what goes on between the teacher and the student. Needless to say, this should be done in an efficient way.

It has been argued that such issues can be dealt with as a technical question, which is not influenced by the basic value problems on what counts as valid knowledge. What matters ultimately is what is going on in the class-room. "The old adage about education is still valid—when the door to the classroom is closed, the teacher controls what takes place" (ADEA, 1996).

Is this to say, that questions about control over education can be left aside, once the basic values and the policy have been defined? The answer may be *yes* in very stable situations. This stability hardly exists anywhere in Africa today.

Decentralization versus centralization

In this situation, the central role of the state in education has been seen by some to imply that a rigid, bureaucratic and authoritarian organization has been built up which is ill suited to the needs of a more pluralistic society.

It has also been argued that an organization that contains all the elements of the Weberian bureaucracy, a hierarchical chain of responsibility, clear division of labour and clear rules and regulations leads to central control and "top-down" approaches.

Such an organization may be well suited to repetitive mass production of goods but it contradicts the very notion of learning as an interactive and creative process. Decentralization, deregulation and a stronger community involvement have been seen as solutions to such problems. We will leave the internal efficiency arguments for and against decentralization aside and instead touch upon two ideological traditions of thought among proponents of decentralization.

One tradition takes the ideal rural community as its starting point. What matters most in education is to strengthen the value systems and social cohesion which are associated with rural communities.

The result is a call for village-based education programmes with strong contacts between the school and the local community. These views formed the background to ideas about education for self-reliance as advocated by Nyerere and before him by Gandhi, Dewey and others. For the Swedish missionaries, who set up schools in Southern Africa at the beginning of this century, the role of education was to strengthen the values and lifestyle of the rural community against social disintegration and the sinful life that characterized mines and urban areas.

Another, much more recent tradition, argues that formal education under the auspices of the state is too supply-driven. Instead it should be demand-driven. Education should be provided as a result of demands of consumers and should be privatized as much as possible. This is the best way to ensure that it meets the needs of its clients. It is implied that the clients should define what counts as valid knowledge.

This contradicts ideas about a national curriculum with detailed specifications of what should be taught. Such ideas reflect a concept of knowledge as essentially consisting of historically determined and universally valid skills. Most national systems have a national education system which is based on this assumption. However, such a system is also necessary for nationally recognized standards which facilitate social mobility and are necessary for the legitimacy of the national system. It should also be noted, as do Lauglo and McLean, that "there are several internationally influential concepts of general education and vocational training and they differ in how far they provide intellectual support for pre-structured universalistic knowledge" (Laughlo and McLean, 1985).

School and community

It goes without saying that teachers are the key to the pedagogical process. But teachers, however qualified and motivated, are dependent on how schools are organized.

What differentiates successful schools from less successful ones is their leadership, the working relationships within the school and the relationship between the school, the parents and the surrounding community.

And yet, so much of the debate about education reform is about physical inputs, such as buildings and school desks. Relatively less attention has been paid to management and organizational aspects within the school, including the relationship between the school and the surrounding community. This can among other things be seen in the support given by outside agencies. There may be many reasons for this, one being that the internal dynamics of the school and its relations to the community are less tangible and more difficult to change than the physical infrastructure.

Education systems include many other aspects that are necessary for the learning process. For some, market solutions may be appropriate. The complexity of this question will be illustrated with reference to textbook provision in Mozambique.

Textbooks, the state and the market in Mozambique

Book publishing can be organized in many different ways. In centrally planned economies it was taken for granted that the Ministry of Education was responsible for production of manuscripts, editing, printing and distribution of textbooks. The main reason was that the curriculum and the books should reflect the ideology of nation building.

Books for the higher levels, which could not be produced within the country, were imported and financed through foreign assistance. This was the case in most African countries up to the middle of the 1980s. It was necessary at that time for the Ministry of Education to have all the necessary expertise within the ministry. As a rule, the system did not work well.

The institutional framework changed when countries began to move towards a market economy. It was argued then that publishing and distribution of textbooks should be privatized, i.e. that the monopoly of the state should be abandoned and that production should be subject to national and international competition.

Developments in Mozambique are a case in point. The government decided to review its policy. Market solutions to publishing, printing and distribution had to be found. At the same time it was necessary to ensure that there was an effective demand for books even from poor students. Household studies showed very clearly that the great majority of parents could not afford to buy books at market prices. A system of state subsidies was introduced which meant that schools were given funds to pay for those students who could not afford to buy the books.

At the same time an independent publishing company was built up, that was expected to operate under commercial conditions. Distribution would, whenever possible, be done through private booksellers. The problems were that they were mostly located in the towns. For the rural areas only the Ministry of Education could provide an effective channel for distribution.

It was also vital to give the new and fragile publishing company a chance to compete with the international companies. Almost all books were financed by international agencies such as the World Bank and Sida. It turned out that the rules and regulations of international competitive bidding, though neutral in theory, mitigated against the formation of a national publishing capacity. The reason was that most orders placed by the World Bank were of such magnitude that small companies could not compete.

For the Mozambican government it was very important to have some capacity to publish books from manuscripts written by people in the country. This was seen as the only way to make sure that the books, the language, as well as the illustrations, genuinely, reflected the culture of Mozambique.

This shows that solutions to the problem of textbooks are more than a question of cost-efficiency. The national policy had to find a way to combine cost-efficiency in production with the overriding national objective which is to also provide books for those who cannot afford to pay. At the same time, the policy wanted to ensure that some local capacity was maintained.

Many actors were involved including the World Bank and Sida. One result was that the World Bank agreed to modify its procurement procedures to make it possible for the small Mozambican company to compete.

Diverse training needs

The teacher is the key to successful education. This is too obvious to be mentioned. A good teacher is someone who knows the subject matter and who has the ability to communicate this to students in such a way that they are motivated to learn. The teacher is also an organizer of the learning process.

This was realized very early on. The development of systems of mass education in the industrialized part of the world was accompanied by the setting up of institutions for teacher training and in-service training schemes. This was also the case in Africa. Teacher training became a state responsibility after independence.

The fact that education systems also comprise leaders of schools, administrators, statisticians and planners in need of professional training was recognized at a much later stage.

The UNESCO Institute of Educational Planning, IIEP, was established in 1963 to train a professional cadre of planners for Africa, Asia and Latin America. It was created at the time when many countries decided to expand their systems.

When the Institute celebrated its 25th anniversary, it had become obvious that the economic crisis had altered the context of planning and the concept had to be reviewed. The need for planning was stressed but it had to take on a less technical and more of a normative character, giving the framework for possible future scenarios.

Concurrently, UNESCO had built up regional programmes for training of statisticians and of educational administrators in Africa.

Planning is only one of many tasks which require specialized and professional staff. There are general administrators at central, regional and district level, there are accountants, statisticians and so on. The most important group is the school principals.

Training programmes have been developed for the different categories of staff, within countries and as cooperation between countries. For example, UNESCO has for many years been organizing regional programmes for educational administrators and statisticians in Africa.

As from 1988, the training of statisticians has developed into a more comprehensive programme for capacity building within Ministries of Education in Africa. This has taken place as part of the work of the Association for the Development of Education in Africa, ADEA, a collaborative joint effort between African Ministers of Education and organizations which support education in Africa. A network of national teams has been built up in collaboration with UNESCO and some other funding agencies, including Sida, the French Ministry of Cooperation and USAID.

Today, ADEA's working group on education statistics works with 32 countries in Africa. The strategy for capacity building is to provide professional support to the national teams which should be based on a national diagnosis of information needs.

Modules for the different stages of the process of collection, analysis and dissemination of information have been developed. Not only does this imply a move away from traditional models of outside technical assistance running training courses but it has also meant that the system of data collection in the countries is being reorganized.

Concluding comments

Education systems are complex structures with many categories of staff. Their ultimate task is to provide a framework for the learning process.

Institutional development in this case implies building consensus about the basic values and policies that should form the basis of these organizations and of the work of the staff.

A strategy of change has to take the complexity of an education systems into account. A comprehensive approach is important. This is not to say that the best way is large-scale organizational reforms. Institutional development should be an in-built activity at all levels and in all areas of the system.

Ingemar Gustafsson is Head of the Policy Secretariat of the Department for Democracy and Social Development at Sida. His professional background is in international education. He has headed the Education Division of Sida, worked as an educational planner in Botswana and has served as Chair of the Association for the Development of Education in Africa, ADEA. His Ph.D. thesis in International Education is about the relationship between education and work with examples from Southern Africa.

References

Association for the Development of Education in Africa, ADEA, 1996, *Formulating Education Policy: Lessons and Experiences from Sub-Saharan Africa, Six Case Studies and Reflections from the DAE Biennial Meetings.* Paris: UNESCO.

Gustafsson, I., 1987, *Schools and the Transformation of Work,—A Comparative Study of Four Productive Work Programmes in Southern Africa.* Stockholm: University of Stockholm, Institute of International Education.

Lauglo, J. and M. McLean, 1985, *The Control of Education*. London: Heinemann Educational Books for the Institute of Education, University of London.

Temu, E., 1995, *Successful Schools in Tanzania—A Case Study of Academic and Production Programs in Primary and Secondary Schools*. Stockholm: University of Stockholm, Institute of International Education.

UNESCO, International Institute for Educational Planning, 1989, "The Prospects for Educational Planning", A Workshop Organized by the IIEP on the Occasion of its XXVth Anniversary. Paris: IIEP.

UNESCO, International Institute for Educational Planning, 1997, *Functional Analysis (Management Audits) of the Organization of Ministries of Education*, Written by Richard Sack and Mahieddine Saidi. Paris: IIEP.

UNESCO, 1997, "Economic Globalization and Educational Policies", *Prospects*, 1997, Vol. XXVII. Geneva: International Bureau of Education.

Management and Private Enterprise

Björn Mothander

Private enterprise assumes very different guises

This article is based on experiences from eastern and southern Africa. These experiences may only have limited relevance to conditions in other parts of the continent. In western Africa, for instance, there is a much longer unbroken tradition of domestic enterprises than in eastern Africa. Here, Indian and (in Mozambique, Portuguese) traders arrived and formed part of the colonial system and, on the whole, came to replace the former traders.

Privately owned companies represent different company cultures with great differences amongst them. In Kenya, for example, a number of companies have been established because multinational companies of primarily British and American origin have chosen to invest there. There is also a very large group of companies with what is rather vaguely called Asian origin, which have strong ties to India, Pakistan, Iran or one of the Arab countries. These companies should also be regarded as multinational, even if they are usually held together by family ties. There is often a family base in the country of origin, but the group of companies may well have branches in Canada, England, other African countries, etc. This category also includes companies owned by Ishmaelites, who owe allegiance to the Aga Khan, even in economic matters. There are other companies that have been built up in Kenya by Europeans or Indians who have lived there for several generations. A growing number of companies are of purely Kenyan origin, in other words, they have been started and are run by Kenyans. In general these companies are very small. A final category of companies which exerts a strong influence on the pattern of company management and the existing market, encompasses the parastatals.

This pattern of enterprises is found in most countries in eastern and southern Africa.

South Africa is, however, unique, since it has the largest market and is also the most industrialized country in the region. In the first place, there is an exceptionally strong sense of domestic enterprise which originates with the entrepreneurs who came to the country in the nineteenth century and made their fortunes in the mining industry. These groups of companies are closely interlinked and dominate the stock exchange in Johannesburg which, in terms of turnover, is the tenth largest in the world. They must be regarded as part of the industrialized world even if their base is in the Third World, since they resemble large multinational companies. In South Africa there are also a large number of subsidiaries of multinationals. During the past fifty years, in competition with companies of Jewish and British origin, a network of companies owned by Afrikaner families has been established. These enjoyed patronage by the Afrikaner dominated state apparatus. Like in other countries in the region, many companies have strong ties to India and Pakistan. Small businesses within the trade and service sectors are often owned and run by Portuguese or Greek families. Parastatals are also robust and have been politically favoured in South Africa. There are, in contrast, very few African enterprises in the formal sector. During the apartheid era, blacks were forced to limit their enterprises to trade of different kinds and to more or less illegal bars or shebeens.

This mix of Asian family businesses, multinational and mainly raw materials based large companies, "development" companies controlled and favoured by the state and small domestic African firms occurs in all countries in eastern and southern Africa.

In an open market, this multiplicity of company cultures might have created a dynamic situation of strong competition, where impulses would have been exchanged to increase the competence of company management. A certain interaction does occur, but the cultural and social differences, and in many cases even state regulations, have hindered such developments. Throughout the seventies and eighties, parastatals have been given the greatest advantages and have therefore set a pattern. The lack of business sense in these state companies has resulted in an appalling waste of resources and serious stagnation, often even declining output, within the industrial sector. The question is whether the negative influence of the state can be limited quickly enough to achieve the change that is needed to create what the World Bank calls *the supply response* to the structural adjustment programmes, i.e. that companies find it profitable to increase their production and become more efficient under new market conditions.

Which companies are successful?

An important point of departure when discussing company management is to find out which companies have "succeeded". Which companies make a profit (even if they do not show it) and have the potential to survive? We know very little about this when it comes to private companies in the region. Generally it can be said that companies in the trade and service sectors have much better prospects than industrial companies, since the macroeconomic situation with rapid and uncontrolled inflation and frequent devaluations has made it almost impossible to make a profit on investments in any field other than minerals exploitation. To put it incisively—a criterion of good business sense is not to invest under the uncertain conditions that have prevailed and largely continue to exist in these countries. Only in ventures where the turnover of goods is very rapid and where capital can be moved from one country to another without delay, is it possible to maintain invested capital intact. Asian companies have shown that they have an exceptional capacity to manage such *hedging*. Otherwise we know very little about how these companies are run and led. On the other hand, we do know that almost no state-run company in the region (with certain exceptions in South Africa) has been successful.

State subsidized companies

In actual fact, our knowledge about how private companies are run primarily comes from those firms that have received state support in one form or another, or that have been financed through state institutions. In most cases, there have been donor funds behind such inputs and it is through evaluations and assessments of the projects that this knowledge has been gained. The purpose of such international assistance is to create industrial (rather than commercial) growth and thereby create jobs in the recipient country. Swedish development assistance was based on the premise that this would be accomplished through development of entrepreneurs, that is, managers of businesses who have their own interests in the operations. Donors have wanted to participate in creating a domestic business class by assisting potential business owners to start their own companies. An implicit aim has in most cases been that these businesses should be able to compete with other, non-domestic companies in the country. The latter have thus *a priori* been excluded from the assistance.

These development assistance projects have resulted in a terrifying number of bad experiences, but also some good ones, and thus it ought to be possible to learn something from them.

Some observations and lessons

What follows refers in the first place to privately owned domestic business enterprises. On the whole these companies are small. In fact, so-called micro-companies are the most common. They are usually run by one person or only employ family members. In such cases it is hardly meaningful to talk of company management. The companies dealt with below employ at least one person.

An important observation supports the above thesis that a good entrepreneur does not invest money under the unfavourable conditions that prevail in these countries. Successful entrepreneurs who have received different forms of support often have several strings to their bows. They use the surplus generated in one business to start another, which often gives a more rapid return on their money (buses, hotels or bars, for instance) or is more permanent (agriculture). It is easy to get the impression that the goal of African entrepreneurship is to create resources to invest in agricultural companies. The African entrepreneurs who followed their own convictions on this question during the 1980s were more farsighted than their foreign advisers, who wanted them to reinvest in their industrial companies. The winners in the structural adjustment process thus far are the farmers.

Thus capital is used to create quick profits, or is invested where it is regarded as secure in the long-term. This cannot be regarded as anything but astute company management.

In addition, it is essential when discussing entrepreneurship and management to consider the social dimensions. To own a company both raises ones status and involves weighty obligations. Irrespective of what a businessman does, he is a visible person who can count on support from the community in exchange for various services in return, not least through employing people who have contacts in influential circles.

This is reinforced by cultural factors that interact with what is mentioned above. These cultural factors are presumably not a constant from one country to another, but nevertheless are very real in many of the countries. A sense of belonging is important in everyone's life. Thus people's loyalty is directed in the first place towards their own families, their clans and tribes, perhaps to old school friends or members of the same faith, etc. Loyalty to an employer in an abstract sense (the company where one works) is consequently low on the scale of loyalty priorities, since it is such a new loyalty. This is particularly obvious in all official business (and it is surprising that so much effort is expended on educating state employees without even touching on the question of loyalty). A private business manager can reduce exposure to risks by employing staff with whom he has previous social connections and whom he can trust. Professional competence takes second place.

These factors are basic to the typical way of running private businesses. The manager of a business has direct and very strong control over everything that happens in the business and he takes all the decisions himself, even regarding small details. The hierarchy is even stricter than in the parastatals.

Since a manager of a business is also a leader in the traditional African sense, he demonstrates by exercising such a strong influence, that he assumes responsibility for the company and the employees. In this way he creates security.

One effect of the business manager's visibility in the community is that he is always exposed to pressures from those around him. Many people claim connections and influence which they do not, in fact, have. A great deal of a business manager's time must be devoted to such people. The state control apparatus, with its complicated regulations and controlling officials, in this way becomes an important external factor which must be very carefully handled by the business manager. Civil servants contribute to maintaining the societal status of the manager. But since they have power, they also have the possibility of making demands on him, both as representatives of the state and for their own benefit.

This social pattern entails that a great deal of time is taken up by receiving and meeting different people. Politeness requires that they are received when they show up, whether or not they have given prior notice. The head of a business spends a considerable amount of time on such meetings with people from outside expressing interest in the business.

From our western perspective of business management, these aspects of African business management are serious weaknesses which will doubtless make further development of businesses more difficult. Yet in order to be able to adapt the usual tools of company management to the African reality, knowledge and understanding of the cultural and social situation must be acquired.

The African business manager must, like all other managers, learn to handle insecurity. To him, the unpredictability of the environment is of decisive importance, both socially and economically. He solves problems through acting in the short term, i.e. he takes decisions determined by the day-to-day situation without binding himself to long-term plans. Even if he draws up such plans (because of demands made by the state financiers) he apparently does not feel controlled by them in any way. The plan exists independently of reality. This is probably rational. Instead he attempts to create stability by taking snap decisions. The problem is that such quick and short-term decisions on a range of detailed questions mean that the management of the business will lack flexibility. This is where he is vulnerable. His long-term thinking is thus not directed at the operative questions of the business, but at investment of the profit (and, unfortunately, often also the surplus liquidity).

African business managers often have a very strong customer orientation. Customers' wishes and demands are satisfied in ways that often conflict with rational business practice. This is of course socially conditioned, but is also related to the avoidance of risk and insecurity. No one wants to lose a client and therefore it is impossible to say, "This is my product. Take it or leave it". Negotiation is always an option.

The small business man does not invest in large stocks, since he knows that there is always a risk that they will remain unsold. This behaviour has been learned from traders.

Salary levels in smaller African companies are also strongly influenced by social patterns. The great number of people who work on the basis of mutual favours require reasonable pay. Irrespective of the strength of the trade unions, and in general it is not great, those in private employment are in a different situation to state employees. They can seldom leave their place of work to attend to small businesses of their own and cannot use their positions to acquire favours of one sort or another. In general, they must make do on their own salary and thus their demands for pay are high, but economically realistic. The head of a business finds this situation unavoidable. In addition, the tax system in many of these countries , like the value of the currency, does not keep pace with development. Tax becomes virtually confiscatory, even on relatively modest incomes, so people do not take out compensation for their work as salaries, but in other, nontaxable forms.

The salary and the tax system create an attitude to all forms of accounting that entails constant work with "double book-keeping". This system is like a cancer growth: more and more people know that this is what happens and have a hold over entrepreneurs. It is not merely the tax system that reinforces this behaviour. Other regulations — remains of attempts to plan economic development — also force the businessman to work and trade outside the law.

The acquisition of capital is one of the major obstacles for smaller businessmen. Banks are also business enterprises and must ensure that they do not lend money to uncreditworthy borrowers. Securities are often inadequate and the poorly functioning judicial system means that in many countries it is almost impossible, or at least very expensive, to recover a debt through the courts. (This also affects business behaviour; suppliers find it equally difficult to collect debts.) The businessman must thus find other ways of financing his activities. Usually friends and relatives help with the financing, but they can or will seldom contribute sufficient capital, since the risk is far too great for them. The informal loan market is too expensive for anything other than short-term loans. This entails that entrepreneurs who have come into a project supported by foreign assistance, will have great difficulty in getting out of it. The project is often the most important source of financing and, in addition, conditions are a great deal more advantageous than a regular financier would offer. The problem is that aid projects are involved in spoon-feeding, i.e. funds are handed out in small portions, since the donor does not trust the abilities of the entrepreneur. We rarely know whether such a business could function on proper market terms and it is doubtful whether assistance designed in this way has any chance of achieving the goal of creating a domestic class of businessmen.

The conclusion is that the African business manager needs to develop tools to help him to cope in a flexible way with the very insecure world around him. Since rapid changes to the social realities cannot be expected, it must be assumed that the African manager's most important functions will continue to be socially oriented, rather than narrowly directed towards leading the company. It is not likely that focused business support, whether it concerns planning, marketing or financing, is of any help in this respect. Only the efforts of the business manager himself, based on the intrinsic economic soundness of the firm, can lead to success. The donor can contribute by encouraging the government to create greater predictability of the market by reducing regulations, improving macroeconomic stability and in general creating an *enabling environment*, in the true sense of the term.

Sustainable economic development in the modern sector can only be achieved through the interaction between such stable and predictable surroundings and long-term investments in well-run businesses. It is thus necessary for the attitudes and behaviour of all participating actors to change in a radical way. Within their own cultural and social situation, business managers in the private sector must therefore, develop know-how which is directed above all at the care and survival of the company itself, on the basis of the resources and potential of the business and not of the donor. Greater openness between various company cultures would certainly contribute to this.

Björn Mothander is the principal of a law firm in Stockholm, mainly oriented towards questions relating to international development assistance. He has previously worked as a legal advisor to Sida, to a development corporation in Swaziland, and to Alfa-Laval. He has been engaged in the establishment of a consulting company in Tanzania and in industrial development in Sweden at the National Board of Industry. He has managed consulting firms in the field of international development assistance since 1986.

Entrepreneurs and African Businesses

Anders Grettve

Introduction

This is a collection of short stories which I think gives some idea about the reality in which African entrepreneurs are working.[1] What sometimes appears to be irrational behaviour, can be understood only if it is placed within the social and economic context of many African countries. The stories are taken from different parts of Africa although mainly from Eastern and Southern Africa, and represent a variety of business situations. The cases are :

- The Ice-Making Machine, about risk-aversion among poor micro-entrepreneurs.

- The Grocery Shop Owner, about access to information and networks.

- The African Elders as Entrepreneurs, showing how the elderly traditional elite may affect new businesses.

- Junior Sisters, about the new well-educated owner/managers in small business.

- The Troubled Start of African Management Services Co (AMSCO) and African Capacity Building Foundation (ACBF), illustrating dilemmas in organizing technical assistance in management development.

The Ice-Making Machine—about the risk aversion of a poor micro entrepreneur

When I lived near to the centre of Dar es Salaam, Shaban and his young, poor family were my neighbours. Working long hours, Shaban sold cold drinks in the streets and squares of the town. He would pull

---

[1] My experience of African business management and entrepreneurship stems from 25 years in project financing, management consultancy, small enterprise development and in giving advise to and making appraisals of African investment banks.

his cart with three aluminium containers, chilled by blocks of ice and covered with jute sacks.

He bought the drink concentrate from a wholesaler. The water came from a public standpipe. The ice also came from a wholesaler. In the hot humid climate, the ice blocks were his highest single cost.

We came in contact with each other and talked about his business. I suggested that Shaban might try a simple cooling device instead of the expensive ice blocks. This could be developed at a low cost, based on salt and a simple arrangement which I had read about in handbooks on applied technology.

Shaban was sceptical. After some reflection, he refused to go ahead with such a perilous, uncertain project. This typical poor micro entrepreneur did the same as all the other hundreds of the city's cold drink vendors: he used familiar equipment and well-known suppliers. He was simply not interested in testing new, unknown suppliers or means to cool and transport his product.

Why? Shaban worked with extremely small margins. His constant financial problem was to find working capital for the next day's juice concentrate and ice. The wholesalers were reluctant to give him credit, and if they did it was at interest rates of up to 25 per cent—per day!

Shaban was restrained by his own poverty and lack of capital other than the cart (which many of his colleagues would not own but had to rent for a daily fee). Considering the risks with new technology that no one had seen being used on the streets (and which I honestly knew very little about in this particular context), his attitude was presumably rational.

As the head of a family and owner/manager of a micro business, Shaban followed the only business strategy that seemed reasonable to him: to reduce the following day's risk at all costs!

The Grocery Shop Owner—about information and networks

There was a wide variety of goods in the little supermarket across the road. You could get most things, from fresh pawpaw (papaya) to milk, soap, oats, frozen foods, washing powder, all enveloped in the heavy smell of mothballs and disinfectant.

The owner had noticed what I bought in the first few weeks for our relatively large household. Would I like to buy on credit? It would be both practical and profitable. At the end of every month my account in the shop would be paid with a decent discount directly to a bank account in London.

Why? My shopkeeper had seen the opportunity to take advantage of one of the major loopholes in the heavily regulated African economies of those days; this was the gap between the real and official value of an overvalued local currency. This gap could be bridged profitably for both of us, if part of my salary in hard currency went directly into his London account.

My shopkeeper was not a typical African businessman. He belonged to one of the minorities that dominated trading in many African countries. As owner/manager of a family business with ties to relatives in less regulated industrial nations, he had information on the discrepancy in the currency and access to a network that made it possible to open an account in London.

Did I accept? No. My good income and my position as an official foreign aid worker meant that I could afford to have high ethics and abide by the prescribed code of conduct.

The African Village Elders as Entrepreneurs—how the traditional elite may affect new small businesses

There is a shortage of land on the fertile slopes of the great mountain. A disproportionate number of the mixed coffee and banana farms are owned by elderly men with their several households living and working there. Ten to fifteen years ago, some of these elders saw to it that they became beneficiaries of new business development programmes. The common form for this was soft loans and subsidies from government support schemes. The elderly elite saw an opportunity to complement their traditional investments in bars, small shops and perhaps a minibus taxi company with new ventures in modern production.

To compensate for their lack of formal education, these mature gentlemen went into partnership with younger educated people (nearly always men) who, though they had no money, had degrees in technical and/or economic fields. The owner combination of some investible capital and an academic background met the formal eligibility criteria for small business support.

The outcome? Unfortunately it was generally discouraging. In the mechanical workshop, the dominating elders diverted most of the income by privately selling the company's products on the black market without recording this in the books. Bankruptcy followed, but only after all equity and most borrowed capital had already been drained from the company.

The younger, better educated partners could not stand up to the elders, although the latter lacked any knowledge about the financing of a modern company or insight in corporate financial discipline. The traditional respect for elders contributed to the situation, as did the fairly generous small business subsidies. Emptying newly started businesses was all too profitable and relatively risk free, given the poor local controls.

The elderly African entrepreneurs, in particular the traditional elite of rural societies, regarded it as perfectly natural to enrich themselves first. The alternative of consolidating something as impersonal as a corporate business entity with several partner/owners, was not a natural notion to them.

Junior Sisters—about the new well-educated owner/managers in small business

There is a new generation of African entrepreneurs. Many who applied to the small business and entrepreneur development programmes with subsidized financing were remarkably well-educated. Academics became brick makers and civil engineers run quite simple production units.

Why? The children of the elite may have had the best connections, or it might simply be that those with better education have an advantage in seeking out new opportunities. In any case, networks and the ability to identify new opportunities are prerequisites for a good entrepreneur.

These patterns became evident in to the so-called Sister Industry Programs in Tanzania and Zambia. Both received several years of official Swedish support. The new local entrepreneurs selected were known as "junior sisters". Their owner/managers often had tertiary education and many had previously worked in large companies. The programme linked these entrepreneurs to Swedish "senior sisters", firms in the same industry. The latter were selected to transfer know how in the particular industry, for a fee from the programme

How did the first generation of "junior sisters" succeed ? Not always so well. The level of subsidy made for prolonged incubator starts. Later on many companies did not survive new competition resulting from macro-economic structural adjustment programmes with liberalized imports, markets and market lending rates. Many units with low productivity dragged on rather too long. The survival rate remained high until the market was finally allowed to perform a natural selection and the high effective loan subsidies ceased.

The African "junior sister" entrepreneurs were intended to become a model for other indigenous would-be entrepreneurs. Were these African owner/managers performing worse than their European or Asian colleagues? My experience is that the answer is no. The small proportion of " junior sisters" who finally survived the steel bath of liberalization, is about equal to the survival rates in similar support programmes in countries like Sweden and India.

The better educated African entrepreneurs in larger towns and cities were able to extricate themselves more easily from one important handicap than those with lesser education, active in rural areas. There is great social pressure on successful businessmen in most African cultures to share profits with the extended family and clan. To maintain corporate discipline and to keep the company's finances separate from the demands of the extended family and its elders comes easier for new African entrepreneurs who may have established a certain cultural and perhaps geographic distance to the old norms.

The Troubled Start of AMSCO and ACBF—dilemmas in organizing technical assistance for African management development

Despite several decades of technical assistance, a desperate lack of good indigenous leaders to foster economic development still prevailed in new African institutions and businesses. This led to two new initiatives in the mid-1980s and early 1990s.

One was African Management Services Co. (AMSCO), an initiative led by the International Finance Corporation (IFC), the United Nation's Development Program (UNDP) and others. The purpose was secondment of experienced business leaders to African enterprises. Local African colleagues would be trained in the process. AMSCO received bilateral support from institutions such as Sweden's Swedcorp and a total of US$15 million in initial funding. About 30 large private companies became shareholders. These were the intended base for recruitment and their involvement would foster an early commercial orientation.

The other initiative, with roughly the same sponsors, was the African Capacity Building Foundation (ACBF) with US$100 million committed. ACBF, based in Harare, would help develop indigenous African macro-managerial competence. The target group was African leaders and specialists. They would represent policy and planning institutions and the educational system on the one hand and the private commercial sector (i.e. enterprises) and its support institutions (chambers of commerce etc.) on the other.

It is a historical irony that both AMSCO and ACBF themselves had troubled starts. Both had their implementation shaken at the outset by internal management and leadership crises. It also appears that flaws in the early plans (emanating largely from the Western supporters) were at the heart of the problem. Neither case had weak African leadership as the prime stumbling block. The goals and objectives were not sufficiently clear or adapted to the problems. None of the institutions were created from the inside, i.e. from an African perspective. They become another link in the chain of largely failed technical assistance for improved indigenous African management. AMSCO did not even have its office on the African continent, but was based in Holland.

What has happened since the rocky starts of AMSCO and ACBF?

ACBF has succeeded in launching a series of interesting programs, e.g. for organizations in the area between macro-economic and institutional studies and management development programs. It has initiated Master Programs for new business leaders and for those involved in regulation and supervision of a functioning market economy. A number of collaborations with universities on the continent are reportedly yielding increasingly positive results.

But the institutional dominance of ACBF remains. It might have been an alternative route to support ACBF with some sort of "twinning" arrangements instead of the present heavy institutional dominance from ACBF's peers. In corporate management this could perhaps have been through contracted back-up from an institute for enterprise management development. Focusing in this direction could have enabled more effective support to leadership development for African private enterprises at the micro-level. It could perhaps also have added commercial colleges and polytechnics to the present main academic orientation. Programs aimed at improved governance at macro-levels, such as in policy making and regulating bodies for a market economy might have had a similar support arrangement, perhaps organizationally separated from the corporate management programs.

The AMSCO crisis has not yet been overcome. It was difficult to recruit customers and leaders. The localization in Amsterdam created more problems than it solved, amongst other reasons because the clients did not make a priority of payment claims from AMSCO for its services but instead of creditors that were geographically closer. Some Swedish consultants have launched and won support for a pilot program that aims to shift AMSCOs centre of gravity. The future ought to entail a considerably increased emphasis on seminars for process support, directly to the management of African companies, adapted to their own business strategies and operation problems. In this way AMSCO should be able to put some distance between itself and the classical technical assistance models which have had such limited success. But will AMSCO's battered business concept of requesting payment for technical assistance, survive?

The domination of aid institutions among AMSCO's founders and the fact that private business leaders from industrialized countries appear to have mentally written-off their shares, continues to be a source of concern.

Does the above reveal any patterns or lessons?

Gunnar Myrdal's concept of vicious circles is valid here. Poor people do not become innovators. Simple new technology for refrigeration in the informal service sector (street vending of cold drinks) might be good for Shaban's business and would reduce energy use in society. But Shaban has no margins within which to invest in any new technology which he has not even seen. Such a demonstration might be provided by aid programmes, or perhaps more efficiently by a new generation of small African capitalists?

The shopkeeper with roots in the East had better information and a better international network than his African competitors. Thus he was able to take advantage of the overvalued local currency. Deregulation of today's African economies ought actually to contribute to reducing such disadvantages of indigenous African entrepreneurs and managers as local markets start functioning better.

Small business support to new companies in northern Tanzania could not break the conservative power of some local elders. The separate corporate entity is an abstract, but necessary new institution. The finances of a business must be separated from private funds. This is one of the major challenges to corporate management programs in Africa and is equally relevant to small businesses as to many large enterprises.

During the European depression in the 1930s, a German author and sceptic said of psychoanalysis that it was the disease of its time that regarded itself as its own cure. AMSCO and ACBF aimed at alternatives to decades of largely failed technical assistance in management development. Both experienced governance and management problems with troubled starts, just like Dumont's *L'Afrique. Noire est mal partie*. The old truth remains that management solutions in a society should be bottom-up and indigenous rather than top-bottom with entirely external designs.

Anders Grettve is a consultant in business development and financing at HIFAB International AB Sweden. He has long experience of small business development and financing in Sweden, Eastern Europe and in Africa. He also contributes to management development programmes.

The Agricultural Sector—Management of Natural Resources

Nils-Ivar Isaksson

In most developing countries, the agricultural sector is dominated by small farmers, primarily subsistence producers, with low productivity. It is often the largest sector in terms of contributions to the national product and employment. Within the industrial sector, the manufacturing of agricultural inputs and processing of agricultural produce are often the largest subsector. Overall the agricultural and agriculture related sector not only includes activities at the level of the individual farm or firm, but also at the sector/society level.

It encompasses not only the production of foodstuffs, but also the production of raw materials for industrial processing and export.

It encompasses not only biological production, but also the supply of inputs (fertilizers, seed, machines, credit, etc.) as well as marketing and processing of the products.

It is not only carried out on a subsistence level in a very large number of widely dispersed small family firms (where income from the firm must be complemented with income from other activities) but also as large-scale, mechanized, commercial production.

The production can be based on a single crop or type of animal, but also on a complicated combination of crops and animals.

It includes private firms (inputs, farms, processing), but also co-operatives and parastatal companies and government organizations.

It includes significant activities in the fields of education, research, extension and regulatory services.

The development of the sector presupposes the existence of well-functioning organizations and efficient management at micro and macro level. As for all other activities, political stability and good macro-economic management are basic preconditions.

The author wishes to thank Bengt Nekby and Johan Toborn for useful discussions and viewpoints on earlier drafts of this manuscript.

The objective of this chapter is to highlight the complexity of management in the agricultural sector. The focus of the chapter is on the political, social and economic context of agricultural production and how it affects the practice of good management. It is less concerned with specific management systems or techniques.

Traditionally, the *agricultural sector* encompasses the subsectors of *agriculture, fisheries* and *forestry,* where agriculture includes both *crop* and *animal production.* Within the individual farm, activities from different subsectors are combined and may include, for instance, agroforestry or fish-farming in rice fields. The common denominator is biological production using land as an input.

In addition to the horizontal division into subsectors, the agriculture related sector can also be divided vertically into subsectors for means of production, farms, extension services, processing, distribution etc. The boundaries between the various terms are often hazy. It is difficult to strictly define boundaries between industry and agriculture, farming and forestry, etc. In the following, the term agriculture will be consistently used to include related industry.

Features of the agricultural sector that affect management

The scope of the agricultural sector and its heterogeneous structure, mean that the various management and organizational factors have varying significance in different contexts. Some of the most important features are described below.

Biological production is the basis

Production in the agricultural sector is based on biological production where renewable natural resources are utilized. The natural conditions during the various phases of the growing period—soil structure of the ground, topography and nutrient status, access to water, rainfall, climate, etc.—affect production. Biological production is spatially and geographically widely dispersed. Unplanned and external influences that are difficult to predict—droughts, diseases, pests—make planning difficult and the outcome unpredictable. Even if human actions can affect natural preconditions to some extent, local and regional variations lead to substantial differences in both the quality and quantity of the yield, the choice of product, variety, type of animal and method of cultivation. Diversified production in turn requires a complicated supply of production inputs as well as collection, transport and processing of the products. During recent decades, attitudes to biological production have changed dramatically from the green revolution's orientation towards commercial means of production and technology designed to increase yields to today's, as yet inadequately documented, investments in *sustainable low cost input* production.

Integrated production

Due to its biological dependence the agricultural sector is characterized by a high degree of integration as well as variation in the possible combinations between the means of production and the product as well as between the products and the types of production. Products and waste from cultivation are used as inputs in animal production; manure and animal traction are used as inputs in crop production; the same animals are used for the production of fertilizer, traction power, milk, meat, skins; on one and the same field combinations of trees and crops can be cultivated for the production of food, cash crops, fodder, fertilizer, wood; the farms, particularly the subsistence farms, are simultaneously production and consumption units; extension services, credit facilities and access to means of production must be coordinated, etc.

Time and timing

Time is an important variable in biological production. Different crops require different lengths of time to mature from a month or two to several hundred years and this period can only be influenced to a limited extent. Production cannot be scheduled according to a fixed timetable nor can the volume be determined by planning, as production is dependent on a range of external factors over which farmers have little influence, primarily temperature and access to water (rainfall). Climatic factors (water, temperature) restrict the use of the soil for production to certain periods of the year. If the requisite measures are not taken at the right time in the biological cycle, they will not have the desired effect and can often not be compensated for by other measures later. If, for instance, delivery of concentrated fodder is delayed, the cow's production of milk drops and can later, during the lactation period, only be increased to a very limited extent.

The structure of the sector

The agricultural sector consists mainly of a very large number of individual agricultural production units (farms), which are also consumption units, i.e. households. In Africa most of these production units are very small and are often of a subsistence nature. At the same time, the family needs extra income from work outside the farm in order to support itself. The increase in population, along with low levels of productivity in agriculture and low employment levels in society as a whole, leads to increased fragmentation, overexploitation of public land, cultivation of marginal and ecologically sensitive areas, migration, etc., leading to conflicts between users and ethnic groups, wars, poverty and starvation. Family members usually have low levels of education and may lack formal schooling altogether. Land and user rights are uncertain and show considerable variations.

Parallel to these small units, there is a modern agricultural sector with vast land holdings, using modern technology and producing for the market. These holdings are often owned by industrial companies—private or government—or by people with economic and political influence.

In the 1970s and into the 1980s production and distribution of agricultural inputs, processing and collection of products, provision of extension and other services, etc., were run by the government, co-operatives or parastatals. Prices of inputs for staple and export crops were often determined by the state. Since the advent of the structural adjustment policies of the 1980s the role of the state in these activities has become less prominent, while the emphasis of donors and the IFIs has been to promote the role of the private sector.

Many groups of actors with different knowledge, competence and power

The sector is characterized by a large group of different actors: farmers, local, national and international civil servants, experts and organizations, politicians and donors.

Most people in the very large group of peasant farmers in Africa belong to a hierarchical social system—a system whose features vary from society to society. Farmers often have thorough knowledge of local conditions, not least on production and the utilization of natural resources. They are not particularly inclined to take risks, but they are prepared to try new methods that may increase production. Their preferences and decisions are often based on a complex analysis and the balancing of many different factors.

African public administration is characterized by high, often forced, staff mobility, low salaries, emphasis on quantity at the expense of quality, low relevance in education, outdated administrative systems and structures. For these reasons civil servants are thus often poorly motivated which is detrimental to innovative thinking as well as continuity and stability in the work. New approaches to agricultural development, such as systems theory, popular participation, sustainable production, are accordingly disseminated only slowly.

Other national civil servants and experts, including researchers, entrepreneurs, consultants and officials of co-operatives have more varied, and possibly more relevant, experience and competence. Thus their services are in demand, not least from non-state and donor organizations. Their availability to the state is thus limited. The state administration may also be reluctant to utilize their services, because they often have new attitudes to many questions and demand high fees.

Even among international experts and administrators of development assistance there are significant differences in attitude, competence, experience and realistic approach. The specialist competence may be high, but the individual expert often acts without an institutional context thus reducing continuity.

Policy and institutional framework

The formal structures, organization and administrative regulations of the post-colonial state apparatus are often inherited from the colonial era and were introduced to control and exploit. In spite of the rapid expansion of the post-colonial state apparatus, the centralized administrative colonial structures and systems were retained. This has contributed to the creation of central powers that in periods of stagnation and crisis have hindered broad basal development.

The pre-SAP economic policies were on the whole directed at meeting the demands of urban dwellers and, in combination with the economic crises of recent decades, this has led to an impoverishment of agriculture. Above all education, research, extension services and control functions have suffered during the two last decades. This has led to a reduction in the legitimacy of the nation state for the rural population. Most African countries have not been capable of developing and adapting practical policies, organizations and management to the new political situation. Nor have development and educational needs received sufficient attention.

The content, form and organization of development assistance

Although development assistance only contributes marginally to the total input of resources, donors have great influence on national and sectoral development policies. The proportion of assistance to the agricultural sector does not match its importance neither socio-economically nor as a motor for national development. Donors give priority to investments in facilities and equipment, where the agricultural sector, particularly peasant farmers, has a low absorption capacity. Donor countries also tend to favour short-term projects. Staff changes in donor agencies, from the highest executives of the World Bank or Sweden's Sida to officials in the agency office or the project, lead to changes in the content, form and organization of development assistance and individual projects.

Development assistance to the agricultural sector appears to have been exposed to greater and more rapid changes in method and approach than other sectors. This is partly a result of trying to find new forms for development and support to the sector, since the desired development has not been achieved.

During the 1980s and 1990s, the following changes and transitions have occurred:
- from project/programme to support for macro/sector policies, building up institutions, structural adaptation, *governance*;
- from growth to distribution, environment, *gender* etc.;
- from large integrated programmes to projects for the development of methods and building of institutions;
- from substantial input of donor agency staff to training and short-term consultants;
- from development to disaster relief, rehabilitation and conflict resolution;
- from central strategic planning to pluralism, participatory aspects and democracy;
- from state ownership/implementation to privatization; and
- from substantial independence of projects to donor control, *monitoring* and feedback.

Experiences of organizational development and management within the agricultural sector

Hjelm (1993) suggests that the objectives of western management literature are to try to capture a picture of the *forces that affect development* in general within commercial sectors and above all in the agricultural sector. The same driving forces affect development. In developing countries many similar forces are at play, but factors in the surrounding world, developmental level, circumstances specific to each country, etc., entail that the importance of different factors varies, the level of competence differs and the impact of increasing knowledge is slower.

Organizational development and management have long been bottlenecks in development co-operation. The main part of the *World Development Report 1983* (World Bank, 1983) is devoted to efficiency and improvement of developing countries' management of their development efforts. The report deals with management questions at different levels, particularly the role and activities of the state, and touches on all social sectors.

In a macro-economic study (Svedberg, 1995) on the lack of economic growth in Africa, it is said that empirical cross-sectional studies support the hypothesis that state direction and regulation have had a paralysing effect on growth. That this is particularly applicable to the agricultural sector seems likely, keeping in mind the importance of the sector and the fact that, more than any other, it has been the object of state direction and regulation.

Management problems in Africa, in the agricultural sector among others, have long been considerable. Moris (1977) notes that studies of the situation in East Africa during the 1960s and 1970s indicate that this is a long-term problem and

> ... these nations must cope with a systemic and persistent malfunctioning of their internal administrative machinery, most notably in the crucial fields of their agricultural, educational, and health services.

Unsuccessful development assistance is regarded as a major cause of the decline in development assistance to the agricultural sector, especially in Africa, during the 1980s. These problems remain today. Cleaver (1993) identifies five areas of priority in a strategy for the sector, but adds:

Success in each of the five priority areas ... requires the building of African capacity to manage agriculture, at the farm level, the enterprise, the co-operative, and in government. ... A major shift is required in the direction of building African capacity to manage through expanded training, support to educational institutions in Africa, and support to learning by doing.

Rondinelli (1986) developed a structure for the evaluation of the management of individual agricultural projects in Africa. Seven main groups of factors were identified:

- organizational and institutional structures;
- administrative processes and procedures;
- management of input factors;
- staff management;
- the context in which the project is implemented;
- factors which determine the design of the project; and
- policy factors.

In the evaluation these factors are brought together in four sets of factors: political, design, context and management factors.

Rondinelli's empirical study verifies that the model is very useful for assessing the potential for development project management capacity and adds:

Because development management is a system of dynamically related factors that affect each other in complex and subtle ways, development management capacity consists of the ability to deal with all the four sets of factors. Although the cases showed that not all of the factors are equally important and that some factors affect implementation differently in different projects, the implication is that development managers must be able to cope with all four sets of factors. Therefore, all the factors and the relationships among them should be given attention in the design of projects, training programs for development managers, evaluations, and research on managerial and institutional development.

Rondinelli's study concludes that the four sets of factors had a decisive significance for how well the project was implemented, an experience supported by previous studies of a similar nature. Together the factors form a dynamic system, where each set influences the others and, together, the result of the project. Nevertheless, it is difficult to draw general conclusions from this, since the various management strategies function differently in different environments. It is also important to differentiate between the aspect of management which is composed of leadership, discernment, experience and creativity, i.e. the human aspect, and the aspect that consists of systems, procedures and regulations, i.e. the institutional aspect.

Fowler et al. (1993) identify ten different subsystems that can be included in what Rondinelli calls the institutional aspect. These subsystems complement and support, but do not replace, the human aspect, i.e. organizational culture, leadership, management style, etc.

> An organization's *structure*, i.e. the way that work is split up and recombined with associated authority and responsibility, provides the basis for how systems interrelate, and is a strong factor in determining effectiveness. Organization development may involve changing a combination of structures, systems and (human) resources.

> The systems view makes clear, for example, *that training and human development cannot simply be equated with institutional or organizational development*. Training can only tackle a limited number of systems and is biased towards a limited type of change, that of people's knowledge and skills.

Within Swedish agricultural assistance to Africa, the CADU project in Ethiopia developed a complete and efficient management system in the 1960s, which was also used in the national extension services. A management culture was created which continued to work well long after Ethiopian personnel had taken over the project. It was only slowly undermined by the turbulence of recent decades. An important reason for the success is probably that CADU had strong administrative, planning and evaluation units which continually supplied the leadership with information on the ongoing work. Unfortunately these experiences have not been utilized in subsequent development work. Planning and evaluation in development assistance has increasingly changed from being an instrument for management of the project to becoming an activity that lies outside the project and functions as an instrument for the donors' control and follow-up.

The general experience of integrated rural development projects is, however, not regarded as being positive. The complicated nature of projects easily leads to organizational and co-ordination problems. According to Birgegård (1987) experiences indicate that planning ought to be broadly done, while implementation can with advantage be divided up into individual or packages of similar activities. The question that must be posed is whether this solves the problem? These, individual or packages of similar activities, must be co-ordinated somewhere and this capacity is obviously missing. Is it perhaps so that insufficient resources have been allocated to the development of management capacity in general and to integrated projects—among them agricultural projects—in particular?

Shortcomings in education have previously been mentioned as an important reason for the low efficiency. Moris (1977) notes

> ... management has been the missing function in the education of the service professionals, just as rural development has been the missing sector in management education ...

> Outside the professional sphere—where, admittedly, the doctors, agronomists, engineers, and resource scientists have missed any such training—the problem is rather that amidst a large volume of formal instruction aimed at conveying management skills, management *as such* receives only small emphasis.

A contributory factor to the limited effect of education in the national administration is that the state has had problems retaining well-educated personnel. Cohen (1992) presents experiences from Kenya, where a large number of Kenyans who acquired higher education abroad, rapidly moved to other jobs, primarily outside the public sector. The huge wage differential—between five and ten times higher salaries—but also better career opportunities are the most important reasons for this.

Attempts to improve the situation regarding the lack of staff with good management training have, however, been limited. The World Bank's *Agricultural Sector Review* (WB, 1993) mentions that the review was conducted because of concern over the results of World Bank loans to the agricultural sector. Through structural adjustment, countries were expected to improve management of the economy within society in general as well at the sectoral level. Experiences from 900 projects, financed by the bank, are examined, but nowhere does the review deal with the need for measures to improve management *as such* (cf. Moris, 1977). In FAO (1993) management aspects are not even touched upon.

Concluding comment

In a sectoral and national development perspective, there are important management aspects at the farm, business, project, sector and national levels. Despite the great national significance of the sector, despite defects in management at all levels and despite the fact that the problems have long been known, there are few studies that describe and analyse management and organizational problems within the agricultural sector or propose measures to tackle these problems in a systematic way. The efforts made to deal with the problems have been limited, poorly co-ordinated and short-term.

Nils-Ivar Isaksson is professor emeritus of agricultural economics at the Swedish University of Agricultural Sciences (SLU) in Uppsala. He was the head of the International Rural Development Centre (IDRC) at the Swedish University of Agricultural Sciences from 1978 to 1996.

References

Birgegård, L-E., 1987, "A Review of Experiences with Integrated Rural Development (IRD)", *Issue Paper*, No. 3. Uppsala: IRDC, Sveriges Lantbruksuniversitet.

Cleaver, K. M., 1993, "A Strategy to Develop Agriculture in Sub-Saharan Africa and a Focus for the World Bank", *World Bank Technical Paper*, No. 203. Washington DC: World Bank.

Cohen, J., 1992, "Foreign Advisors and Capacity Building: The Case of Kenya", *Public Administration and Development*, Vol. 12, No. 5. London: John Wiley & Sons.

FAO, 1993, *Strategies for Sustainable Agriculture and Rural Development (SARD): The Role of Agriculture, Forestry and Fisheries*. Rome: FAO.

Fowler, A. et al., 1993, "Institutional Development and NGOs in Africa", *IRD Currents*, No. 5. Uppsala: Sveriges Lantbruksuniversitet.

Hjelm, L., 1993, "Att generera ekonomisk tillväxt och utveckling inom näringslivet, särskilt i jordbruket" (Generating economic growth and commercial development particularly in agriculture), *Småskriftsserien*, nr 78. Uppsala: Institutionen för ekonomi, Sveriges Lantbruksuniversitet.

Moris, J.R., 1977, "The Transferability of Western Management Tradition into the Public Service Sectors, an East African Perspective", in L. Stifel et al. (eds.), *Education and Management for Public Sector Management in Developing Countries*. New York: Rockefeller Foundation.

Rondinelli, D.A., 1986, "Development Management in Africa: Experience with Implementing Agricultural Development Projects", *AID Evaluation Special Study*, No. 44. Washington DC: USAID.

Svedberg, P.S., 1995, "Kan bistånd till Afrika bli effektivt?" (Can development assistance to Africa become efficient?), *Ekonomisk Debatt*, 6. Stockholm: Nationalekonomiska Föreningen.

World Bank, 1983, *World Development Report 1983*. Washington DC: World Bank.

World Bank, 1993, *Agricultural Sector Review*. Washington DC: World Bank.

Identifying the Missing Links in HIV/AIDS Prevention and Control

The Role of Community Based Groups in Health Promotion, Counselling, Care and Social Support

Gunilla Krantz and Frants Staugård

Problems, challenges and opportunities

A multitude of organized prevention and control efforts have been planned and implemented at the national, district and local community level in third world countries ever since the HIV/AIDS epidemic became visible there.

Recently, however, it has become painfully apparent that those organized efforts and the development of a super- and infra-structure for HIV/AIDS prevention and control has only to a limited extent been effective at the grassroots level in terms of changing attitudes and behavioural modes of average members of the population. Problems have become particularly evident in the area of care, counselling and social support for persons with AIDS and their relatives at the local community level.

A well defined gap can now be documented between the national structure for HIV/AIDS prevention and control on one side—and the tangible problems, facing the most vulnerable groups of the population particularly in the sparsely populated and remote areas of many third world countries on the other. Consequently our interest and efforts should be focused on the development of innovative and culture specific strategies for health promotion, counselling, care and social support in the local communities, which are now suffering from the devastating impact of the AIDS epidemic.

Through reviewing two case studies from Tanzania and Uganda the authors wish to draw the attention to current gaps in AIDS prevention and control efforts—and to highlight some gap-bridging initiatives, which have been initiated by members of the local community themselves and ought to be promoted and strengthened.

Through doing so the authors wish to make their general point: that the HIV/AIDS epidemic is a human and societal disaster and a tragedy, particularly tangible for the most vulnerable groups in the most vulnerable communities. However, the epidemic should also be seen as a catalytic factor for innovative thinking and for a revival of the essential elements of the primary health care strategy and the new public health approach, which so far has been more visible in conference rooms and glossy publications—than in the local communities in third world countries.

The role of multi- and bilateral organizations

The World Health Organization (WHO) responded fairly slowly and with some hesitancy to the global HIV/AIDS epidemic. But when the visibility of the epidemic became higher—particularly in the affluent, western societies due to the outbreak of the epidemic in groups of predominantly white, homosexual males—the response became structured and powerful and quickly spread to the international donor community.

WHO's Special Programme on AIDS (later renamed Global Programme on AIDS—GPA) was established as late as February 1987 (WHO, 1987). Among the most important initiatives of the WHO/GPA was the support to the elaboration of national AIDS control programmes, integrated in local primary health care strategies and coordinated with the global control efforts (WHO/Global Programme on AIDS, 1989). During the period 1987–1990 the role of WHO in global HIV/AIDS prevention and control focused on global strategy development and policy formulation, on epidemiological surveillance and research development and on the coordination of support to national AIDS programmes.

Those national AIDS programmes in the majority of countries assumed a role of national super-structures for a number of vital elements in prevention and control. They were made responsible for national policy formulation, for national epidemiological surveillance, coordination of external and national support to the programme and for the establishment of functional infrastructures for safeguarding the blood transfusion system, for the protection of health professionals in institutions and for the organization of care and health education for the general public.

The role of the bilateral donor agencies in this early phase of the epidemic focused on supporting WHO as the global lead agency and through WHO also on supporting the development of national programmes. In addition—and increasingly so over time—bilateral funds were spent on the development of "own" projects within the general framework of the national programme structure and also on support of internationally and nationally active non-governmental organizations (NGOs) (WHO, 1989).

With hindsight and with our current knowledge at hand, it is easy to criticize many of the initial efforts, planned and implemented by multi- and bilateral agencies and national governments. They may be characterized as far too vertical, as culture-insensitive and stereotypical in the development of prevention and control projects and as very top-heavy in the administration and implementation of these projects. But in the view of the authors of this article this initial and vertical phase was a necessary—albeit evidently not sufficient—precondition for a future process of horizontalization in all HIV/AIDS related interventions and a true integration of such efforts into the primary health care structure at the national and local levels.

So the problem is not so much the vertical character of projects, and the lack of "bottom-up" approaches in the early phases of AIDS programme development in the majority of societies—but the fact that a true horizontal perspective and integration of activities in primary health care and local community resources never really materialized as originally foreseen.

The role of non-governmental organizations

From the early days of the HIV/AIDS epidemic NGOs have activated themselves at the district and local community level in relation to the epidemic—often as an extension of already ongoing health related work. This applies particularly to the many NGOs with a missionary background, which are contributing significantly to the maintenance of a health care structure in sparsely populated areas in third world countries and among the most marginalized and underprivileged population groups, constituting the "fourth world" globally.

But a wide range of new NGOs have also been formed in direct response to the epidemic and serve the local communities in highly prioritized and often less glamorous areas such as appropriate, home based care and other support for persons with AIDS (PWAs) and their families, especially the orphans. A number of studies have high-lighted the significance of such NGO efforts, without which the national governments and local populations would have suffered even more from the impact of the epidemic than is now the case (Esu-Williams and Staugård, 1992; Staugård and Westphal-Victor, 1993).

The main features and characteristics of many of these NGOs are that they act through a fine network, staffed by dedicated personnel, that they are particularly well qualified to deal with extremely sensi-tive issues in relation to prevention and control of HIV/AIDS and that they are firmly rooted in the local community, where sustainable, cul-turally and socially appropriate strategies for small-scale interven-tions can be developed (Staugård and Westphal-Victor, 1993). These features could also be defined as the comparative advantage of NGOs in relation to multi- and bilateral agencies and national governments.

Recognizing these facts many agencies and organizations have in-creasingly paid attention to and supported NGO activities in relation to HIV/AIDS. Currently there is a tendency towards allocation of in-creasing proportions of national and international resources for HIV/AIDS prevention and control to NGOs. Following a WHO re-commendation, for example, many national control programmes have decided to allocate 15 per cent of their total financial resources to NGO projects. But there are not only positive features on record. A summary of five country studies on the role of NGOs in HIV/AIDS related work characterizes the majority of activities as sporadic and uncoordinated, as lacking in long-term planning and clear objectives, as developed in isolation and lacking in monitoring and evaluation criteria (Rockefeller Foundation, 1992).

The existing gaps in HIV/AIDS prevention and control

Against the background of the above observations it is possible to define a well documented gap between the existing national super-structures for policy formulation and national programme implemen-tation, supported in many cases by multi- and bilateral agencies, on one side—and the reality at the grassroot level in the local communi-ties on the other. Many of the HIV/AIDS related prevention and con-trol efforts, generated at the national and district levels, fail to reach the local community, where the needs are most pronounced. And if such efforts do indeed reach out to the local community—they are not always sufficiently culture-specific and appropriate to alleviate the plight of the local population or affect its behaviour, where that may be needed.

Somewhat simplified the existing gap in AIDS programme delivery in a typical third world country could be described as in Figure 1.

The question, formulated in Figure 1, should not be misread to indicate that the local population has to await initiatives from WHO—or from any other multi- or bilateral organization for that matter—in order for them to witness effective gap-filling strategies being implemented. But who, then, can contribute to solving the most burning questions in current HIV/AIDS related work in the third world and be instrumental in providing support to those population groups, suffering most from the impact of the epidemic?

Community based groups in health development in Tanzania

The Government of Tanzania has always maintained a very open and constructive attitude towards community based groups and non-governmental organizations. The basis for this exceptionally positive attitude appears to be the recognition by the government of the major contributions, made by the non-governmental organizations, to the early development process in Tanzania, in particular by small religious and often health related groups, which have dedicated themselves to community oriented development work. Tanzania is still heavily dependent on the contributions of non-governmental organizations to its health sector.

The non-governmental sector in the country is multidimensional and represented by an estimated 200 individual organizations or bodies (Esu-Williams and Staugård, 1992). To this figure should be added a substantial but unknown number of community based groups and loosely structured associations, which remain unregistered and are active at the regional, district or local community level.

Some, but not all non-governmental organizations are affiliated with umbrella organizations which aim at coordinating and facilitating the work of the individual groups. Specifically referring to the area of HIV/AIDS prevention and control, a large number of groups have already become involved in direct activities and the potential for future involvement appears to be vast, provided that the government and external donors decide to play a proactive role in order to mobilize and strengthen the capacity of these groups for an active involvement.

Figure 1. *The gap between national programmes and HIV/AIDS prevention and control at the local community level*

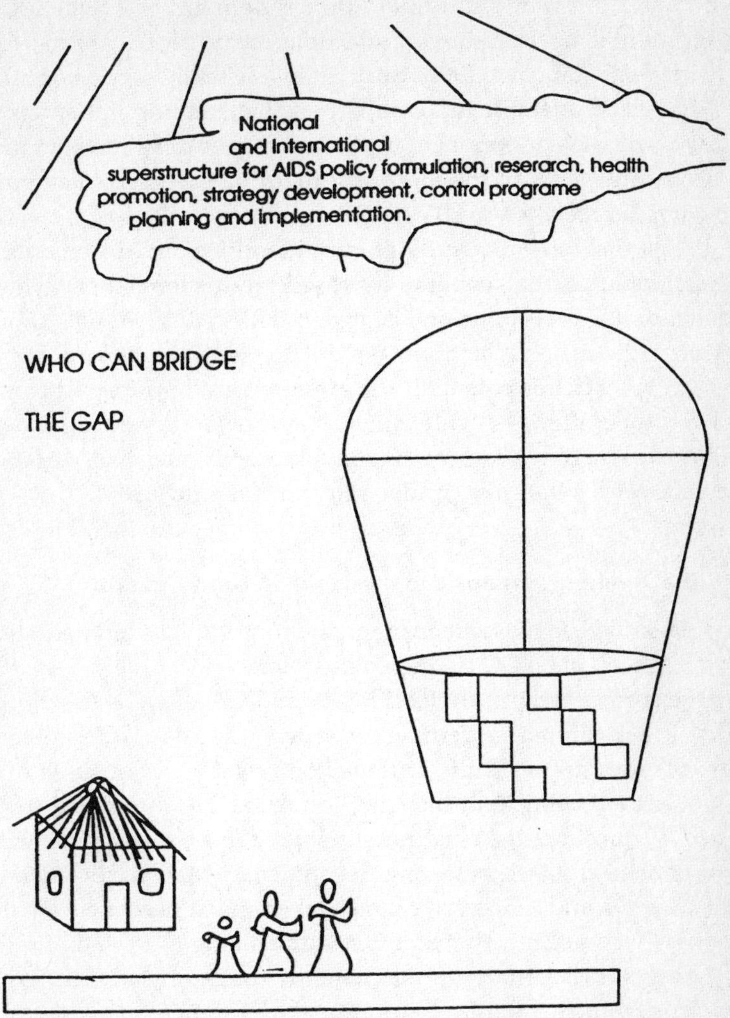

National and International superstructure for AIDS policy formulation, research, health promotion, strategy development, control programe planning and implementation.

WHO CAN BRIDGE

THE GAP

The Tanzania case study identifies the HIV/AIDS programme components of health promotion, care, counselling and social support as particularly relevant and important areas for involvement of non-governmental organizations and community based groups (Esu-Williams and Staugård, 1992). Such an involvement should primarily be targeted at unemployed youth, marginalized population groups and women with no formal education or means of supporting themselves, as members of these groups might be categorized as potentially at risk in relation to HIV/AIDS.

While the Tanzania study readily identifies and documents the vast potential of small community based groups in relation to necessary action for prevention and control of HIV/AIDS—it falls short of identifying sustainable management systems for the necessary strengthening of this potential. The grassroot groups often act in isolation and their efforts—highly valuable as they are for the local population—suffer from a lack of coordination with other HIV/AIDS related activities in the area (Andersson and Staugård, 1986).

Informal women's groups and networks in rural Uganda

Uganda is still heavily dependent on the contributions of international as well as national NGOs to its health sector.

The current activities of local NGOs and CBGs can be described as sporadic and limited concerning the state of the HIV/AIDS epidemic. The activities are a result of understanding the seriousness of the HIV/AIDS epidemic and the need to take action to prevent further spread of infection, the need for support to those infected as well as for orphaned children following the epidemic. Many of the activities which NGOs and CBGs have undertaken, have been tied to funds provided for specific activities, often with no long-term commitment.

Many of these groups, predominantly formed by women, experience constraints such as limitations of financial and technical resources, as well as lack of special training and supervision. Limited managerial and administrative capability and capacity of some women's groups also prevent them from fully utilizing their potential for a full and effective participation in the national AIDS control programme (NACP).

Current role of women's groups in health promotion, care and community support activities

Rural women organized in women's groups perform health related activities such as health education directed towards the youth, mainly orphaned girls. Women occasionally take part in educational campaigns promoting the use of condoms for specific target groups. There are different kinds of home based care programmes directed towards persons with AIDS and their families. Some are highly specialized while others are mainly based on social support, not being able to offer any medical advice or treatment.

Some women's groups receive basic training from NGOs and are on a voluntary basis, visiting persons and families affected by AIDS in their homes, offering social support. Sometimes they are able to provide some basic products to alleviate lack of food. These women, organized in community based groups, are not trained in counselling or on health matters, but perform supportive activities out of sheer commitment. Women organized in informal women's groups perform community support activities by engaging in income-generating projects, vocational training activities for orphaned girls and by providing and caring for orphans.

Women organized in women's groups face severe constraints in all their efforts. They experience lack of continuous financial support, lack of training in managerial and administrative skills, and also a shortage of materials and utensils to be able to extend their activities as well as difficulties in finding a market for their products. The small income generated makes it possible for the women's groups to support persons and families affected by HIV/AIDS and is often transformed into basic needs like soap, seeds, and blankets. It also enables the women to care for a limited number of orphaned children, making it possible for some of the children to attend school.

A number of women's groups are engaged in activities concerning orphaned children such as caring and giving social support, providing scholastic materials and basic necessities, for example clothing, food, and shelter. The NGOs and community based women's groups which are involved in orphan support activities, are confronted with a number of problems. The main problem is lack of funding as well as lack of building materials, transport and equipment.

The above mentioned health related and community support activities, performed by women's groups, are generally of limited coverage and lacking in long-range planning. They are only to a limited extent effective in preventing the further spread of HIV—not only due to limited geographical coverage but also to the uncoordinated nature of the efforts.

Potential role of women's groups in health related and community support activities

Because of the magnitude of the HIV/AIDS epidemic in Uganda there is a need to encourage and support greater participation by groups outside government for HIV/AIDS prevention and control. There seems to be an obvious possibility to enhance the participation of women's groups in HIV/AIDS programmes, with only a minor increase in assistance, to make women's groups effective collaborating partners with the primary health care sector in their mutual struggle against the HIV/AIDS epidemic. Women's groups might contribute to filling the gap between rural people and the National AIDS Control Programme, which the primary health care sector alone is not able to do at present.

Health promotion is a crucially important area in prevention of HIV transmission and there are numerous groups to be reached with appropriate HIV/AIDS education and information. Community based women's groups can actively participate in educating young girls within and outside of school. It will be desirable for educational activities to be linked with training for skills for income generation, in order to give young women an opportunity to stay economically independent, thereby reducing their risk of being HIV infected.

Programmes for youth and adolescents are important areas where women's groups could make a contribution. By involving traditional sex educators (aunts, elderly women, traditional birth attendants—TBAs), it might be possible to incorporate HIV/AIDS education within puberty rites and the education of girls.

Special emphasis should be put on TBAs as they are key figures in the informal women's and girls' networks in many societies and may access these networks with relevant, culture-specific information in relation to sexual behaviour and HIV/AIDS. In their role as informal community leaders and guardians of social norms and rules, TBAs could be trained to channel educational messages to the local population on HIV/AIDS issues. Household members could be approached with HIV/AIDS educational messages by community health workers/women's groups while performing caring activities to a sick member of the family. Orphans, both boys and girls, are often cared for by women organized in women's groups and therefore can be addressed with educational messages concerning HIV/AIDS.

The level of literacy is in many respects decisive for how educational messages will be received. The importance of children and youth attending primary school cannot be sufficiently emphasized.

Selected women organized in women's groups could be trained as counsellors in a more comprehensive training scheme with the goal to have one well-trained counsellor in each village.

As regards caring for persons with AIDS it is obvious that women's groups constitute a not yet fully utilized resource, assuming that a considerable number of community based women's groups could be mobilized to perform home based activities. Women in the local community possess good knowledge of households and their respective needs. A prerequisite is that basic training, refresher courses and supervision from health staff will be provided. Through mobilizing women's groups, a good coverage within the district will be secured concerning home based care for AIDS patients and their families.

The promotion of non-health related activities such as training for vocational skills and income-generating projects, like organized farming activities within villages and towns, may act as the basis for the economic and social development of many communities. This approach, which should also consist of HIV/AIDS education, forms the basis for primary prevention and control of the epidemic. This strategy is of particular importance for reaching young people in villages, as their migration into cities may increase their risk of contracting sexually transmitted diseases.

Today women's groups are engaged in income-generating activities to raise funds to be used as a contribution to community development. This type of activity could be further developed, assuming that training and funds are provided for a more extensive and long-term engagement. A crucial point is to find new products and to increase quality in produced articles, as a way of finding a market. Activities such as growing mushrooms and keeping silk-worms for silk production have been suggested as small-scale business opportunities.

Caring for orphaned children and ensuring their school attendance make an important contribution to social and economic development of the community. An extended family/kinship-oriented project that will ensure stability and long-term sustainability for orphan care has been proposed by Rutayuga (1992). It is stressed that the traditional system should be supported with financial assistance and social services to overcome the problems created by the large number of orphans. The children could be helped within the family system rather than in institutions. This would benefit the children psychologically, and give hope for stability in their future lives.

Many women's groups are already, on their own initiative and on a purely volunteer basis, engaged in supporting families and caring for orphans but they need further technical assistance and fund raising possibilities to be able to enhance their activity.

Preconditions for grassroot involvement in HIV/AIDS prevention and control

Discussions and interviews with representatives of already established women's groups as well as with local community members, reveal that there is an expressed interest and potential for becoming involved in HIV/AIDS related activities. It is emphasized though, that a necessary precondition for inputs by community based women's groups, is support in various forms such as training, education, coordination and funds.

The needs for support can be summarized and described as a need for support from local institutions and donors, need for support from and communication with other NGOs/CBGs and need for support from the health care sector/NACP. The need for support from local institutions and donors, expressed as a need for financial support as a precondition for initiating or consolidating already ongoing HIV/AIDS related activities, is stated by women's groups and key persons in discussions. The need for training in the fields of administrative and managerial skills as well as in project development is of vital importance.

Women in Uganda, according to current legislation, are prohibited from ownership of land, resulting in lack of security. Government and donors, including internationally active NGOs, may create a fund to which women's groups can apply for time-limited loans. Tentatively, the funds could be managed by a suitable umbrella NGO.

To secure more sustainable activities, conditions such as continuous financial support to women's groups guaranteed for a period agreed upon, tentatively two to three years, and micro-credit schemes without interest should be specifically designed for women organized in groups.

Donors should take responsibility for training in administrative and managerial skills as well as in project development skills. The training should be looked upon as part of any future grant to projects performed by women's groups.

The training should be of the nature of a training of trainers and at least comprise areas such as administrative procedures, accounting, book-keeping and reporting procedures. Also of vital importance are basic training in management, target setting, monitoring of activities, evaluation, policy and ethical issues in order to enable women's groups to develop their projects.

Women organized in women's groups need collaboration with and support from the health care sector. Staff at health facilities throughout the district form a potential resource when it comes to training, supervision and support to women's groups engaged in health related activities.

A collaboration between the formal health care sector and community based groups, including women's groups, involved in health related activities, could be a mutually beneficial opportunity to enhance the activities performed and a way to increase resources at a low cost.

However, it is important to point out that it is a question of exchanging knowledge and experiences, a two-way communication, that is desirable. There is an obvious risk that women organized in women's groups as well as traditional health practitioners will be subordinated to the health care staff and that the organization will be over-bureaucratized. The spirit and the initiatives of the grassroot level groups risk being suppressed in an extended organization, something that must not happen.

Summary and conclusion

As indicated by the two case-studies from Tanzania and Uganda there appears in some African countries to be a gap between the policy formulating and technical advisory bodies of the ministries of health and the AIDS programme's regional and district implementing bodies on the one hand—and the local communities on the other. Consequently some of the strategies for HIV/AIDS prevention and control which have been formulated within the health care structure, are failing to reach, or affect the attitudes and behaviour of, the population at the local community level.

The wide range of non-governmental organizations and community based groups in the two countries studied represents a major potential and might become mobilized in order to fill the present gap between the existing national super-structures for HIV/AIDS prevention and control and major population groups in the villages and rural areas.

Health promotion, care, counselling and social support appear to be particularly relevant and important areas for involvement of community based groups in HIV/AIDS prevention and control. Such an involvement should primarily be targeted at marginalized population groups and women with no formal education or means of supporting themselves.

To secure an efficient and effective contribution by existing community based groups to the national HIV/AIDS control programme— and to facilitate the mobilization of additional groups who have a major potential for such a contribution—the administrative and managerial capability of non-governmental organizations and community based groups must necessarily be strengthened.

The two case-studies, summarized in this paper, conclude that specific action should be taken by the national governments and by external donors in order to facilitate the mobilization of a wide range of non-governmental organizations and community based groups for future participation in health promotion, counselling, care and community support in relation to HIV/AIDS and to strengthen the capability and capacity of these groups in order to sustain the necessary initial financial and technical support, rendered to them.

One way in which the management of support to small, community based groups, could be designed, is the establishment of a "five-tier-system" for the flow of funds from donors to recipients and for the organization of necessary educational initiatives (see Figure 2).

The "five-tier-system" could consist of an external donor agency at the first level and a national non-governmental umbrella organization at the second. At these levels, funding would be generated and educational arrangements concerning the strengthening of administrative and technical skills be organized.

The third and fourth levels in this system would consist of national non-governmental organizations, active at both the national and local levels. And, finally, the fifth level in the system would be represented by the small community based groups, where the capability in terms of administrative and technical skills might initially be low but where the capacity appears to have the potential to make a difference.

Figure 2. *A proposed five-tier structure for funding and management of community based small scale health projects*

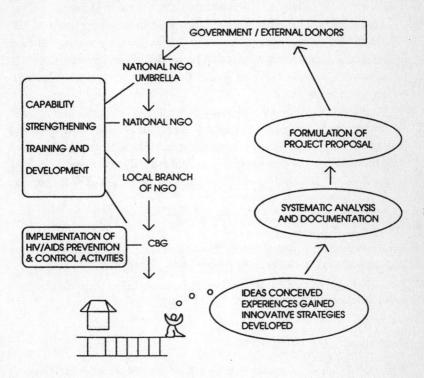

Using this "five-tier-system" for the channelling of funds and training—from the external donors through to small community based groups—would enable all participating parties to respect legitimate demands for accountability while at the same time focusing on the long-term sustainability of the efforts initiated.

This part of the "five-tier-system"—used to channel funds and technical skills from the external donors and national umbrella organizations through to small community based groups—will, of necessity, have a top-down orientation. But the "bubbling-up" potential of the system—enabling non-governmental organizations, national governments and external donors to collate, analyze, and utilize highly valuable experiences from the grassroot level in the development of innovative, national strategies for future HIV/AIDS prevention and control—is even more exciting than the potential for establishing a functional system for administration of funds and skills. This model for strengthening community based groups has now been launched as part of the Rakai district Development Programme in Uganda.

The energy, enthusiasm, and readiness to take necessary action has been convincingly documented in the studies on women's groups in local communities in Central Africa. But those groups urgently need material support and technical skills in order to ensure sustainability of their efforts.

It is the obligation of national governments, regional and district administrations and external donors to respond to this challenge and provide the necessary support for the multitude of community based groups, which have the potential to make a difference for a population facing the devastating consequences of the HIV/AIDS epidemic.

Gunilla Krantz, MD, DPH is Acting Senior Lecturer in Community Health at the Nordic School of Public Health, Gothenburg, Sweden.

Frants Staugård, MD, MPH, Dr Med Sci, is Professor in International Health at the Nordic School of Public Health, Gothenburg, Sweden.

References

Anderson, S. and F. Staugård, 1986, *Traditional Midwives*. Botswana: Ipelegeng Publishers.

Esu-Willams, E. and F. Staugård, 1992, *Community Based Groups and Non-Governmental Organizations Concerned with HIV/AIDS. Country Needs Assessment Tanzania*. Rockefeller Foundation, New York/University of Calabar/University of Gothenburg.

Rockefeller Foundation, 1992, *Initiative to increase international assistance to developing country groups outside government concerned with HIV/AIDS. Five country studies* (Côte d'Ivoire, Egypt, India, Mexico and Tanzania). New York: Rockefeller Foundation.

Rutayuga, J., 1992, *Assistance to AIDS-orphans within the family kinship system and local institutions. AIDS education and prevention*. New York: Guilford Press.

Staugård, F. and B. Westphal-Victor, 1993, *Evaluation of Danchurchaid's AIDS Sector Support 1987–1992*. Danish Church Aid, Copenhagen; and Nordic School of Public Health, Gothenburg.

Ukimwi Orphans Assistance, Mission Statement, P.O.Box 29 074 Washington D.C., 1994.

World Health Organization, 1987, *Resolution WHA 40.32 of the Fortieth World Health Assembly*. Geneva: WHO.

World Health Organization, 1989, *Resolution WHA 42.34 of the Forty-second World Health Assembly*. Geneva: WHO.

World Health Organization/Global Programme on AIDS, 1989, *Progress report submitted to the Global Management Committee Meeting, 6–8 December, Geneva, 1989*.

Urban Management and Democracy

Ann Schlyter

My interest in urban management derives from research that I have done on housing and on urban services in housing areas. Since 1968 I have followed the development of a peri-urban area in Lusaka called George compound. I have studied upgrading, community organization, housing, and family survival strategies, as well as the rights of women heads of households and married women. At the moment I am engaged in a study on young people, gender relations, everyday life and politics. This paper is based on partly unpublished material from fieldwork that I carried out during 1994 and 1995. I will discuss local organization as a complement to local authorities, with examples from Southern Africa, particularly Zambia. In addition to this, I will demonstrate that economic and political reforms do affect people's everyday life to a much greater extent than is normally acknowledged in discussions about aid, democracy, and development.

Politics and management on a communal level

Within the public sector, management refers to both administration and political governance. In the anthology *African Cities in Crisis* (1989), Stren divides the concept of management into local government, which is the decision making authority, and local administration, the unit that provides the urban services. This he does for analytical purposes only; in African local authorities there exists no explicit division between the decision making and the executive bodies.

In Africa, local governments have never been independent but rather been regarded as executive branches of the central government. This applies to the earlier British colonies and, probably to an even greater extent, to the French ones. In South Africa, Zimbabwe and Namibia (the "white") local governments had a higher degree of independence, probably due to Dutch and German public management traditions.

Generally the city councils consist of both elected and centrally appointed members. There are variations, but for the most part local governments come under a ministry and have limited economic independence. The revenues derive mainly from charges for communal services and taxation of real estate. For investments, say in infrastructure or housing, local governments are dependent on loans and allocations from the central governments.

In the literature, urban management is often limited to the reference of urban service such as physical infrastructure, notably water and roads. The responsibility of the local government is defined in different ways in different countries. Caroline Moser (1995) from the World Bank suggests that local governments should take on greater responsibility for social issues. She presents this as a new idea, which it may be from a World Bank, and possibly from an African, but certainly not from a Nordic, perspective.

The divided town

During the fifties, the British colonial administrations started to extend the cities and their service systems. A new era demanded skilled labour instead of unskilled rural migrants coming as guest workers to towns. Local governments built housing areas for a permanent industrial labour force, and for a limited, newly created, African middle class working in the public sector. With small but important privileges the urban population was expected to become a politically stabilizing force.

The new, independent states continued the colonial urban policy. According to the prevailing modernization strategy, the focus was on industrialization and high standard urban housing was developed. However, the problem was that the number of houses that were actually built did not cover even the needs of the expanding middle class. Hence, divided towns were created, consisting of high standard planned areas and illegal squatter areas.

For as long as possible, the local governments tried to ignore the expansion of these illegal shantytowns, as did the development agencies, which regarded the urban poor mainly as a result of unsuccessful rural policy. Frequent cases of demolition actions created a sense of insecurity among the shantytown dwellers. In many towns the majority of the population lived in unplanned areas without any service at all.

Within the legal town, i.e. the part of the town existing on the map, the local government was generally effective and maintained order according to the regulations laid out in a zone plan. Premises for crafts and business, for example, were only allowed in certain districts. Even during the eighties, local officials in Zambia and Zimbabwe destroyed maize fields, planted by town dwellers to increase their food supply. The rules were there to be obeyed, even though their origin, as in this case, was colonial. This particular rule was supposed to be a health regulation with the motivation that the maize fields were breeding mosquitoes. In reality the regulation originated in a policy of migrant labour and influx control, and it aimed at making it impossible for people to live in the cities without salaried work.

It took some time for the young African nations to develop a local competence within urban management, and much of the planning was performed by consultants. Gradually a small, professional group of planners and technicians was established, proud of their skills, and not inclined to discuss other and more simple, local solutions with the poorer part of the population. Nor did the politicians think that they had anything to gain from talking about reduced standards of living. Simple squatter upgrading was no political showpiece.

Not until the development aid agencies intervened in urban policy and management during the seventies were squatter areas legalized, and basic site-and-service areas were provided for self-building. In many cases, however, the projects were brought about by separate administrations set up by the aid agencies. Often the local government officials felt neglected, and looked on enviously as these development projects got past otherwise impenetrable obstacles.

Informal management and self-management

Ever since the seventies, when the concept informal sector was formulated, it has been criticized. This has not prevented the concept from surviving. Now, there is an on-going discussion on how to bridge the dualism between the formal and the informal city, or how to integrate the informal sector into the formal one, by using different kinds of regulations. However, the difficulties are many. For example a great number of informal businesses would not be able to meet the costs of formalization.

In general, the urban management is only responsible for the formal city. The dominance of the so-called informal sector becomes evident from the fact that half of Zambia's population lives in towns, but less than ten per cent of the country's labour force works within the formal sector. From the viewpoint of urban management, the informal sector is a problem which makes it difficult or impossible to collect taxes and charges, maintain norms according to zone plans or public health rules, and much more.

The boundaries between the informal and formal do not always coincide in various departments of the city administration. Shops in squatter areas may, for instance, be equipped with electricity, and public buses may run within areas where neither garbage collection nor water supply exist. Public health regulations may be maintained at certain shops, but not at other work places.

The inhabitants co-operate in different ways to organize and manage their immediate common environment. For an urban area to function, there is work to be performed, and this work is often done by women although men are usually seen as the leaders. The management of the local community is such an important part of women's daily life that Moser (1993) in her handbooks on gender planning, has identified the work within the community as one of the women's three most important roles. The other two are within the production and reproduction spheres.

Informal management of an urban area may be performed in many different ways and with varying degrees of participation. It can, for instance, be organized by, or in co-operation between, churches, political parties, and non-governmental organizations. Often, organization for the urban environment functions at its best when the environment is threatened, or when prospects of improvement are present. In between, however, management of this kind often functions badly. It easily becomes individualized and invisible.

In countries with a one-party system the boundaries between formal and informal management may be blurred. So, on the one hand, Lusaka City Council maintained a strict division of the town, and did not accept any responsibility for the management of squatter areas. On the other hand, these areas were planned by local leaders, elected within the framework of the one and only party. Within the one-part system, the party, and the local government merged in such a way, that the local party organizations were perceived by the urban inhabitants as the lowest levels in the urban management hierarchy.

Change of system—with problems

At present many countries in Africa are changing from a one-party system to a multi-party system. The case I refer to in this article is a peri-urban area in Lusaka but Zambia's system, with sections that consisted of 25 houses, did not differ in any decisive way from Tanzania's system of ten cells, the *kabeles* in Ethiopia, or from the so-called dynamization groups in Mozambique and Angola. The local party organizations took responsibility for local management, even in shantytowns considered illegal by the formal urban management. For people living in the shantytowns this was the very structure that incorporated them into society and politics.

The local party organs obtained authority and legitimacy, partly because people found it quite natural that the responsibility held by a village headman, in the town corresponded to the responsibility of a leader within the party—a kind of urban headman—and partly because these leaders were elected among the people in their own community. The leaders had the double task to, on the one hand, advance their district's cause upwards within their party, and, on the other hand, to disseminate information from above to the people. Elections to local women's and youth organizations were also carried out. The women performed a large amount of unpaid social work in the community, while the young men kept law and order.

The local party structure in George compound in Lusaka strengthened its position during the seventies, when the compound was legalized and improvements were made (Schlyter, 1983). The local leaders, who had long been struggling for improvements, took credit for the project, and were also deeply engaged in its implementation. For the community this development was a big step forward, but in spite of the legalization Lusaka's urban management never established any additional service in the area, nor did it take any responsibility for its maintenance.

During the eighties, when the population's economic situation and living conditions deteriorated drastically, the party gradually lost much of its credibility. This applied both to the central leadership and the local organizations. Some of the leaders, especially among the women, kept up the social and conflict-solving part of the activities, but now more in their capacity as trusted citizens.

When the one-party system was abandoned in the 1991 elections, the entire local party structure disappeared as if by magic. Many inhabitants felt a new freedom when the formalized social control maintained by the party disappeared. At the same time, they expected that the new governing party, MMD, the Movement for Multi-Party Democracy, was going to fill the seats in the local organization, which was perceived as their level of local government. When it became evident that the MMD had no intention to establish such a system, many were disappointed (Schlyter, 1996). Now the people living in Lusaka's various areas were left with only one formal link to the urban democracy, i.e. their councillor. And the councillor who was in charge of the central parts of George compound did not even live in that area, but in a middle class area at the other end of Lusaka.

A system with one councillor who speaks for his area in the corridors of power may be as effective as when the grassroots views are advanced gradually within the party hierarchy. But such a system does not create a framework for local responsibility and initiative; instead, a patron-client relationship easily develops. Occasional projects initiated by international development agencies or charitable institutions cannot replace a permanent local organization. Many people find their way to the churches, and a church may function as a social organization for its congregation, but no single voluntary organization will be able to represent everybody living in the area.

The situation in Lusaka four years after the election was such, that the local government had been unable to budget for any services whatsoever in the poor communities. The government had to rely wholly upon the population's own efforts and external help. Development agencies from the entire world appeared with their various projects for water, drainage, etc., and the local government tried to take care of the co-ordination.

The local officials told me that they had initiated the establishment of Residential Development Committees (RDCs) in the different areas. The idea was that they should be independent of party politics. One RDC has functioned well and succeeded in improving a small peri-urban area, and now it remains to be seen if this idea can be implemented on a larger scale. George and adjacent compounds with more than 100,000 inhabitants have been divided into zones, and in December 1995 the elections started. But the situation was very confused. Nobody seemed to know how the elections should proceed. Many mistook the RDC committees for the "water committees", being elected at that time to supervise the installation of new water pumps with Japanese support.

Urban development assistance

Swedish development assistance has been directed mainly toward rural areas, and support aimed at urban areas is almost non-existent. An exception to this is administrative aid which has also reached urban areas. In Botswana and Zimbabwe among other countries it has focused on land issues and physical planning (Karlsson et al., 1994). During certain periods it has involved direct staff assistance for town planning.

Other development organizations have wider experiences. In 1972 the World Bank published an Urban Policy Paper, and during the seventies it also embarked on a series of projects including not only management support, but also investments in the development of urban areas. The majority of projects were evaluated as successful as far as the population's everyday life was concerned, but were considered unsuccessful when it came to financing. According to the Bank's cost-recovery policy, the total development costs should be met by charges paid by the poor communities themselves. However, it seemed impossible to make upgrading projects in poor areas self-financing. Consequently, the projects had very few offshoots, and the result was renovated islands in an ocean of unplanned housing without any service.

The criticism against project-orientation in urban aid led to a switch toward a more pronounced policy- and management-oriented assistance. The idea was that towns should be improved by strengthening their management resources. House-building should be stimulated by support to institutes for the financing of buildings, and other institutes and companies. But this kind of assistance has also been criticized and called "housing without houses". Furthermore, it has been asserted that management reforms were not always carried out to the same extent or with the same degree of commitment due to the often contradictory advice of different development agencies.

Like most things development assistance and politics are subject to trends. Decentralization has been a political and developmental catchword in many countries but often things have turned out as they did in Tanzania. In the beginning of the seventies, Nyerere launched a decentralization policy aimed at strengthening local and regional management and public authority. According to Stren (1989) his reforms in fact led to the opposite result.

The urban management assistance lost impetus when the main focus was placed on the structural adjustment programmes. Support to the public sector was not in line with structural adjustment policy. On the contrary, this meant cutting down on urban management resources, which often led to urban services almost collapsing. Subsidies were abolished, and charges were introduced for education and health, changes that hit the urban poor hard.

Everyday life in poor urban areas has been affected in a very negative way by the economic reforms. Unfortunately, the political reforms aimed at democratization have also had a not entirely positive impact.

In large areas of the towns urban services that we consider as normal: water, roads, garbage collection, schools and so on, are non-existent or non-functioning. It has been calculated that within the next thirty years Africa's towns will have a population growth corresponding to the entire present population of the continent. There are no contingency plans for this, but in the wake of all evidence of urban impoverishment during the structural adjustment period, there is a growing interest from donor countries to take an active part in urban development.

In conclusion

Today democracy is both a goal and a condition for assistance, and currently many countries are experiencing a transition from a one-party system to a multi-party system. During this transition more attention must be paid to the impact this change has on ordinary people's daily life. When party structures for self-management disappear, urban politicians and officials must take full responsibility for urban management.

Non-governmental organizations, local as well as external, may be able to take over some parts of urban management but they cannot be expected to take full responsibility, and from a democratic point of view they should not do so. In order to develop new methods for collaboration within urban management, new democratic forms of cooperation between local governments and various community based organizations must be found.

In African countries there is no clear line of demarcation between politics and management. Therefore as development aid to urban management entails direct intervention in local politics, the democratic aspects must be especially considered by donors.

The urban areas are today divided into formal and informal sectors. A large part of the towns' development and activities take place within the informal sector. In Zimbabwe and South Africa, the One City Concept was used when merging the black and white parts of town under joint management. Similarly, a deliberate policy is imperative here, to bridge the gap between formal and informal urban areas and activities.

In a negative sense the gap has narrowed since the urban services have to a great extent collapsed, even in the formal parts the of towns. The aim is now to find a level where all urban activities may be integrated, and in such a way that services and protection may be provided even in informal areas, but at the same time without stifling ongoing activities.

In a situation when the central government as well as the local authorities have abandoned their responsibilities for urban management, perhaps more attention ought to be paid to how the towns actually function. Diana Lee-Smith and Richard Stren (1991) formulated the issue as follows: "A new approach to the study of African urban management needs to start with the state of society, rather than with the society of the state".

Dr. *Ann Schlyter* is a senior researcher at the Nordic Africa Institute in Uppsala. Her research centres around urbanization, housing and gender in Southern Africa.

References

Karlsson, Anders, Arne Heileman & Eliese Alexander, 1994, *Shifting the Balance? Towards Sustainable Local Government, Decentralization and District Development in Botswana*. Stockholm: Sida.

Lee-Smith, Diana & Richard Stren, 1991, "New Perspectives on African Urban Management", *Environment and Urbanization,* 3(1):23–36.

Moser, Caroline, 1993, *Gender Planning and Development. Theory, Practice and Training*. London and New York: Routhledge.

Moser, Caroline, 1995, "Urban Social Policy and Poverty Reduction", *Environment and Urbanization,* 7(1):59–172.

Schlyter, Ann, 1983, *Upgrading Reconsidered—The George Studies in Retrospect*. Gävle: The National Swedish Institute for Building Research.

Schlyter, Ann, 1996, "Urban Community Organization and the Transition to a Multi-Party Democracy in Zambia", in L. Rudebeck and O. Törnqvist (eds.), *Democratization in the Third World. Concrete Cases in Comparative and Theoretical Perspective*. Uppsala: The seminar for Development Studies, Uppsala University.

Stren, Richard E. and Rodney R. White (eds.), 1989, *African Cities in Crisis. Managing Rapid Urban Growth*. Boulder, San Francisco & London: Westview Press.

Aid Management

Jan Valdelin

This article is concerned with *aid management* or the question of how international development co-operation is best managed. The purpose is to illustrate what experience from Africa has taught us about official development assistance (ODA), as well as to draw conclusions from these lessons about what is needed to make future aid generally more effective.

Introduction

By way of introduction some characteristic features of international development co-operation should be pointed out. Among these is the fact that the nature of bilateral co-operation is extremely political. This is in actual fact obvious, since it involves the relationship between two governments. Thus, assistance cannot be reduced to purely economic or technical issues, although such concerns are in the forefront of this article.

An extension of this political aspect is that international assistance produces a special relationship between two parties. The *aid relationship*, which exists between governments, also occurs in administrations and projects where foreign advisors are working. It does not function in the same way as trade relationships or general business relations. Aid relationships are different, which is revealed simply by the terms *donor* and *recipient*. We have finally recognized this, but what aid relationships lead to has not been adequately considered. British historians have pointed out that trade is one of the few human activities that has been able to develop its own system of rules, quite independently of nations and states. For the bilateral aid relationship, the position is reversed: it *only* exists within the framework of a system of rules established between the contracting governments.

The text is translated and edited from original Swedish version.

Projects supported by donors consequently operate within the framework of a political agreement and as part of a special aid relationship. The two most important parties in the management of aid are the donor and the recipient. This applies to the bulk of bilateral assistance as well as to multilateral aid.[1]

In addition to the above-mentioned actors, a number of others, such as public authorities, non-governmental organizations, companies, and staff employed by either the donor or the recipient country to implement projects, also participate in aid-created relationships.

In a recent study,[2] an analysis was made of stakeholders in Swedish aid. The authors claim that some of the most important aid stakeholders are the very people who in different roles and various forms manage or work with aid. This *group of people with personal stakes* includes representatives of both the donor and the recipient country. This may entail that these stakeholders only rarely subject aid to critical review. It may be difficult to create changes in established aid relations from within this group and they may make it even more difficult to achieve changes from the outside.

The existence of stakeholders creates a challenge to those who design policies and to those who are in charge of their implementation. For a policy to be able to make a breakthrough, it must be understandable and possible to implement. Even so, it will not actually be implemented unless the managers are made accountable and subjected to repercussions if the policy is not followed. Unless both of these conditions—accountability and sanctions—are met, aid projects tend to be routinely run by stakeholders, without specific legitimacy.

The following presentation is divided into the donor's methods of managing budgets and the recipient's management of foreign aid. Most aid relationships are dominated by the donor and the collective view of the donor community over time is what exerts the strongest influence over methods and management.

---

[1] We omit assistance channelled through private agencies, e.g. non-governmental organizations, as well as the relatively modest part of aid that goes directly to private organizations in recipient countries.

[2] Schill, G. and J. Valdelin, *Countering the Conveyor Belt*. Stockholm: Sida.

The donor's management of development co-operation funds

Country programming

In the early 1970s, country programming was introduced as a method of allocating and managing aid. The concept was introduced by the Johnston report commissioned by UNDP. The method was based on the donor selecting a number of programme countries. One of the criteria of selection (by some countries, e.g. Sweden) was that the country should have adopted policies that aimed at economic and social equity. Such policies were to be expressed in a development plan that the donor would support by giving assistance to the recipient countries' planning and budget systems.

The ideology underlying country programming contained several components; the most important of which included *trust in the political leadership* of the recipient countries and *faith in planning as a tool* for economic and social development. A feature of the thinking of the time was the bundling together of most poor countries in one category, where the individual characteristics of each country had to give way to common features, such as planned economies. Another sign of the times was the efforts to increase (Swedish) aid to the level determined by parliament, i.e. one per cent of GDP. Annual funding increases were thus very large and the main problem in managing assistance was to find sensible uses for the funds while maintaining the level of disbursement.

Country programming as a model survived for quite a long time at a formal level, but led only in exceptional cases to a free transfer of resources to the development budget of a recipient country. In Ethiopia, to take one example, the model was about to be applied, based on detailed knowledge of how the two countries' planning systems could be linked up with each another, when doubts began to arise about the new regime's development policies. Sweden therefore continued to demand control over the use of Swedish funds and country programming became nothing more than a channel for inputs to projects, each of which was to be approved by the donor.

During the 1980s, aid in the form of inputs into defined projects predominated. In those cases where sector support to programmes for the development of a sector occurred, it often consisted of a range of projects collected within an overall framework. Within a decade, the pendulum had in practice swung from country programming to project programming, even if the country programme still existed in the planning cycle. It was realized that trust in the capacity of the recipient country to plan and implement development projects had been exaggerated in the country programming model. However, caught in the trap of project aid, disbursement rates and transfer costs became serious difficulties.

Bypassing

In extreme cases, project aid went so far as to consciously plan projects as a *bypass*, simply to avoid the public sector in the recipient country. In a bypass, aid funds are controlled from start to finish by the donor, or at least by companies that are the direct agents of the donor. This model is in many ways the ultimate expression of a lack of trust in the recipient's ability, in combination with a lack of faith in the long-term possibility of improving capacity in the recipient's public sector.

Sometimes the bypass is quite simply a way of avoiding flagrant corruption. Within the Swedish support to the provision of water in Kenya, virtually a full-time position was required for a while, merely to keep an eye on the chequebook. At the time, the crisis of African states was a well-known fact. The question was no longer how great a trust one could have in the ability of the governments, but instead how assistance could be given *despite* the weakened administration of African states.

At about the same time we began, however, to see examples of African states which had succeeded in creating an efficient public sector and which, in addition, had resources of their own as an alternative and complement to donor funds. Botswana was a country that had succeeded in its macroeconomic policies and its budgeting system and was able to make demands on donors instead of the other way around. Aid to Botswana was becoming increasingly more like a genuine country programme: support to the country's own budget. After independence, Namibia was aware of the dangers involved in becoming dependent on aid and it tried to counteract this tendency. Mauritius and South Africa are other examples.

In a comparison between country programming and the extreme of bypassing, the direct costs of administration differ noticeably. In country programming, a cheque is sent to the country's budget, while in project aid the funds are retained by a foreign advisor until it is time to pay each individual cheque. Underlying each of these models is a different ideology and above all different assessments about the recipient country's capacity to use the funds. It is important to find a balance between these extremes and based on this to determine guidelines for how to implement bilateral support in each case. Clearly, there is a middle road that is more appealing to both parties in an aid relationship.

Structural adjustment programmes

In the mid-1980s, the "World Bank's" structural adjustment programmes were well established and macroeconomic conditions for support had become the rule within the donor community. Structural adjustment programmes led to the end of all national development plans, as the donors all put their faith in the "market". Macroeconomic balance became the crucial criterion when it came to confidence in a government's possibilities to use foreign aid effectively. The state was replaced by the market as the impartial distributor of resources.

Bilateral support, including that from Sweden, began to be adapted to the World Bank's conditions for credits in public commercial sectors. Planning even began for markets which did not exist. The well-intentioned purpose was to attempt to emulate market conditions to achieve the best possible developmental effect.

An important theoretical objection to this way of working is that competition on the market contains both substitutes and complements. The so-called free market is full of ties in the form of rigid relations that complement each other's goods and services.[3] Often these conditions are so different on a new market in a developing country that the entire exercise of emulating so-called free markets in the developed economies becomes a meaningless—but unfortunately not always harmless—exercise. Furthermore, the donor country's competence in this subject is often limited.

One ought to feel somewhat perplexed by the tremendous enthusiasm shown when arguing for the "market economy" as an isolated means of economic development in Africa. The market economy has existed since time immemorial in Africa too. Yet, the institutions that make up the requisite superstructure had not been developed there at

---

[3] In Sweden Lars-Gunnar Mattsson has carried out research and published material that sheds light on these relations.

the beginning of the colonial era. I think that this should therefore be borne in mind when analysing organization and management in Africa.

To what extent do development efforts take place within the framework of organizations and institutions that are African?

It is important to reflect upon the fact that only very few organizations which are included in the African development package have any roots in African history.

Why is there in the context of development, more often talk about how Asian historical institutions can be utilized rather than about corresponding ones in Africa? In Vietnam, it is nothing out of the ordinary among aid workers to refer to an ancient form of credit association that is established among neighbours, friends and colleagues. How many times have we heard about the corresponding institution in Ethiopia, for instance, which is almost identical to the Vietnamese one?

I fear that Eurocentrism in business and aid circles is greater when it comes to Africa than Asia. Sometimes the discussion about the need for *management* in Africa almost assumes colonial proportions.

Actually, the 1997 financial crisis in the south-east Asian "tiger economies" is a good case in point: after years of extreme economic growth rates and market orientation it turns out that the institutional superstructure has great flaws. The market needs those institutions for sustainable growth.

The 1980s became the period when assistance to non-governmental organizations increased dramatically, which can partly be seen as an expression of wavering faith in the efficacy of government to government assistance. Among other things, Sweden, for example, channelled support to an increasing extent to non-governmental organizations through so-called apex organizations, which distributed the funds to their member organizations. This form of assistance was, in terms of trust, the direct opposite to government to government assistance to recipient countries: here the Swedish authorities had very little insight and the opportunities for control were delegated to the apex organizations. There was almost complete trust, although it was already a well-known fact that some non-governmental aid organizations had misused state funds.

Reporting results

In Sweden, suspicions about ineffective government to government assistance were also voiced by the government in the early 1990s, when the demand for tangible results was repeated in several government bills. Reporting and monitoring became the new theme in Swedish aid and thereby attention was moved from the field to the authorities in Sweden. What became important was not what happened in the recipient countries, but how well the Swedish authorities could report concrete results from the field. Subsequently a planning model was introduced which had long been used by other donors, the *Logical Framework Approach* (LFA). Improved project planning was seen as a condition for better reporting of results.

In a sense, the increased emphasis on reporting results was a logical consequence of the Swedish state's transition to results-based budgeting in all areas. In the first crisis package of the 1970s, the Department of Finance had begun its work of changing the budgeting system. In the new system, results analysis is the very core of budgeting. This is meant to lead to new objectives on which resources are to be allocated.

Unfortunately, there is one catch in this system when it comes to government to government assistance: co-operation is based on negotiated frameworks about the amount of funds, an amount which is determined by the Swedish parliament and is part of the agreements. Thus, in practice, it is impossible to adjust the aid budget for a country during the time that the agreement is in force. This has led to result-based budgeting being replaced by reporting of results only. In my view, this is something that must be corrected. An *interface* must be introduced between the Swedish result-based budget system and the recipient country's budget system.

The emphasis on results analysis has had a number of side effects. The intention of the new budget system is to enable monitoring of the fulfilment of the objectives. A project is to be managed, monitored and evaluated in relation to objectives—not in any other way. By focusing on results, projects became oriented towards outputs in the LFA sense, sometimes even at the level of activities. Consequently aid officials became overwhelmed by details, as they were tempted to monitor the activity planning of those who were implementing the projects. This is a waste of time. The whole idea is that guidance and follow-up should be directed towards objectives and objectives only. How those who are responsible for implementation achieve these objectives within the framework of the budget is solely the concern of those who do the implementing. The donor's focus should be on the achievement of objectives. Management by objectives must be given a genuine meaning, by putting an end to control of activities.

The recipient's management of development assistance funds

As mentioned above, over the years most recipient countries have had to accept the necessity of adapting their methods to the donor's management needs. During the era of country programming, the responsible party in the recipient country was a development unit within the planning or finance ministry, created to plan for the co-ordinated use of foreign aid. With increased project aid, the significance of these units has declined in favour of project management units, with whom the donor discusses aid matters directly.

The development co-ordination units in recipient countries are nowadays usually passive recipients without any greater influence on the design of aid use. However, some countries make demands on donors and succeed in having their ideas accepted. Usually they are countries which are restrictive to foreign aid and have the economic base to be so, such as Botswana and Namibia. Among the poorer countries, Eritrea has become known for questioning donors when their suggestions are not acceptable to the country's government.

One pre-condition for the successful management of aid funds is a working system for overall planning and budgeting in the recipient country. In such cases, the recipient's management of aid funds will also be efficient. Inversely, a weak administration often goes hand in hand with low efficiency in the use of foreign aid.

The classical foreign aid issue in recipient countries is how assistance from the various donors can be co-ordinated to achieve the best developmental effect. One example of this problem is the multi-donor support that is sometimes mobilized for emergency aid when famine strikes. During the famine in Ethiopia in 1974, an expatriate advisor was employed and placed in Addis Ababa to co-ordinate the various donor inputs. Much of his time was spent on such trivial but important matters as trying to convince donors that spare parts for trucks of a certain make did not necessarily fit those made by another manufacturer. This type of unnecessary problem always arises when there is poor co-ordination. Donors prefer to supply products made in their own countries.

There are few successful examples of recipients' co-ordination of donors over a longer period. Usually there are limits in the recipient's capacity to co-ordinate, but the main problem is that donors are reluctant to be co-ordinated on the conditions of the recipient.

What happens is rather that donors collaborate with each other to advocate ideas or policies which the recipient is unwilling to accept. During a recent assignment for Sida, I worked parallel to a World Bank mission, which was conducting a study in the same sector. We met the WB team more often and under more relaxed forms than we met the recipient's aid co-ordinating unit in formal meetings. Naturally, the result was that the two mission reports submitted at the same time presented common solutions to several important issues. What could the recipient do then?

The question of how a recipient co-ordinating unit can be effectively organized to give the recipient country better control of foreign aid would require an article of its own. This was, however, done well in a study led by Ernst Michanek on how to make aid management and aid relations more efficient in Tanzania. The study, from the early 1980s, later led to the development of a manual for the co-ordination unit in the ministry of finance.

I would like to emphasize here the importance of a responsible and well-staffed recipient unit in the aid relationship, that can assist, support and supervize all the internal actors in the recipient country. The unit must create order among the enormous number of donors and donor-supported projects that each country is offered. According to statistics from Kenya, more than 2,000 donor projects are implemented annually. The manual mentioned above shows in detail what a unit of this nature ought to focus on and how it should act. Again, management by objectives is more important than detailed control. It is important that the initiative comes from the recipient rather than the donor (in the final analysis, the development of the recipient country is at stake), and that the recipient carefully scrutinizes all agreements concerning aid in order to co-ordinate inputs and, as discussed above, takes the initiative for all donor co-ordination.

In conclusion, I would like to recall the lack of institutions within public and business life in many African countries. The task of managing foreign aid in an economy where large sections lie outside the monetary economy and thus far beyond the reach of the state is beset by difficulties. Individual projects outside the formal organization easily become isolated from economic development, particularly considering how little we know of the connection between the micro and the macro levels. What can lead to greater impact, despite everything, is for the recipient countries to identify clear priorities and development objectives, as well as to create a functioning structure within their institutional frameworks to receive aid, obliging donors to fit in with the country's own efforts. In many countries, donor co-operation could probably play an important role in this regard.

Management of scarce aid resources

Below follows a summary of the lessons which the article suggests can be learned from the past, as well as ideas for research:

- Research on the consequences of the aid relationship as such could give rise to institutional reforms of aid management.
- There is a great need for increased accountability of aid officials and stakeholders.
- In the absence of both political trust and belief in planning as a tool for development, foreign aid programming becomes intolerably difficult; at least one of these two has to exist for development to occur as a result of foreign support.
- In the balance between trust in the recipient and methods of bypassing the recipient's public sector, we have learned that the attitude of the recipient is crucial: if an input cannot be effected without the recipient having total responsibility *(full ownership)*, no support at all should be given. Aid ought not to be used to evade and maintain institutional problems in the recipient country.
- As assistance shifts from state to market, we ought to remember that seeing these two as direct opposites involves a serious oversimplification. The introduction of the market economy entails far more than deregulation of the old state planning system. Building up institutional prerequisites for economic development is instead an important area for co-operation, which must be based on the specific historical conditions of each country.
- Result-based planning demands new forms of links, an interface between the decision making and budget systems of the donor and recipient countries that allows for an allocation of aid funds

based on past performance. Without a new interface, management by objectives cannot be implemented.

– The new (Swedish) planning model for international co-operation should be monitored and evaluated at the level of objectives; all forms of donor monitoring and management at the activity level must be stopped.

– International co-operation should be oriented towards strategic inputs, including an often overlooked institutional task, namely the recipient's co-ordination of international aid. At a time when a sector-wide approach is emerging as a donor favourite, support to donor co-ordination by the recipient is an essential area for foreign aid.

Jan Valdelin is a senior lecturer in business administration and has worked as an adviser on international development co-operation for over twenty years.

Successful Capacity Assistance for Sector Development

Poul Engberg-Pedersen

Foreign assistance is increasingly aimed at the development of entire sectors such as agriculture, health or education. "Sector investment programme", "sector programme support", and "programme approach" are some of the names given to this form of development cooperation, which is likely to dominate in future, particularly in small and medium-sized low-income countries.

The aim of this article is to examine two cases of successful approaches to foreign assistance aimed at the development of national capacity. Both cases cover the water and sanitation sector. One case describes a multi-year, bilateral donor involvement in the sector, making use of all types of assistance in a flexible manner: the assistance by the Norwegian Agency for Development (NORAD) to the Government of Zimbabwe under the National Rural Water Supply and Sanitation Programme. The other case describes the use by a major multilateral donor (the World Bank) of an international consultancy company (COWI, Copenhagen) to support Malawi's national water and sanitation authorities in the preparation of a long-term sector development plan.

The reasons for the move towards the sector level as the target and context for much development assistance are both ideological (emphasis on national ownership and responsibility), practical (increased chances of institutional sustainability), and strategic (the most effective level of intervention in development). In terms of the history of development cooperation, it reflects a move from focused trickle-down projects in the 1950s–1960s and integrated basic needs projects in the 1970s; through macro-economic adjustment conditionalities in the 1980s and human rights policies in the early 1990s; to the institutional governance issues in the mid and late 1990s that are focused at a meso level of society (i.e. neither macro nor micro) but reach vertically from sector policies and programmes to the service users and beneficiaries.

Sector capacity, as applied in this article, covers the way in which the main stakeholders in a particular development sector (whether economic, social, or infrastructural) assess, debate, form policies and strategies, manage and implement programmes and support initiatives at all levels of society. The stakeholders are the national authorities (typically involving a line ministry and local authorities), private and non-governmental actors, the direct beneficiaries, as well as foreign donors.

Following a summary of the dilemmas faced in the provision of capacity development assistance, the article explores how recipients and donors in the two cases managed both to develop sector capacity and to provide critical foreign inputs. The final section discusses three gaps in the current assistance for public sector reform and institutional development. Despite, or because of, an institutional reform mania among donors, critical determinants of the performance of public sector institutions are still being neglected.

Dilemmas in capacity development assistance

Most development assistance continues to be based on a relationship between states. This covers all official bilateral assistance as well as the aid provided by donor governments through multilateral agencies. In the 1990s, state-to-state cooperation must address at least three critical institutional dilemmas.

Demanding both national ownership and a particular governance model

The first dilemma concerns competing and even contradictory demands by donors on recipient governments. It is impossible to combine respect for the national sovereignty of developing countries and a desire for national ownership of development activities on the one hand, with the insistence on state protection of universal human rights and Western forms of multi-party elections, democratization, decentralization and financial and political accountability on the other. While the 1980s saw the global imposition of a specific market-economic model, through uniform stabilization and adjustment programmes, especially in the low- and lower-middle-income countries, the 1990s have seen the imposition, though through more diverse means, of a specific political-administrative system that resembles that of the West. Both impositions are aimed at deregulation and the establishment of a liberal economic and political system.[1]

This dilemma has been highlighted by the widely recognized fact that structural adjustment programmes actually contributed to an erosion of state capacity, due to ideological attacks on the state, privatization schemes, cut-backs and lay-offs, the removal of revenue sources, etc. The attempts to safe-guard, restore and build capacity came several years later.[2]

The dominant approach to overcoming this dilemma has been to emphasize *dialogue* between donor and recipient states, although a dialogue between unequals tends to have a strong flavour of monologue, which in this case takes the form of conditionalities. The advantage of the increased focus on development cooperation at sector level is that the dialogue also allows for demands to be made on the donors to commit themselves to long-term support to national policies and programmes. Capacity development assistance is long-term in nature, which ought to reduce the option available to the donor of ad hoc selectivity in aid allocations and sanctions in response to non-performance by the recipient.

National ownership and capacity development vs. targeting and goal achievement

The second dilemma is related to the tension between process and output. Urgency is almost always the enemy of capacity development. Accountability to the donor can often work against general transparency of public activities. The concern about efficiency and accountability, even in the context of good governance, implies a pressure to produce, deliver and show results. Developing national capacity and ownership requires a donor approach which is quite different

---

[1] It is interesting that the validity of the uniform economic model (as promoted by the IMF and, to a lesser extent, the World Bank) is only now being questioned by mainstream economists as it seems to contribute to the depth of the crisis in south-east Asia in 1997–98. The political and economic interests underlying the uniform model become exposed when the model is being imposed on the strong Asian economies, rather than when the weak African economies were left with no choice but to adjust.

[2] Poul Engberg-Pedersen, Peter Gibbon, Philip Raikes and Lars Udholt (eds.), 1996, *Limits of Adjustment in Africa. The Effects of Economic Liberalization, 1986–94*. Oxford: James Currey and Centre for Development Research.

from rigid donor insistence on reaching particular target groups and achieving specific goals, often within unrealistic time-frames.

This dilemma is seen in each and every interaction between donors and recipients. A famous example was found in UNICEF's extreme preoccupation with the 1990 target of 90 per cent immunization of children against a range of diseases. Specific targets were set in New York for individual years and countries, and the UNICEF country offices had to reach these targets almost at all costs, irrespective of government policies and the priorities and capacities of national health systems. UNICEF landrovers were sent out on sweeping campaigns far into the bush with temporary cold chains, staff and resources. National and local capacity was not only neglected, but actually eroded as UNICEF made little but highly selective use of local institutions and resources.[3]

At the other end of this dilemma, NORAD has probably been the donor agency paying the greatest political attention to national ownership under the concept of "recipient responsibility". Recognizing the dilemma, NORAD has sought to combine recipient responsibility with a strategic choice of sectors and programmes that Norway would be prepared to support. Selecting target group-oriented programmes in the social sectors, Norway sought to minimize the need for donor-controlled targeting.[4]

Given the complementarity of aid and national resources (the so-called "fungibility" of aid) and the institutional weaknesses also in the social sectors, it has long been clear that the selection of "progressive sectors" is not enough to overcome the dilemma. Due to the aid allocations to the social sectors, recipient states can use their own resources on military adventures, prestige projects etc. Even within the social sectors, the donor must address the inappropriate and ineffective use of resources, which makes it impossible to rely only on "recipient responsibility".

All donor organizations have, through their project assistance and insistence on attention to their own particular activities and procedures, contributed to the erosion of state systems and capacity in

---

[3] COWIconsult & GGI, 1992, *Strategic Choices for UNICEF: Service Delivery, Capacity Building, Empowerment.* Evaluation of UNICEF—Synthesis Report, prepared for the aid organizations of Australia, Canada, Denmark and Switzerland.

[4] Asplan Analyse & COWIconsult,1993, *Capacity Building in Development Cooperation: Towards Integration and Recipient Responsibility.* Evaluation Report 4.93, Royal Ministry of Foreign Affairs, Norway.

developing countries. The most widespread example of this is the hiring of national government employees to staff donor-supported projects, including the paying of topping-up salaries to national civil servants. OECD's Development Assistance Committee, the Special Programme of Assistance to Africa, and other donor bodies have all issued guidelines on how to minimize these practices, but with little effect.

The complexity of these issues is seen in the almost perverse effects of an otherwise laudable attempt to rely more on national staff at the donor representations in developing countries. The EU delegation in an African country once, with pride, told the present author that they had both increased their efficiency and involved national capacity by offering officials from the Ministry of Finance much higher salaries for them to move from the Ministry to the delegation where they continued to handle the same work tasks of getting EU-supported programmes through the national bureaucracy! Many donors, including for example Denmark, experience the ironic situation where nationals of the developing country, say Tanzania, are employed at the Danish embassy to undertake policy dialogues with the line ministries of the Tanzanian Government that may often be represented by sector programme advisers from Denmark!

A starting-point in unrealistic government plans and budgets

The third dilemma concerns the mismatch between plans and resources. Development needs drastically exceed government resources and capacities in developing countries. At the same time, donors demand plans and programmes with highly ambitious objectives and targets. Hence, the institutional objective of full integration of aid programmes into national investment plans and budgets is often unrealistic right from the start. The aim of institutional integration of aid should be to promote realistic priority-setting and decision making in and by national institutions. The size and mode of operation of foreign assistance implies, however, that decision making traditionally has been removed from line ministries to levels "above" (viz. in donor organizations) or "below" (viz. in project organizations) their regular planning structures. At best, institutional integration has resulted in decision making which is strongly biased in favour of the donor-supported programmes.

The first serious attempt to overcome this dilemma was the public expenditure analyses promoted by the World Bank and taken up by a range of recipient and donor governments. They reflect a necessary move from the preoccupation of adjustment programmes with macro balances to a concern about the distributional effects of government budgets. The new mechanisms of sector investment programmes and sector programme support emphasize aid coordination at sectoral level in a form which takes the availability of national resources and capacities into consideration. The donor community is, however, still looking for success stories in this field.

Capacity development in the water and sanitation sector

A history of increasing institutional complexity

Aid to the (drinking) water supply and sanitation sector has seen an increasing institutional complexity, which is typical of the history of much development cooperation. In the 1960s, donors wanted to install as many pumps as rapidly as possible, for which purpose they relied on a combination of contracts with the private sector and heavy funding of government ministries of water that were staffed and managed by engineers. In the 1970s, it was recognized that safe drinking water in itself did not improve the health of the target group. The building of latrines and the provision of health education were both added to the programmes which were still implemented by engineering departments. This led to gross inefficiencies in the form of unused latrines, overstretched engineers, and confused service users. The response was to expand the institutional scope of the water and sanitation programmes by involving health and social mobilization departments in planning and implementation. The result was another type of inefficiency: the programmes had heavy administrative overheads and coordination costs and suffered from communication and collaboration problems between the engineering and social departments.

By the 1980s, it was realized that the complex programmes could not be maintained by either the government departments or the beneficiaries. User participation and cost-sharing became key objectives, which received ideological support from the promotion of privatization in the late 1980s, and the emphasis in the early 1990s on water as an economic good and decentralization of water resources management to the lowest appropriate level. The water/engineering departments, which first had to learn to collaborate with social departments, now had to be both decentralized and restructured to act in a more supportive role in relation to private and non-government actors. Given these continuous shifts, it is no wonder that the water departments tend to suffer from reform fatigue and institutional confusion.

New instruments of capacity development assistance

In parallel with these changing institutional objectives, the instruments of capacity development assistance have also changed. Until the 1980s, they took mainly three forms: human resource development (formal and in-service training, scholarships, etc.) aimed at skills upgrading; secondment of experts and the use of advisers and consultants to develop local skills and find operational solutions to specific problems; and support to the establishment of new organizations, which led to institutional proliferation within the public sector in developing countries.

In recent years, new forms of capacity development have taken root, including: participatory capacity assessments to identify and address strengths and weaknesses; funding and facilitating workshops and seminars for all stakeholders; funding and assisting in information collection and the analysis of development scenarios and policy options; support for procedural development for planning, priority-setting, implementation, etc.; and support for the introduction of staff incentives and performance-based financing.

The Zimbabwe case presented below shows how a donor can use these multiple instruments flexibly and effectively over 10–15 years. The Malawi case shows how even a one-year consultancy can aim to develop capacity through some of these instruments.

The National Rural Water Supply and Sanitation Programme (NRWSSP), Zimbabwe

Institutional strengths and weaknesses

Norway's support to rural water supply and sanitation in Zimbabwe has had several very impressive features with respect to institutional capacity development at central and local levels of government.[5]

---

[5] The account is based on field-work undertaken in 1992–93, as reported in *Asplan Analyse & COWIconsult*, op.cit., Annex 3. Unfortunately, it has not been possible to undertake follow-up visits in recent years, where both the programme and the Norwegian support have faced problems in the expansion of the programme coverage to more and

Norway has shown *continuous commitment* to 15 years of sector development in cooperation with all the relevant central government departments. Norway has also shown *adaptive flexibility* in the provision of financial and technical assistance that has responded well to the changing context for rural development in Zimbabwe. This was seen in four partly overlapping phases of Norwegian support:

1. Post-independence rehabilitation and establishment of a service delivery capacity to benefit the hitherto neglected communal areas;

2. Master planning and establishment of inter-ministerial cooperation mechanisms in the context of central planning for social development;

3. Mobilization of civil servants at all levels for effective, integrated service delivery and establishment of team-spirit at district level; and

4. Generation of commitment for devolution of decision making powers to rural district councils, and provision of Norwegian assistance as basic sector support.

During these phases, Norway interacted well with the Government of Zimbabwe, particularly the Ministry of Local Government, Rural and Urban Development (MLGRUD). NORAD supported the changing emphases between phases, but it encouraged government ministries to take the lead in redefining programme strategies and institutional approaches.

During 1986–87, following a master planning effort for the sector, the *basic institutional model* of the NRWSSP was chosen: inter-ministerial coordination, bottom-up planning, and multi-legged implementation through several line departments. NORAD accepted this as the politically most feasible model, and facilitated its adoption through financing of both a range of head offices projects and integrated, district-based projects.

The Norwegian support reached an unusually high degree of *institutional and operational integration* into Zimbabwean government bodies and procedures. Although programme-specific planning and budgeting procedures were established, these were developed for a

more districts in Zimbabwe. It appears that capacity development efforts in recent years have shifted from the central to the local level, which may be appropriate in itself, but which is not sustainable without continued improvements at central government level.

national programme, and they were applied by regular government staff at central, provincial and district levels.

Norway may have gone too far in demanding institutional integration of the NORAD-financed national coordination unit into the MLGRUD. The success of this unit, particularly in the early years of its existence, was due to its perceived neutrality in the inter-ministerial disputes and its catalytic role in supporting districts vis-á-vis central government line departments. Such tasks are probably best handled by an independent unit.

There was much emphasis on *capacity development* in government institutions. Still, the long-term and immediate programme objectives aimed directly at the health and standard of living of the target group: institutional development was a programme strategy, not an explicit, formal objective. The capacity development efforts seemed to achieve *effectiveness* in programme implementation. They also succeeded in generating *participation* by all government departments, though less in involving sub-national political bodies in priority-setting and decision making. The instruments were less effective with respect to *sustainability* and *accountability* in programme implementation.

As a consequence, the Norwegian support and the NRWSSP as such had not, at the time of evaluation (1992), reached a situation of contributing to a more *participatory governance* system. There was much capacity development in the public administration, particularly at local level, but the NRWSSP was only then moving towards real decentralization to the rural district councils. Programme objectives aimed at community participation in implementation, not in priority-setting; thus, empowerment of the target group had not been a programme objective.

Finally, both the government and NORAD made a major effort to involve other donors to the rural water supply and sanitation sector in concerted support to the NRWSSP under a National Action Committee. The mechanisms for improved *aid coordination* were available in the form of clear national policies, programme objectives, coordination structures, and review instruments.

There were also *weaknesses* in the Norwegian support to the NRWSSP. Thus, there could have been more active NORAD participation in the *choice of institutional arrangements* for the sector programme supported by it. A donor agency can and should play a crucial role in the process of screening and choice among institutional options, because the involved national institutions naturally will have a number of legitimate organizational interests in this respect. Even within the political-institutional context in Zimbabwe in the mid-1980s, NORAD was too hesitant with respect to examining the possibility of further decentralization of authority for programme implementation as an institutional alternative to the centralized, multi-legged implementation structure. Also, attempts could have been made to use the sector as an entry-point in area-based empowerment programmes. NORAD chose instead—quite legitimately—to give priority to high quality in service delivery (through the specialized line departments) and capacity development at central government level.

Another problem was that NORAD accepted the separation of authority for planning and budget preparation from authority for implementation and budget execution. This separation was inherent in the multi-legged institutional model chosen for the NRWSSP. Its key weaknesses were:

- The district sector teams were mobilized during planning and budgeting, but given no power or direct access to resources to ensure implementation; hence, they became the victims of non-adherence to the plans by the centralized line departments.

- Communication and reporting lines were very complex because of the different decision making structures of the involved line departments.

- The system for requesting release of funds from the Ministry of Finance (and hence from NORAD) was equally complex because budgets were based on a matrix of individual districts and individual line departments (as well as individual activities).

- Progress monitoring and expenditure accounting was difficult for the national coordination unit, which relied on data from districts that did not themselves receive adequate information and feedback from the central line departments.

- The model required active interventions (in the form of facilitating interventions during day-to-day operations) by a coordinating body at central level. The national coordination unit could live up to this as long as few districts were involved and communication lines were direct and inter-personal, but the quality of such support inevitably diminished as the national programme expanded.

NORAD had for too long accepted the weaknesses in financial accountability that were the result of the multi-legged implementation model. NORAD had not been able to secure timely transfer of funds from the Ministry of Finance to the implementing bodies, nor secure agreement between Finance, the implementing line departments, and the national coordination unit on actual expenditure incurred.

These weaknesses in institutional development and financial management were not unique to Norwegian assistance. Hence, from an evaluation point of view, they did not detract decisively from the general assessment of an impressive NORAD performance in the institutional aspects of Norwegian assistance to the NRWSSP. The point is not whether the successes and failures of the programme were the result of NORAD interventions, but whether NORAD managed to interact in a capacity developing manner in relation to government policies and stakeholder interests.

NORAD's use of capacity development instruments

NORAD's performance under the NRWSSP in Zimbabwe could also be assessed in relation to an effective and flexible use of seven capacity development instruments:

1. *Organized and in-service training*: Priority was given to in-service training of staff in almost all the line agencies and programme participants at all levels, from pump minders and communities, to extension workers and higher level officials. However, implementation of the training measures was generally slow.

2. *Provision of advisers*: NORAD went from heavy reliance (in the first half of the 1980s) on international consultants and expatriate advisers, to a large complement of expatriate and national advisers, and on to a situation of mainly Zimbabwean advisers. This gradual change led to good use of national consultants as the providers of capacity development assistance.

3. *Establishment of new institutions and structures*: This was the preferred approach to the management of the integrated programme and promotion of inter-ministerial cooperation. The institutions that were established all dealt with coordination, centrally and in the provinces and districts. At province and district levels, the sector-specific coordination mechanisms were new institutions, but they were closely attached to existing coordination structures. They involved all relevant line departments, including Finance and Planning at national level. While the national action committee was essential for policy-making and harmonization of ap-

proaches, the district committees were critical for local mobilization and implementation support.

4. *Financing of workshops and seminars*: Generating commitment from all parties to NRWSSP objectives and strategies was achieved through an impressive use of policy-making and coordination workshops at critical times in the development of the integrated approach, complemented by support for information dissemination. These workshops which were financed by NORAD and other donors lasted up to one week and were organized approximately every two years.

5. *Analysis of policy and strategy options*: The NRWSSP was literally flooded with policy-oriented studies addressing options for institutional arrangements (including different forms of decentralization), for cost recovery, for the organization of operations and maintenance, for community participation and mobilization, etc. The policy-oriented studies were instrumental in improving the quality of programme design and management and in generating commitment and a strong sense of national ownership of the programme.

6. *Development of new planning and priority-setting procedures*: A bottom-up approach to planning and budget preparation was a key institutional achievement of the NRWSSP. With technical assistance from NORAD, guidelines on district planning and implementation were prepared; however, through standard programme designs these set rather strict limits on the room-to-manoeuvre for local decision making.

7. *Provision of flexible funds*: NORAD used this mechanism of capacity development in two ways. Firstly, NORAD financed head offices projects that provided all central government line departments with an incentive to participate in the programme; hence, the flexibility with which these projects were used was partly intentional. Secondly, NORAD sought, at the time of evaluation, to go far in terms of offering financial support to the sector whose actual use would be determined annually through the programme's bottom-up planning procedures.

These diverse instruments could only be made use of because the NORAD Mission in Harare included a series of permanent NORAD staff, who managed the Norwegian support for the programme. Over the years, they were active in the use of all capacity development instruments, and their efforts included active engagement in the solution of administrative problems, constraints on financial management etc., in the Zimbabwean government bureaucracy. At the same time, the NORAD staff members seemed to be able to know when to withdraw to the NORAD Mission and the Norwegian Embassy, letting the Zimbabwean government agencies adapt the solutions to the organizational culture of the government, which of course included sorting out amongst themselves the unavoidable inter-ministerial struggles over spheres of competence and access to resources. Occasional, well-timed withdrawal of outsiders seems just as important as their active engagement.

Water Services Sector Study, Malawi

In 1993–94, the World Bank financed an international consultancy for the Water Department of the Government of Malawi, aimed at preparing a long-term plan for restructuring the national water and sanitation services sector, including a detailed, multi-year investment plan. COWIconsult won the international tender for a multi-disciplinary project, which ran for approximately ten months.[6] Considering the fact that Malawi had just emerged from decades of extreme political oppression and suffered from continuous poverty and very limited capacity for public sector planning, the project could have ended up in just a neat consultancy report for the World Bank and other donors to carve up as nice investment projects among themselves. The project design was traditional in that it excluded all forms of end-user participation in planning and decision making. Thus, the scope for innovative capacity development was very limited indeed.

However, the Water Department management insisted on a participatory approach, which led to *five phases* in the interaction of international consultants and national bureaucrats that can be deemed as successful in terms of capacity development at the level of sector management.

1. *Problem identification*: The consultants visited all the organized stakeholders (five line ministries; finance and planning departments; water boards; local authorities; private contractors and

---

6 COWIconsult, 1994, *Water Services Sector Study*, Summary Report (42 p) and Main Report (297 p), Water Department, Ministry of Works, Government of Malawi.

consultants; and donors), to inquire about sector objectives, goals, plans, conflicts, constraints, resources, etc. The consultants made use of three simple "capacities": they were outsiders; they covered all relevant disciplines; and they "represented" both the government and the World Bank. This phase lasted approximately one month.

2. *Scenarios and options:* The consultants prepared a 60-page policy report, describing the existing sector challenges and management structures and weaknesses, and outlining four scenarios and policy options for the future development of the sector. Each scenario covered the legal foundation; different water and sanitation services standards and technologies; an appropriate management structure for the sector as a whole; staff requirements and qualifications; and sources of finance (public, private, user).

3. *Stakeholder workshop:* Two months into the project period, the Water Department and the consultants organized a one-day workshop for approximately 40 representatives of the main government stakeholders: line departments, water boards, and local authorities. After three hours of traditional consultant presentation, the Malawian civil servants took over, demanding group work on the scenarios presented in the policy report. The civil servants had an impressive capacity to sit in working groups (with representatives from all different levels of the government staff hierarchy) and discuss the pros and cons of various rather complex institutional options. This reflects the advance in education all over Africa, as well as the tremendous capacity to deal with the constant institutional turmoil, which all public sectors in low-income countries have been exposed to for decades.

At the end of day one, the consultants were asked to summarize the recommendations of the working groups and to look for some commonality, which combined elements of the scenarios in a new manner. The following day, the consultants presented a two-page outline of the common recommendations on the future structure of the water services sector in Malawi. The plenary meeting of the workshop, guided by an extremely able and democratically-minded head of the Water Department, then made decisive changes in the outline and produced a new outline based on a consensus, which participants later referred to as the "workshop spirit". The workshop had clearly led to a reform process owned by the various levels of the government bureaucracy.

4. *Assimilation and adaptation:* After the workshop, the consultancy team stayed away from the institutional issues for 1–2 months, allowing time for inter-agency consultations and assimilation of the workshop recommendations. This period proved to be too short, however.

5. *Feasibility study:* Upon their return to Malawi, the consultants were meant to be informed about the government's policy decision on the future institutional structure, technologies, and finance of the water services sector. For some time, no clear decision was made public. Then a decision was made by the government, which was different from the recommendations made by the workshop. The reason was that the relevant Minister and Permanent Secretary insisted on a less radical institutional change. In itself, this proves that local participatory processes and capacity development efforts can be undermined by political decisions. This is unavoidable and, to a large extent, a positive reflection of the primacy of political decision making.

The consultants were told to make a detailed feasibility study and implementation plan for the new official solution. They tried, however, to prepare their detailed report in such a way that it incorporated both the official policy and the workshop recommendations. This proved to be wise, since the Minister was replaced a few months after the submission of our report, and the workshop recommendations returned to the policy agenda.

This simple case shows that it is possible to combine an external specialist input with systematic stakeholder involvement; capacity development through transparent policy analysis and participatory decision making; national ownership of sector reforms; and a national political process. The limits of the process are clear, however. There was no scope for beneficiary involvement, and the national political process could turn the whole thing over.

Capacity development—three critical links

The development of institutional capacities for sector management is situated between three fields: public sector or civil service reform;

sector development (e.g. health or agriculture); and capacity development assistance. The above analysis has focused on capacity development assistance to the water supply and sanitation sector. This section discusses sector capacity development within the context of public sector reform.

The public sector reforms advocated by most donor agencies have shifted from a Weberian ideal to "new public management": a market-oriented public sector, based on a limited role for the state (provision of well-defined public services), services-based performance assessment (user or client satisfaction), and performance-based promotions and salaries. As usual, there is much to be said about retaining some of the old ideals: Weber should not be thrown out with the bath water! Capacity development assistance at sector level should address and incorporate at least three critical links between *institutional capacities* and *sector resources*.

Firstly, the national and local *political processes* should explicitly be involved in the reform and capacity development efforts. This is required not just to avoid later political "surprises" (as in the Malawian case), but more importantly to promote clear, consistent and transparent political goal-setting. All institutions—from the state as such to the individual department and local authority—serve as a platform for political conflicts in society. The public sector reflects and expresses current power relations. These should be openly recognized, not isolated under the disguise of rationality and modernity, as is usually done by for example the World Bank.[7] Politics must be considered as and turned into a constructive force in the development of society.

Secondly, the emphasis on public services must coexist with a concern about *public revenue*. The economic room for reform must be considered in all sector programmes, with its implications for the choice of service level and technologies. Introducing cost consciousness and the need for revenue-based strategic choices is obviously made difficult by the continued flow of aid to line ministries. Linking services and revenue through user-payments and a decentralization of the right to retain collected user fees (e.g. by local authorities) *may* provide useful incentives, but it risks fragmenting public expenditure

---

[7] In the *World Development Report 1997: The State in a Changing World*, the World Bank presents a reform approach and sequence aimed at minimizing the role of political discussion and priority-setting. Politicians are mainly referred to in the context of corruption, and the political system is almost considered a "constraint".

and revenue management in a new way which is just as detrimental as the old "projectitis" caused by donor pets and procedures. Priority-setting on the level and composition of public expenditures and revenues must be undertaken both for the public sector as a whole (through the national budget process) and for individual sectors and institutions.

Thirdly, the logic in the *present mode of operation* of the civil service and public sector in general must be analyzed and understood in its specific context, before capacity development and public sector reforms are launched. All public institutions in low-income countries have, due both to their continued resource crisis and to the constant changes and reforms that they have been exposed to, developed a "survival practice", which should be considered a necessary and often effective point of departure for change. Quite often, the removal of simple constraints (in relation to the Weberian ideal), including basic resource deficiencies, can enable the public administration to operate more freely and effectively. At the same time, outsiders such as donor agencies must recognize that they cannot fully understand the organizational culture and survival practice of their partners in the bureaucracies of developing countries. The two cases showed the crucial importance of withdrawal: providing time and space to the bureaucracies to assimilate, absorb and adapt the capacity development assistance provided by donor agencies.

Poul Engberg-Pedersen is currently director at the Centre for Development Research, Copenhagen, Denmark. He holds a Ph.D. in international public administration. His work as a consultant and researcher has focused on institutional issues in development cooperation, related in particular to the effectiveness of UN and other multilateral aid.

Public Administration Reform in Namibia

Tor Sellström

Background

That studies of economic development should also include an analysis of the state and its operations is nothing new (Lundahl and Vedovato, 1986). However, the structural adjustment programmes (SAPs) worked out by the World Bank (WB) and the International Monetary Fund (IMF) and implemented in country after country in Africa, in the 1980s gave the place of honour to "pure" economics. This approach had widespread negative consequences. The SAP theoreticians regarded the state as an obstacle to economic growth and wanted to prune it down as much as possible. Reforms of the state apparatus—often in the form of more or less arbitrary quantitative cut-backs—became an important part of adjustment programmes.

An effect of these *Civil Service Reforms* (CSRs), as Johnston and Wohlgemuth (1995) have observed, was that the administrative machinery supposed to implement the economic reform programme, was, in most cases far too drained to manage the task. By weakening the public institutions responsible for economic recovery, the SAPs threw the baby out with the bathwater. This is *one* important reason why the structural adjustment programmes under the WB and IMF in Africa did not create the conditions for sustainable economic growth predicted by the advocates of the SAPs.

At the same time in the early 1980s, it was clear that the civil service which had mushroomed since independence in many African countries had become a great burden. It swallowed increasing amounts of the shrinking economic resources and was often poorly adapted to meet the challenges the countries were facing. A reform of the civil service was therefore essential. One conclusion to be drawn from the first SAP programmes was, however, that this reform should not simply be regarded as a biproduct of the purely economic measures. On the contrary, it was a prerequisite for success. A reform of the public service had to be planned and implemented as part of an overall reform programme and in harmony with it. Johnston and Wohlgemuth emphasize that at least two basic conditions must be met for growth to occur, namely

- a favourable macro-economic environment, and
- a competent and legitimate government.

Development theory must thus go beyond the bounds of pure economics and include disciplines such as political science, organization theory, sociology, etc.

Like other donors, Sida initially concentrated its assistance to public administration on educational inputs. A large part of the support went to the building of educational institutions for public sector employees in the recipient countries. During the 1980s—and particularly against the background of the SAP programmes and their effects—Sida began to realize the limitations of this perspective (Dyrssen and Johnston, 1991).

If assistance to a public authority was to bring about the desired results, i.e. create better conditions for sustainable economic growth and social development, it was necessary that two conditions were met, namely that the support

- was integrated in the administrative structure of the recipient country itself, as well as
- contributed to making the central functions of the state apparatus, such as economic planning, budgeting, financial administration, civil administration and local government, more efficient.

Educational support in the area of administration was consequently transformed into support for organizational development or *institution building*.

This, in turn, required greater knowledge of the entire public sector—how it was built up and operated, both horizontally and vertically, how resources were divided, what the decision making processes were, how appointments were made and salaries determined, etc. In brief, greater demands were made upon Sida to get to know the public sectors in the recipient countries as holistic organisms.

Such a perspective also began to emerge within the World Bank to some extent during the 1980s as it initiated or implemented *Public Expenditure Reviews* (PERs) in a number of countries. However, they focused primarily on the administration of public funds and paid scant attention to questions of an institutional and personnel nature. Against the background of what has been pointed out above, Sida saw a need to go further. On a trial basis, a *Public Sector Analysis* (PSA) was in 1986–87 carried out in co-operation with the Mozambican government. The attempt was successful and has subsequently led to other similar studies. One such study was conducted in Namibia at the beginning of 1994.

How is a Public Sector Analysis carried out? What results are obtained and what lessons can we learn concerning the possibilities and the conditions for administrative reform in an African country? These are the two main questions that this article attempts to answer.

Namibia

In all countries, the public sector has special characteristics, which in turn make different demands on the sector analysis. After a long and difficult liberation struggle, Namibia achieved national independence as recently as March 1990. Prior to that, the country was governed as a province of South Africa and lacked at independence not only a national administrative tradition, but also a number of central government functions, such as a public planning authority, a central bank, a statistical office, reliable national accounts, a university, a unitary regional and local administrative structure, etc. In addition, due to South Africa's apartheid policies the African majority had a very low educational standard, while the white minority, because of its favoured position, controlled the country's economy and occupied all senior positions. Furthermore, on the eve of independence, SWAPO, the liberation movement that won the 1989 elections, was forced to accept a stipulation in the Namibian constitution that civil servants with permanent jobs before 1990 could not be dismissed.

This meant that SWAPO could only appoint ministers, deputy ministers, permanent secretaries and a few other senior civil servants within the former South African provincial structures, which now were transformed into national departments. In addition, the governing party could, of course, appoint civil servants to the new administrative structures that were created. As a result, from the start Namibia's public sector was not only very divided, but also unnaturally large. When the analysis of the public sector was done, the number of civil servants was no less than 66,000 people out of a population of 1,4 million. Nearly one in twenty Namibians was thus employed by the state. The costs for this corps of civil servants can be illustrated by the fact that more than half of the public income was spent on salaries to the state's employees.

The cake previously reserved for a minority had after independence to be shared among the whole population. Yet SWAPO was in a precarious position. The attitude of the corps of civil servants which was to implement the transformation from apartheid to democracy and economic development for all was not merely luke-warm, but often prejudiced against such a transformation. In addition, it was this very corps of secure officials who consumed the major part of the government's resources.

Against this background, it was highly motivated to put the question of a review of the public service on the political agenda, although Namibia had no agreement with either the World Bank or the IMF on a structural adjustment programme. At the end of 1992, the government decided to implement two measures. Vacant and new posts would not be filled for a two year period from February 1993 and a rationalization plan would be worked out to make the existing administration more effective. The purpose was to increase productivity, improve the decision making processes and bring the various parts in line with each other.

The rationalization plan began to be implemented in 1993. In the absence of a single central supervisory and decision making authority, each ministry was individually given the task of rationalizing the administration within its area of responsibility. The sector analysis subsequently noted that this in several cases led to increased centralization, rising costs and considerable duplication of functions between the ministries. Each ministry was bent upon increasing its own capacity and one hand literally did not know what the other was doing. Thus at an early stage it was clear that the rationalization plan as a whole would not lead to the intended increase in efficiency, decentralization and cost-savings. On the contrary, the formerly weighty Windhoek-based administrative apparatus became even heavier and less suited to implement development policies, at the price of increased rather than decreased costs. The need for a comprehensive inventory and analysis of Namibia's public sector remained.

Faced with an increasing budget deficit and an administration that greatly encroached upon the nation's finances, in 1993 the Namibian government decided to conduct a *Public Expenditure Review* (PER) in collaboration with the World Bank and Sida. The WB had since independence been pressing Namibia to do such an analysis. The Namibian government was, however, reluctant to permit a one-sided WB exercise over which it could not exert sufficient influence and where it could have difficulty in endorsing the resultant conclusions and recommendations. A number of examples of World Bank intervention in other African countries with inadequate local participation reinforced this view. With the support of Sida, which contributed both funds and personnel, a group of World Bank economists was instead invited to add experience and expertise under the leadership of the Namibian government and in co-operation with a local NGO, the *Namibian Economic Policy Research Unit* (NEPRU). The ownership of the PER-analysis thus remained with the Namibian government and the Prime Minister was asked to lead a specially appointed steering group. The Public Expenditure Review was carried out during 1994.

The Public Sector Analysis (PSA)

It was, however, necessary to complement the financial data of the expenditure review. There were also flaws in the comprehensive analysis of the rationalization plan of the Namibian public service. Sida and the *National Planning Commission* (NPC) thus agreed in early 1993 to conduct a *Public Sector Analysis* (PSA). The analysis was doubly motivated since Swedish assistance to Namibia to a large extent already went to the public sector in the form of support to the central bank, statistical development and—at the preparation stage—to public auditing. Further, an agreement for a new period of Swedish-Namibian development co-operation was shortly to be signed and the National Planning Commission was, in addition, engaged in working out the country's *First National Development Plan* (NDP1).

The overall goals of this joint public sector analysis were

- for Namibia, to identify strengths and weaknesses in the public sector with the aim of harmonizing the development plan with essential public sector reforms and improvements;
- for Sweden, to place its bilateral support to Namibia in a larger context, particularly the support to public sector development, and in this way improve planning for future assistance; and

– for both parties, to create a common frame of reference for dialogue about future development co-operation.

On behalf of the Namibian government, the National Planning
Commission is responsible for contacts with donors, while overall responsibility for the country's public administration lies with the *Office
of the Prime Minister* (OPM). When Sida and NPC had agreed on the
sector analysis, the go-ahead was given by OPM, which was in close
contact with the PSA team during the work and contributed with information and advice which otherwise would have been difficult to
access.

The Swedish-Namibian group which in January–March 1994 con-
ducted the public sector analysis consisted at most of seven people:
one from NPC, two from Sida (one from the administrative division in
Stockholm and one from the development co-operation office in
Windhoek), a senior consultant from the Swedish National Fund for
Administrative Development and three local consultants from
NEPRU, the local organization which at the same time carried out re-
search for the public expenditure analysis.

The team was well-rooted in the Namibian administration and
had through NEPRU good insight into local conditions. Via NEPRU,
it was also continuously informed of the parallel work of the expenditure analysis. One of the most important experiences from the work
with the public sector analysis in Namibia is that a high degree of
political support is needed from the public authorities in the recipient
country, as well as good knowledge of local conditions (including
language skills), so that the doors on which one knocks are opened
and the information received is set in a wider context and correctly
interpreted.

The idea was to conduct the public sector analysis in three stages, or
to

– survey the structure of the public sector in Namibia;

– gather information through interviews at central, regional and
local levels; and

– carry out the analysis proper.

It became, however, evident that the work of surveying the structure
of the public sector—partly because of the changes taking place
within the framework of the ongoing rationalization plan—required

considerably more time and effort than planned. In the event, the survey was undertaken parallel with the main work. Nevertheless, thanks to guidance from the Office of the Prime Minister and the exchange of information with the group reviewing public expenditures, the analysis work and the interviewing were hardly affected by this. In the ideal case, as detailed a picture as possible of the structure of the public sector, the mandates and functions of the various public authorities and institutions, their services and vacancies, staff categories and salary structures, etc., should, however, be available before the interview stage. Experiences from Namibia—with a public sector that by African standards is comparatively easy to work with and get a picture of—show that a survey of the structure requires time and good long-term planning. One reason is that the work involves checking with a number of sources that are often difficult to access, such as budget data, annual reports, auditors' reports, etc.

The interview and analysis work is discussed below. It should first be pointed out that the information about the structure and personnel of the public sector acquired in a survey such as the one outlined above naturally has an independent value. Like a reference work or guidebook, it may be used both to increase general knowledge about the public sector in a particular country and to answer different kinds of specific questions. In the case of Namibia, Sida and the National Planning Commission agreed that the survey would not only be used as background material for the analysis work of the PSA team, but also be presented as a separate addendum to the final report.

The addendum (*A Handbook on the Namibian Public Administration*, Nashitati, 1994)—a comprehensive document of over 130 pages—was worked out at NEPRU, which agreed to update it annually. The handbook should thus become one of the most important reference works about Namibia, both for the government and for international donors and other domestic and foreign organizations.

Interviews—methods and selection

In addition to the survey, the PSA team acquired information for its analysis through a series of interviews with key people in the public sector. As the financial aspects on the whole were covered by the PER group, emphasis was put on questions of an institutional and personnel nature. The interviews followed a guide worked out beforehand

and were so designed that one or more complexes of problems first were defined at the policy level—usually in discussion with the responsible minister, permanent secretary or head of division—to subsequently be followed through the administrative structure down to the level of implementation. Normally, an interview took between one and two hours. The team conducted about twenty interviews at the central level and somewhat more at the local and regional levels. In addition, there were a great number of meetings, shorter follow-up interviews and conversations with various resource people, researchers and non-governmental organizations.

The method of personal interviews (survey questionnaires and other written material were not used) presupposed a relatively limited selection of both interviewees and areas. At an early stage, Sida and NPC had agreed that the PSA group in the first hand would study the ministries/activities that were already recipients of Swedish assistance. The selection could also be regarded as representative and relevant for the various core functions of the public sector.

As pointed out earlier, the finance administration was studied by the parallel Public Expenditure Review group. The Public Sector Analysis focused on

– the Ministry of Works Transport and Communications (the economic sector);

– the Ministry of Justice (the state's controlling functions);

– the Ministry of Education (social development); and

– the Ministry of Regional and Local Government (vertical integration and decentralization).

In addition, there were interviews with the *National Planning Commission* regarding development planning as well as with the *Office of the Prime Minister* and the *Ministry of Labour* on more specific questions concerning the administrative apparatus, the labour market, remuneration levels, training of civil servants, affirmative action, trade union questions, etc.

Interviews within the four main sectors at the central level in Windhoek were followed up at the regional and local level through visits to the regions of Khomas (central Namibia), Hardap (southern Namibia) and Okavango (northern Namibia). These regions were selected since there are very great socio-economic and political differences between them. Local officials could thus be expected to understand and express their interests towards the central administration in different ways. At the same time, the regions were representative of the complex and varied Namibian social formation.

The Khomas region—with the capital Windhoek as its centre—is relatively urbanized, while both Hardap and Okavango are predominantly rural regions. Since colonial times, Hardap has been an area of white settlers, with small urban centres and large commercial farms. Okavango, on the other hand, was throughout colonial history situated beyond the so-called police zone, which was reserved for whites. There are no towns and the region is dominated by small African subsistence farms. At the regional and local elections in 1992, these differences were expressed through a majority for the political opposition in Hardap and in a monopoly position for SWAPO, the governing party, in Okavango.

It is beyond the framework of this presentation to discuss the rich empirical information about Namibia's public sector gathered by the PSA team during the interview phase. The method permitted the team to follow the treatment of a certain question from the government to the local level and within the four main sectors to form a clear picture of the strong and weak sides of the public sector, both institutionally and from the point of view of its personnel resources.

Together with the information about Namibia's public expenditure gathered by the PER group, the interview material formed the basis of the analysis of the public sector which Sida and NPC had initiated. In July 1994 the material was summarized in a report submitted to the government (Johnston et al., 1994). It included conclusions and recommendations for national measures (the government) and proposals for assistance inputs (Sida and other interested donors). After consideration by NPC, the report was at the end of 1994 presented to the Office of the Prime Minister for submission to and decision making by the Namibian government.

Findings of Namibia's PSA

With its conclusions and recommendations, the report discusses both major policy questions at a national level as well as smaller practical questions at the local level. It is a comprehensive document which requires far more space than is available here to do it justice. In addition, such a presentation would demand good general knowledge of the Namibian public service in the early 1990s. The orientation of the report is shown by its contents, which are as follows:

a) The historical background of the public administration in Namibia;

b) The public sector in its macro-economic and sociopolitical context;

c) The public sector and its efficiency
    horizontal co-ordination at central, regional and local levels;
    vertical integration (education, justice and transport and communications);
    budgeting, auditing and financial management;
    civil servants;

d) administrative reforms; and

e) international assistance.

As pointed out above, the impossibility of dismissing civil servants was written into the Namibian constitution. The country (like South Africa during the transition phase 1994–99) must come to terms with a corps of civil servants that according to all observers is far too large and costly. Massive dismissals with the aim of saving money were thus not on the Namibian agenda in the early 1990s, nor an option for the PSA group. The work focused instead on the existing institutional and staff efficiency of the public sector. In other words, the review examined how the SWAPO government would be able to (re)structure the administrative apparatus given the available resources. It was concerned with the mobilization—and motivation—of the 66,000 employees to prepare, implement and supervise directives to transform the society inherited from the time of apartheid and to create the conditions for economic development for all Namibians, including equal access to social services, as well as popular participation in the transformation process.

In this respect, the PSA team noted serious flaws. On the whole, the Namibian public service was found to be poorly co-ordinated, both horizontally and vertically. The centralization to Windhoek under the South African administration had not been dented during the first years of independence, but had rather increased as a result of new appointments and the government's own rationalization plan. The top-heavy public sector had become even heavier and the administrative distance to the local level had become greater.

The government's work on the first development plan was thus, in all essentials, an armchair exercise without roots in the local communities it was supposed to benefit. In both Hardap and Okavango the politically elected representatives experienced that their proposals for local development received little attention from the Namibian Planning Commission, whose planners had not even visited the regions. In Windhoek, the PSA and PER groups found that the distance between the National Planning Commission (responsible for the capital budget) and the Ministry of Finance (responsible for the recurrent budget) was considerably greater than the 300 metres that separated them geographically. The administration of Namibia's finances was permeated by a lack of co-ordination.

In brief, Namibia's public service was a colossus with feet of clay, a drain on the government, the citizens and the budget, slowmoving and inflexible and poorly rooted in the regions. Overlapping between different ministries was common and the farther from Windhoek one travelled, the more tenuous was the tangible presence of the state. It could thus be noted that entire staffs of more or less under-employed administrators were found in Windhoek, while regional and local administrations suffered from an acute lack of fiscally trained personnel. This, in turn, could explain the increase in corruption and mismanagement of state funds.

The Public Sector Analysis gives concrete examples of the phenomena described above, and recommends measures to be taken. One of the most important findings—which also should have relevance in other African countries—is that certain central societal functions must be given due recognition, such as economic and social status, to become attractive and respected. In Namibia, this primarily concerned categories such as economists, planners, bookkeepers, accountants, tax collectors and fiscally trained secretaries. During the colonial times, South Africa had provided these strategic professionals. After independence, they had been neglected and many had left the public service for the private sector, with far-reaching consequences for development planning, social services and financial control.

Conclusion

The structural adjustment programmes initiated in Africa by the World Bank and the IMF were motivated by deep economic crises in several countries. The architects behind the programmes focused on macro-economic questions. In their desire to effect savings, they paid very little attention to the role the public sector must play in a reform programme. Quantitative goals were set up to reduce the public sector and drastic cut-backs were implemented. To quote Sharma, an economic plan

> ... cannot be good if it cannot be implemented or if it is not imple-
> mentable or if it does not contain a plan for developing an administrative
> capacity essential to its implementation or it does not take into account
> the realities of the political system, society, culture and administrative
> machinery (Sharma, 1992).

In 1993, Namibia decided to conduct both a Public Expenditure Review and a Public Sector Analysis, with participation and financing from Sida. Together, the two studies were intended to provide valuable knowledge about the strengths and weaknesses of the public sector in Namibia. The weaknesses were found to predominate. Namibia, which has not entered into a binding Structural Adjustment Programme with the WB and IMF, now faces a new kind of public sector reform, in which qualitative aspects—not quantitative—will hopefully be in the forefront.

Comprehensive empirical PSA studies have, from the late 1980s, given both Sida and the recipient countries detailed knowledge of the role of the public sector in economic and social development. It is surprising that this awareness did not emerge earlier which might have modified the SAP programmes' one-sided economism and negative view of the state and its officials. All too often a country is judged on the basis of its expressed goals, without the tool—the public sector—being taken into consideration.

The analysis of the administrative sector in Namibia once again revealed this to be the case. Development is not merely—and sometimes not even primarily—determined by quantifiable economic data, but also by factors that are usually taken for granted, such as administrative systems, organizational development and management.

Tor Sellström is a political scientist who, since August 1994, has been employed at the Nordic Africa Institute in Uppsala, where he is responsible for a project dealing with the Nordic countries and the liberation struggle in Southern Africa. As deputy director of the Namibian Economic Policy Research Unit (NEPRU), he participated in Namibia's Public Sector Analysis.

References

Dyrssen, H. and A. Johnston, 1991, "Co-operation in the Development of Public Sector Management Skills: The Sida Experience", *Journal of Management Development*, Vol. 10, No. 6.

Johnston, A. and L. Wohlgemuth, 1995, "Civil Service Reforms in Developing Countries", *21st Century Policy Review*, Vol. 2, No. 3.

Johnston, A., J. Basson, H. Melber, L. Gustafsson, T. Sellström and C. Johansson, 1994, "Public Sector Analysis, Namibia: An Analysis of the Resources, Structures, Functions and Activities of the Public Sector of the Republic of Namibia". Stencil (limited access). Windhoek.

Lundahl, M. and C. Vedovato, 1986, "Statens betydelse för utvecklingen i fattiga länder" (The importance of the state for development in poor countries), *Ekonomisk Debatt*, Nr. 1/86.

Nashitati, P., 1994, "A Handbook on the Namibian Public Administration 1990–1993—Post-rationalization 1994". Stencil. Windhoek.

Sharma, K.C., 1992, "Envisaged Role and Nature of Politically Neutral Public Service in Africa's Emerging Multi-Party States: Lessons from Botswana", in Hunter, J. and C. Lombard (eds.), *Multi-Party Democracy, Civil Society and Economic Transformation in Southern Africa*.

Developing Human Resource Management in Mozambique

Lais Macedo de Oliveira and Maximo Loschiavo de Barros

Background — transition to a market-oriented economy

In 1989 Mozambique had been independent for 14 years. After independence, the country chose to follow a socialist route to development led by the liberation movement, FRELIMO. In 1975 FRELIMO adopted a policy to transform the public sector under the slogan of "Break down the state", which reflected a need to make a clean break with the colonial system and create a radical new order. The idea was to use the public sector as an instrument in this process. For numerous reasons this transformation attempt was unsuccessful.

After the Nkomati Accord, signed with South Africa in 1984, the country's political leadership began, step by step, to open up to a market economy. With support from the World Bank and the International Monetary Fund, a structural adjustment programme (SAP, in Portuguese PRES) was introduced in 1987. Economic transformation was a precondition for a political model to meet changes in the international arena. FRELIMO and RENAMO, opponents in the long civil war, signed a peace accord and a new constitution in Rome in 1992. Measures were taken to increase political freedom. This opened the door to democratic change and during the latter half of 1994, the country held presidential elections.

Through SAP, attempts were made to stave off the collapse of the Mozambican economy and to create the basis for a more liberal economy through adjusting the exchange system, foreign trade, the finance and tax systems, the labour market, and the pattern of public expenditure and investment. Yet the structural adjustment programme was to be implemented by a state which had little administrative capacity and with institutions that had been too weakened to manage such a task.

To assist the Mozambican state in this process Sida began in 1987 to co-operate with the newly created Ministry of State Administration

(Ministério da Administração Estatal, MAE). Sida in its turn engaged as consultants a foundation from Brazil, which was involved in the entire undertaking. The aim was to help develop MAE itself, so that it could successfully take over responsibility for building up and re-organizing the public sector. This work began in 1988 with a broad analysis of the public sector in Mozambique, in order to learn about its structures and working routines, and was followed by the launching of a reform project , called "Structuring and Implementation of the National System for Human Resource Management".

The project — goals, theoretical background and working methods

This article aims at analysing the project to support the building up of MAE and initiating the reform of the public sector. The project was revised many times over the years, but the original goals were to:

- introduce a system of human resource management (HRM) for the public sector;

- foster co-operation between the personnel administration sections of the various government departments as well as to build up the Ministry of State Administration (MAE) to function as co-ordinator for the exchange of ideas and information;

- create the technical and operational preconditions for efficient administration of the human resources of the state; and

- develop and apply new regulations for human resource management.

To provide a preliminary overview of the area and to enable the project to continue with a suitable methodology, a diagnosis was carried out. The most important problems identified were:

- a lack of clear organization and routines;

- administrative irregularities because of the rapid turnover of civil servants at middle levels;

- difficulties in designing a consistent policy on salaries, owing to the existence of diverse salary scales, overlapping administrative categories, and incoherent career structures;

- a lack of qualitative and quantitative information on government employees;

- extremely centralized and inefficient political and administrative decision making;

– deficient knowledge about the content and application of the personnel administration law, which meant that many administrative
decisions were, in fact, illegal;
– poor communication between the HRM divisions of the various
ministries; and
– cut-backs in staffing and difficulties in employing certain categories of staff because of low pay.

The project viewed government employment as an administrative
system with the MAE as the central authority and the HRM units in
the provinces and in other ministries as subordinates.

The idea of thinking in system terms was well founded as it was
necessary to ensure a certain minimum of organization and consistency in the HRM area. The diagnosis had revealed that every sector
had its own policies and routines. In addition, the failure of human
resource management legislation largely depended on flaws in the
organization responsible for distributing the tasks and responsibilities
for HRM at the various levels of the administration.

The lack of feedback mechanisms and communication between
sectors , the fragility of the administrative system, the scarcity of staff
and the lack of clear guidelines when it came to applying the regulations which were meant to legalize the procedures, had created an
"institutional vacuum" which now had to be filled by the MAE. Using
the new system, the ministry would be able to cope with basic needs
and deal with organizational flaws.

The new national system for human resource management was built
up of the following units:
– The National Council for Public Administration, composed of the
ministers of state administration, labour, finance, and justice. The
council was responsible for drawing up guidelines and approving
policies, plans and general regulations for public administration.
– The Ministry of State Administration (MAE), responsible for
planning, guidance, follow-up, control and co-ordination of activities within the sector of human resource management.
– HRM units in the ministries and provincial governments, with the
task of co-ordinating and implementing routines and administration at sector and local level. These units report to the MAE,
which draws up the guidelines and controls and does follow-ups
of the work.

The new system is not built up according to classical hierarchical principles. Relations are built around the practical functioning of the system rather than on authority and subordination. In other words, the new system was in contrast to the prevailing thinking at the time, which was characterized by being firmly hierarchical.

The project was implemented by:

– The National Council for Public Administration, which was responsible for political guidance and for approving proposals.

– A steering group, which was responsible for planning and co-ordination, composed of the most senior official in charge of HRM issues in the MAE, the technical co-ordinator of the consultancy organization, and the managers of the HRM units within the ministries that were directly involved in the project.

– A development group, consisting of civil servants from the MAE and the HRM working groups at the ministries who, after a period of training and exchange of experiences with the consultants, in due course took over the work of running the project.

The purpose of this structure — which has not changed during the implementation of the project — was, on the one hand, to guarantee responsibility in the line system while, on the other, to ensure continued integration of local counterparts, so that the mutual exchange of learning between consultants and counterparts could continue.

The approach chosen was the *Action Research* method, based on a mutual exchange of experience and learning. The contribution of the consultants was their knowledge of administrative theory and techniques, while the local counterparts contributed with their experience of how HRM had functioned in practice in Mozambique. The consultants also took the historical dimension into account and placed organizational development in a wider context. The joint conclusion was that proposals and solutions must be deeply rooted and approved at the local level. In this way the group attempted to introduce methods that had greater possibilities of becoming a vital part of the country's economic, political, social and cultural realities.

Another important tool worked out on the basis of the diagnosis was the plan of operation for the period 1989–1992. It specified the goals and expected results of the work for the three years in question and contributed to increasing understanding of the process, since it defined the scope of the work as well as its institutional and technical content. This plan came to play a strategic role in the consolidation of the system.

Project development — strategies and attitudes

The system was defined according to a basic concept. The major question nevertheless remained: how closely could one keep to the basic concept in relation to local realities? This was a crucial question, since it raised the significance of the traditional African culture in this context, a culture which also has its own mode of social organization.

To come to grips with this question it was decided that the project should start with a pilot phase. All the solutions would be carefully tested before they were generalized. To implement this, special pilot units were created in three ministries and one province. The MAE participated in its role of central controlling organ.

The staff of the pilot units carried out all the phases of the project: diagnosis, discussion of alternatives, formulation of proposals, trials, and thereafter, analysis. Not until these trials had been completed did the system begin to be introduced into other departments. The legislation which regulated the national human resource management system was also not approved before the proposals had been discussed by the local managements involved and tested in the trial units.

The HRM system is composed of processes, routines and documents which require participation on all levels: managers, specialists and civil servants. This range, in combination with the lack of administrative procedures and properly trained staff, meant that the project had to be implemented in stages. Thus, it was necessary to start by establishing an operational base and to continue thereafter to other levels. After discussions with the managers of the pilot units and responsible personnel, it was decided what should be accorded priority. Among the many proposed activities, it was decided to begin with the following:

– Creating order among the staff files, the information from which would create the future basis for a HRM system.

– Drawing up detailed routines and instructions so that the different HRM units could supervise personnel activities and guarantee that the administrative work was done in accordance with regulations. Once the proposals had been tested, they were compiled in a handbook for government personnel administration staff.

A comprehensive training programme was worked out, with the aim of spreading and applying the HRM code, first centrally and then in the provinces.

In the initial diagnosis, the issue of the total lack of administrative routines and guidelines had been raised. A great deal of work was expended on laying down a new management culture, based on division of work, distribution of responsibility and fixing of routines as well as setting out written rules on civil servants' rights and duties.

When this was done, the practical work could begin, by putting into effect those measures which the managers themselves regarded as the most important. This strategy contributed to increasing confidence in the project and in MAE. The ministry soon developed the capacity to meet the demands from other organs such as trade unions.

In a country like Mozambique, where reality changes rapidly, processes such as these are very uncertain. Urgent matters often arise and require attention. Sometimes changes of direction must occur as a result of changes in the surroundings. How well consultants succeed depends on their ability to handle these uncertainties.

A good example of this type of urgent matter came up at the end of 1990. The need arose to create a uniform salary scale for all government employees. Yet this scale could not be worked out until a complete survey and rationalization of all the job descriptions had been made, so that all civil servants could receive a title and a salary that matched their tasks. While doing this, for the first time ever it was discovered how many people worked in the service of the state and thus the cost to the state of the entire work force. The importance of information as a tool within the administration was demonstrated and in the process, a personnel information system was created as well as a common salary scale and career ladder.

These experiences showed that the project had the flexibility to change course and was capable of dealing with new situations and uncertainties. It built on successes and gave the participants a clear insight into planning by objectives and results. It managed to create a feeling of ownership among those involved, a consciousness that the project did not belong to Sida or the consultants but to the country.

At the beginning of 1995 an analysis of the results of the project was conducted. The following was noted:

– The organizational basis of the system had been laid and was functioning. The new personnel administration system became law in 1992 and the division of responsibilities between MAE and other organs was specified.

- The MAE had been given the responsibility for co-ordination within the system and the power to exercise its functions.
- The formal structure had been constituted and the staff trained, the basic routines had come into operation and the civil service statute had been applied. The legality of the actions and decisions of the administration had thus been guaranteed.
- The system of human resource management as well as the wage and career scales were in operation.

The project has been continued for the period 1995–1999. A new government policy approved the decentralization of competencies for the HRM area, initiating an irreversible process of administrative decentralization which culminated, in 1996, with the elaboration and presentation of draft legislation on municipalization and reform of local government.

In order to create at local level the new capacity to be responsible for the HRM of almost 70 per cent of all civil service staff, an intensive local training programme for managers and technicians of HRM has started. Thus 1997 was an important year in the process of structuring the National Human Resource Management System. MAE consolidated the results attained during the preceding years and established guidelines to ensure the continuity of the process. After the establishment of the technical and operational base at central level, the process has started to be extended to the provinces and districts.

Taking into consideration the complexity of the task at the local level, due not only to the lack of material resources but above all to the lack of trained personnel, the MAE chose to co-operate in a system of partnership with other strategic sectors in the public administration. An Interministerial Group for the Restructuring of the Public Administration was established. Its main objective was to optimise resources and create a permanent space for an exchange of ideas and for the formulation of plans, guidelines and strategies related to the implementation of government reform programmes at all levels.

The implementation of the new wage scale and career system together with the training and education of personnel has created an important instrument for the process of changing the profile of the public sector staff. This is due inter alia to the new possibilities which have been created for attracting and keeping more highly qualified personnel.

In addition, the establishment of "intelligent partnerships", creating a platform of intersectorial understanding and cooperation, constitutes the MAE's most effective answer for ensuring the system's sustainability and the success of long-term projects and programmes such as the decentralization of the public administration.

Some conclusions and lessons

The implementation of the National Human Resource Management System is playing an important role in the on-going process of modernization and rationalization of the public administration in Mozambique. Its development was interlinked with the changes taking place in the political and socio-economic arena in Mozambique. Whenever possible, the changes were incorporated in the project's structure and methods of steering. In a smooth and gradual way, the system's operational base was built up as a way to fill the vacuum left in the post-independence period.

We consider that the goals established in 1989, when the project started, have been attained. Today the instruments of HRM are in place. It is now time to expand the training to the management staff at different levels of the administration who will be responsible for the planning, organization, guidance and control of the personnel in the public sector. To build up this capacity will be the challenge to be faced in the next century.

We learnt that a process of mutual learning, based on mutual trust, is the only way forward for this kind of reform work. In this way people assume ownership of the process, learn how to deal with insecurity and reach concrete results within the allotted time. The organization of interministerial groups working interactively to develop the national administrative machinery was a key to the project becoming firmly rooted in the public administration.

Nevertheless, this learning process requires a good deal of time, just because it is based on trust. It also requires knowledge about the social and economic characteristics of the environment in which the project is being implemented.

All the proposals were subject to a trial phase. This was the core of the learning process. It also contributed to minimizing the risks when the project was implemented.

In our opinion, it is through co-operation in this form that Africa can build up an administration which is adapted to African conditions. It is also our opportunity to participate in the creation of a democratic society, our opportunity both to make a contribution and to learn.

Lais Macedo de Oliveira and *Maximino Loschiavo de Barros* are both employed by the *Fundap*, Foundation for Administrative Development in São Paulo, Brazil. De Barros has been a member of the board of *Fundap*. He conducted the analysis of the public administration sector in Mozambique which preceded the project and during its entire implementation co-ordinated inputs from São Paulo. De Barros has also participated in the work of developing Sida's strategy for public administration. Lais Macedo de Oliviera was the senior *Fundap* consultant in Maputo during the implementation of the project.

Telecommunications in Mozambique
—More than just Telephones

Dag Sundelin

Introduction

This chapter describes a successful institutional co-operation. It shows that even a country in severe political and economic crisis can develop its institutions if donors and recipients can agree on certain preconditions. In the following case, the most important inputs, from the Mozambican side, were continuity (the two main actors stayed during the total developmental phase), consistency and a serious striving for change. On the part of Sida, there was a long-term perspective and patience. Together the parties developed a co-operation which at first only consisted of foreign experts and delivery of equipment but, over time, a close partnership emerged where institutional development and good leadership were the main goals. These objectives, together with the long-term assistance, convinced other donors to support this sector.

Telecommunications services were introduced in Mozambique as early as in 1908. A colonial directorate was given the responsibility for the postal service, telegraphy, and later on telecommunications. At independence in 1975 most Portuguese, who had until then held all the key positions, disappeared, leaving behind an enormous task for the new nation to try and maintain necessary social services as well as develop new ones.

The telecommunications sector was no exception as far as the state of affairs at independence was concerned. However, during the past twenty years telecommunications has proved to be one of the public services which has led the way in the development of the country.

One illustration of this is that up to the present time the number of subscribers has more than doubled while the number of employees has remained constant. The increase in the number of lines during the last ten years is on a level with the average for the COMESA coun-

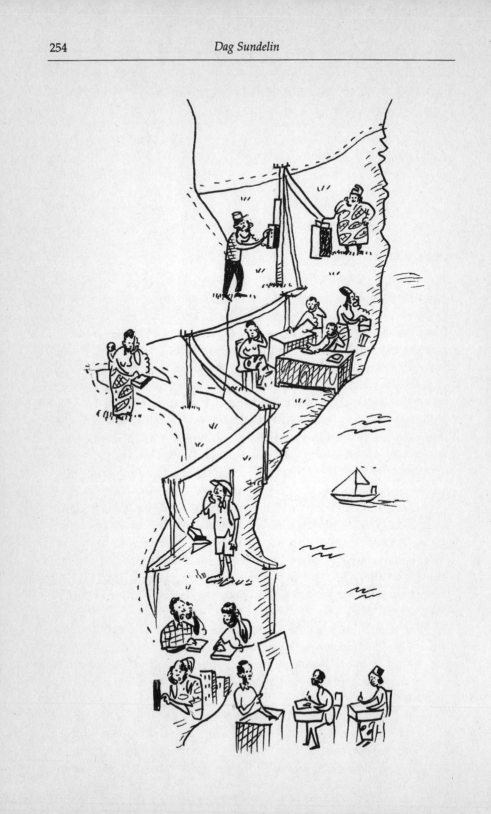

tries, but is considerably higher than, for example, Angola, which has only had a 30 per cent increase.

Telecomuniçacões de Moçambique, TDM, has adopted a deliberate policy of increasing the skills of its staff. Today 162 of its employees are university graduates which can be compared with two in 1976. The organization has undergone a revolutionary change. Formerly a government bureaucracy it is now a commercially sound company in an area characterized by an unbelievably rapid development.

Sida has supported the telecommunications sector in Mozambique since the end of the 1970s. During this time TDM has advanced both technically and organizationally from a very low starting point. This has been made possible by aid made available to TDM by international donors and finance institutions.

Sida's role has become strategically important through the support it has provided to TDM's objective of becoming an efficiently functioning telecommunications operator. In addition to certain investments Sweden has financed consultancy projects in respect of overall development plans, and also consultancy projects designed to improve co-ordination when it became clear that Mozambique had access to financing from different donors. From the beginning of the 1990s the Swedish support has been concentrated on the institutional development of TDM.

The changing role of the government

As early as 1908 a department with responsibility for postal services, telegraphy and telephony was established in Mozambique. In practice the sector was run from Portugal with Portuguese management and Portuguese technicians on site in Mozambique.

During the period from 1975 to the 1990s, Mozambique's development was governed by the fundamental conviction of the governments' leading role, not just in respect of politics but also at operational levels. In 1981 the Mozambique government decided to separate the postal and telecommunications services. TDM was formed as the government agency for telecommunications, i.e. it was directly subordinate to the responsible ministry. This resulted in TDM being under the direct control of both its own director-general and the minister responsible for telecommunications.

For TDM this power constellation proved to be one of the most important factors for expansion. From the creation of TDM until 1994 the same two persons held these two posts.

The transition from a centrally planned to a more market-oriented economy began at the end of the 1980s. The role of the government was to be changed and the different social sectors were to be given a different framework in which to work, although they were still to be governed by overall political objectives. Draft laws were drawn up which had the aim of defining roles, responsibilities, powers at different levels and, above all, a separation of the political and the operative level.

In October 1992 the peace treaty between Frelimo and Renamo was signed and Mozambique stood on the threshold of comprehensive social change including greater democratization and new development objectives for the reconstruction of the country. This affected the telecommunications sector which now faced the new challenge of extending the network to previously inaccessible parts of the country.

A new telecommunications law was passed in 1992 and this, together with a new law for the transformation of parastatals into government-owned enterprises, laid the foundations for TDM to become the first government agency in Mozambique to be transformed into a publicly owned company.

The result of the change is that TDM must follow the policy objectives established by the government, in its capacity as owner of the company. These objectives refer both to development plans and the requirement to remain financially sound. The government is now represented by the Ministry of Finance instead of the sector ministry. One of the most important issues has concerned TDM's financial restructuring. The aim has been to enable the company to draw up a consolidated balance sheet which reflects the company's operational assets and determine whether these debts are to be financed by borrowing or by the owner's equity.

During 1994 TDM, for the first time, produced a profit. That year was an exceptional year with a large UN presence and the holding of the first general election in the country. The forecast made by TDM indicates that profits will decrease. Future profitability will be governed by the decision on the criteria for new investments and changes in tariffs as well as volumes of traffic. Appropriate socio-economic investments, which are not financially sound, must continue in the future to be financed by the government or through different forms of assistance.

The so-called regulatory agency, stipulated in the law passed in 1992, has an important role to play in the telecommunications sector. Within the framework of the approved legislation the main task of this independent body is to co-ordinate and supervise radio frequencies, approve and issue licences and concessions for different operators and, in all other respects, ensure that the parties involved in the sector follow the rules which have been laid down. However, up to the present time the independent role of the agency in relation to TDM can be questioned. Its political independence is also unclear. If the telecommunications sector in Mozambique is to be exploited more commercially, with elements of greater competition, the regulatory body must be empowered in accordance with the intentions of the telecommunications legislation.

Progress towards deregulation is being stimulated by international competition and the aim is primarily reductions in tariffs for international traffic. In a country such as Mozambique the monopoly for basic communications services will probably be more difficult to break in the light of a national market where the great majority cannot afford to pay for these services.

The investment phase

Sida's support to the telecommunications sector started as management support to the telecommunications operator on an ad hoc basis at the beginning of the 1980s. Since 1983/84 some SEK150 million have been disbursed via the country programme, which corresponds to some two per cent of the total assistance payments over the period 1983–1994. In addition assistance has also been provided within the framework of regional support, mainly in the form of a microwave link between Malawi, Mozambique and Zimbabwe (SEK42 million) and an international telephone exchange in Maputo (SEK25 million). In addition telecommunications components have been included within the framework of support for the Beira corridor (some SEK7 million).

At an early stage Frelimo planned for a considerable expansion of the telecommunications sector through an extensive investment programme. Sweden's role was changed to supporting TDM in the revision and co-ordination of the investment plan in a ten-year perspective. High priority was given to the task of linking together the largest cities in the country to make country-wide communication possible.

Sida expressed great doubts about the programme when it was presented, saying that: "Sida's doubts about the project have increased as the economic situation in the country has deteriorated. It is questioned whether it is right to make an enormous investment which would lead to greater indebtedness. It is also probable that the security situation will cause problems". Sida also underlined the necessity of reducing the rate of investments in order to enable TDM to develop into an organization with the capacity and skills to operate and maintain an expanded system.

Consequently Sida limited its support in respect of investments in a micro-wave link between Malawi, Mozambique and Zimbabwe and a new digital AXE exchange to Maputo. This exchange became Mozambique's "window" to and from the surrounding world. At the same time, and despite its doubts about the investment programme, Sida decided to give support to TDM's overall co-ordination of the programme.

TDM and Sida, through the consultancy company Swedtel, co-operated very closely during this phase in order, among other things, to encourage TDM to co-ordinate different donors and finance institutes. Donor conferences were arranged to increase the flow of information and to make the programme clear to all involved. TDM was thus regarded by the donor community as a recipient organization which had taken the initiative. Above all other finance institutes regarded Sweden's support and role as a form of guarantee for both realism in the proposals and perseverance in their implementation.

Due to continued security problems in the country, the implementation of the ten-year plan was drastically delayed. This mainly affected the transmission system and certain changes in priorities were necessitated. In general, however, the original plans were followed even if they were delayed.

During the 1980s TDM concentrated its development work on technology and education and training. Investment capital was made available and the focus was on modernizing the telecommunications system from the very bottom. Sida, as other donors, more or less accepted this strategy even if certain doubts were expressed about the level of investments. Although Sida, quite early on, had adopted a position of wanting to contribute to strengthening the educational and training functions in parallel with the investment programme, it was training in the technical area which dominated.

In connection with a donor conference in 1989 a proposal was presented for a programme (Operational Management Plan, OMP) to increase the skills of the organization and its management, particularly in respect of operations and maintenance. The main aim was to safeguard investments in the network structure. This donor conference was of decisive importance for the development of TDM, both internally within the company and also for the international finance institutes. During subsequent donor conferences the OMP programme focused more strongly on support to general institutional building with comprehensive and long-term organization and management development.

Education and training

TDM and Sida gave priority to technical training in a situation in which there were almost no managers and technicians at intermediate level after the Portuguese had left the country. Sida insisted that it was necessary for TDM to establish, at all project levels, close co-operation with the consultant. It was often difficult to find persons with suitable experience and qualifications in TDM. Nevertheless this requirement was maintained during all phases of the project. TDM actively tried to recruit younger people with a reasonable formal educational background. With a combination of internal training and practical work they would be able to take on a job with greater responsibilities.

A telecommunications school was developed on a Swedish pattern based on the experience of the Swedish Telecom. A relatively large number of courses were developed whose main priority was the different technical disciplines in the field of telecommunications. The premises for the telecommunications school were financed by Italian assistance. The centre is without precedent in Mozambique as regards size and equipment but no more than 15–20 per cent of its capacity is utilized today.

Training activities have often been implemented as a component in the supply of new equipment in connection with new investments. They have, however, also been carried out as a regular skills development process. There has also been training abroad, not least on BITS financed courses in Sweden for TDM employees.

However, it has been obvious that the problems lie in the character of the training system. The rapid organizational development in TDM placed entirely new demands on the internal training function, not least as an instrument in the process of change. Since Sida phased out direct support to the management of the telecommunications school in 1992, the pace of this change has slowed down. The quality of the training and its adaptation to changing needs deteriorated markedly. At the end of 1995 TDM realized that an entirely new strategy must be produced and since then there has been a much greater focus on requirements in respect of the role and responsibilities of management.

From technology to institutional development

In 1989 it was clear to both TDM and Sida that the emphasis needed to be shifted to the administrative areas and management functions. In the light of an earlier decision that the telecommunications sector would not be an area for long-term co-operation, this phase was formulated as a final phase in the co-operation programme.

A new programme of support was formulated by the parties which was expected to lead to a situation in which Mozambique, which even then had a technically modern telecommunications network, would acquire a fully modern telecommunications structure in the organizational and commercial senses as well.

To guarantee future company management with appropriate skills and experience, management training was established for future managers in the company. The development of future managers in the company is considered to be of particular importance for long-term survival. The concept has been copied from the Ethiopian telecommunications company where it has contributed to making the company one of the best managed in Africa.

Today TDM is successful in recruiting many well-educated young people who see an opportunity for their own development in the company. The salary situation is, in relative terms, competitive and career possibilities are considered to be good.

Factors contributing to success

Since independence the political situation in Mozambique has meant that the maintenance and availability of the telecommunications system have been especially important. In the worsening security situation telecommunications were a substitute for physical transportation by land. Telecommunications thus played a decisive role in official and commercial operations as well as in the maintaining of social relations.

Another important factor is the dedicated leadership which TDM has had since 1981. The minister for the sector has given the development of telecommunications high priority. The leadership duo of the minister and the director-general gave TDM a very strong position in relation to both the government and the international donor community. This type of relationship could by no means be found in all sectors of society.

A special situation for Mozambique was the fact that TDM was realistic in its expectations of what international assistance could contribute. TDM had lost more or less all its personnel in leading positions as a result of the Portuguese exodus at independence. It realized that long-term education and training and human resource development was essential. In addition Sida insisted on the need for TDM to work closely with foreign experts and consultants, even in line functions. This insight meant that there was no alienation—instead there was partnership which formed the foundation of close co-operation.

The telecommunications sector has developed very rapidly during the last twenty years and TDM has succeeded in using this development to its own advantage concerning the choice of technology. Unit costs for digital equipment have decreased continuously in real terms and TDM has therefore been able to build up a telecommunications system with a technically impressive performance, even in comparison with many OECD countries.

Political developments in Mozambique have led to TDM becoming increasingly more independent of the political level and developing into a company which operates with a greater degree of freedom and sound commercial principles.

Finally assistance has had a considerable influence on TDM's development for a period of 15 years. Not only technical development has been made possible, even organizational and commercial factors have undergone extensive changes. Sida's support has, over the years, been flexible, and above all Sweden has supported areas which give long-term results. From the end of the 1980s it can be said that Swedish support has concentrated on institutional development rather than technical development, investment co-ordination and education and training. The financing of investments is considerably easier to secure for an organization such as TDM, while support for institutional development requires a long-term commitment and perseverance which, de facto, few donors have.

Challenges and critical factors

Sweden has, via Sida, given long-term support to TDM for just over 15 years. Experience has shown that the question of "partnership" between donor, recipient and consultant has been a central issue. Above all Sida, as a donor, must regularly analyse the role of Swedish assistance to a specific sector, and consequently its decisions must provide a basis for a necessary long-term perspective. It is not easy to achieve a successful partnership, but once it is achieved both parties must take responsibility in a long-term perspective.

Experience gained from the development of telecommunications in Mozambique also shows the different roles telecommunications has in the development of society. The socio-economic benefits of the developments in the telecommunications sector have been, and still are considerable for Mozambique. The requirement in respect of sound finances can be difficult for TDM to meet, in view of the demands made by the government for the extension of telecommunications to areas which cannot bear the costs in their entirety. As international tariffs are governed by the international market, trends show that the scope for subsidizing national traffic by international traffic is decreasing.

During September and October 1994 Sida carried out an analysis which resulted in a decision that support to the telecommunications sector would be phased out by June 30, 1996. This analysis was based on the fact that TDM had then reached a level where the company would be able to develop further without Swedish support of the long-term nature which had been given since 1983. This decision was not questioned by Mozambique and TDM, due to the mutual understanding in which the "partnership" had resulted.

The telecommunications sector in Mozambique will in all essentials need to continue its process of development and its adaptation to the demands placed on it. By definition telecommunications is not only a national concern. Global conditions and demands for access to communications at the right price necessitate greater internationalization. TDM already has some ten subsidiaries which it owns jointly with foreign companies. The operations of these companies are all linked directly to the field of telecommunications, while the core operations have been retained within TDM. It is interesting to note that Swedish Telia, through Swedtel, started a joint consultancy company, Teleconsultiores, with TDM in 1992.

Soon the Mozambique government, as the owner of TDM, and even TDM itself, will need to decide how to proceed. A credible scenario is that, in the medium term, TDM will be partly or wholly privatized. Mozambique will have difficulties in meeting the requirements for greater skills both within sophisticated technologies and business methods through its own efforts. Provided that the sector can maintain commercial profitability, there are in all probability, a number of possible partners who could be interested in co-operation. For Mozambique this is mainly an issue of being able to combine requirements for long-term development goals with short-term profit motives, which are essential to attract internationally active telecommunications companies.

Dag Sundelin is a business economist and has worked for Sida, both at headquarters and in the field (Angola, Mozambique and South Africa) for many years mainly within the fields of telecommunication and energy.

The Decline and Recovery of an African Central Bank

Olof Hesselmark

Introduction

In 1987, the Governor of the Bank of Zambia wrote a letter to Sida in Lusaka with a desperate call for help. The Central Bank was in difficulties, and there was an urgent need for assistance. Earlier in 1987, the external auditors had refused to complete the audit of the bank's accounts for 1986, on the grounds that they were incomplete, partly due to several frauds in the bank. The Bank of Zambia (BoZ) was not to deliver unqualified accounts until 1995.

Since then, the BoZ has gone through a remarkable process of decline and restructuring. In 1989, when the call for help was answered, the BoZ was an organization without focus, weak in resources and capability, and suffering from inadequate organizational structure, obsolete work methods and poor management. It did not perform well as a Central Bank. Accounts were in arrears, the output of economic planning information was very limited, its supervisory performance was very weak, and the foreign exchange control functions were badly managed. Now, eight years later, the BoZ is an altogether different organization, with a clear mission and organizational focus. It is staffed with motivated people and management, and it is fulfilling the role of Central Bank with confidence. The improvements are visible in all areas. Annual reports are produced on time with unqualified audits, the volume and quality of economic information improves continuously, all basic IT systems are in place and functioning, supervision of financial institutions has reached new levels.

Sida has supported the BoZ since 1989, mainly in the areas of computerization, bank supervision and management development. The support has mainly been in the form of technical assistance, over the years totalling about 15 man-years. At the same time, several other donors have supported other areas in the bank. The total external input can be estimated at 50–70 man-years over the last eight years, constituting a very substantial addition of professional and managerial manpower.

But the same amount of manpower has been infused in many other organizations in Africa during the same time, in many cases without any success. In most other cases in Zambia, the supported organizations have been worse off after receiving support. What is the difference in the case of the Bank of Zambia? In this article, I shall try to show and explain the causes of the BoZ success. I shall follow the process from 1987 to 1997, using a sequence of documents produced by some of the different people who have been involved in different capacities.

Zambia's economy

By 1987, when the call for help came from the BoZ, the Zambian economy was in a free fall. During the first ten years after independence in 1964, Zambia's economy grew by an average of 2.3 per cent per year. A sharp decline in copper prices beginning in 1974, combined with increasing import prices, caused rapidly deteriorating terms of trade. Between 1977 and 1984, terms of trade fell from an index of 100 to 62, i.e. nearly twice the quantity of copper had to be exported to finance the same import. The real per capita incomes fell by 25 per cent in the same period, a long inflation period started, and the value of the Kwacha fell to one thousandth of its value between 1983 and 1997. The decline in the economy has continued during the last ten years, and it is only after 1995 that a moderate real growth has finally been achieved.

During this long period of economic decline, all public institutions in the country have suffered from lack of resources, mismanagement and general degradation. It is important to have in mind this fall from a position of moderate well-being at independence to serious poverty 30 years later, when an institution such as BoZ is examined.

Down to the bottom

The Central Bank was no longer capable of performing its duties. Inflation was accompanied by a rapid growth of money in circulation, but the bank did not have the capacity to handle the circulation of notes. Used notes were stockpiled in the BoZ, and a shortage of bank notes occurred at times. The highest denomination note was still K20, which in 1977 had purchased a tank full of petrol. In 1987 it would only buy a few litres.

During the 80s, import and export control, and the control of foreign exchange, had intensified. It had always been strict in Zambia, with its history as a British colony, but now the controls of the Kaunda government increased even more. The control over the allocation of foreign exchange was removed from the BoZ to FEMAC, a new institution in the Office of the President. This did nothing to improve morale in the BoZ, and a number of embarrassing frauds and corruption scandals involving BoZ staff were exposed.

While all this happened, the number of employees at the Bank continued to grow, to a maximum of about 1,350 during the 1989–1994 period. During the good years following independence, many institutions in Zambia added various welfare functions to their organizations. They managed housing for the employees, provided security and health facilities, vehicle maintenance, canteens and sports facilities. A study in 1993 revealed that over 60 per cent of the employees of the BoZ were busy (or rather *not* busy...) in these peripheral functions.

The accounting functions of the bank were also allowed to deteriorate, to the deplorable state that the Central Bank's accounts could neither be audited nor published for a period of six years. An attempt to computerize the accounts started in 1987, and ended three years later in complete failure.

The collapse of the Zambian economy had many negative consequences for the bank. By the end of the 1980s there was no money to pay for the civil servants' salaries. The commercial banks would no longer cash the civil servants' pay cheques, since they would bounce at the BoZ. To solve the problem, the civil service, to the last man and woman, queued up on Cairo Road in front of the BoZ building with their pay cheques at the end of each month. The chaos in the bank was beyond description. Hundreds of people milled about in the lobby and in the bank hall, and all internal security had broken down.

On the whole, the Bank of Zambia did not perform well as a central bank between 1987 and 1993. However, very little else worked well in Zambia's administration at that time, and the question is if it would have been reasonable to expect more from the BoZ in the prevailing situation, than from the government as a whole. Looking at the situation with hindsight, it can be argued that given the macro-economic and political situation at the end of the 1980s, any kind of disaster could occur anywhere in the administration. The BoZ was then—in reality—just another branch of the government, with only little Central Bank independence.

The BoZ Act from 1985, Section 4, gave the bank the power to exercise control over all foreign currency dealings. This power was in practice removed to the Foreign Exchange Management Committee (FEMAC), which was under the total control of Central Government. Also in the area of monetary policy the government had—through provisions in the BoZ Act—full power to finance its spendings through an overdraft at the BoZ, thereby overruling the Bank's objective of monetary stability.

Thus the decline of the Bank of Zambia was not remarkable in the Zambian context at the time. The recovery, however, has been all the more remarkable.

Changes in the environment

The Bank's call for assistance led to Sida's commissioning of a consultant to study the bank and to come back with recommendations for further assistance. A first mission in 1988 was followed by several others. A number of shortcomings in the operations and organization of the bank were identified, and the first project was started in 1991. It was to last for two years, and focused on management development, support for bank inspection and computer services, in total about eight man-years and SEK13 million. In addition to the Sida assistance, several other donors started support activities to the BoZ at the same time. It is interesting to note that the proposals in the first reports focused on the internal situation in the bank. All improvements were to come from better internal management, through training, awareness and computerization. Even if the consultants did realize that the situation in the BoZ was partly caused by its lack of independence, it was not reflected in the reports.

At the end of 1992, the first phase of Sida's project had been completed. In the BoZ, a restructuring phase had begun, to a large extent driven by the expatriate Governor and the large number of expatriate experts provided by the donors. A computer department was formed and staffed; the bank supervision was brought in under the BoZ and made into a functioning unit; a first retrenchment of 280 staff was performed.

The Chiluba government had now been in power for a year, and a new economic environment was beginning to take shape in Zambia. During 1992, the first step towards making the Kwacha convertible was taken. Bureau de Change offices were introduced in October 1992, and most foreign exchange transactions were moved away from the BoZ. In addition to this change, the procedure for the financing of the budget deficit was changed. Instead of using a simple overdraft in the central bank, the government started to issue treasury bills through the Bank of Zambia. This introduced the market as a third party in the financing process, and interest rates shot up. The cost of financing became manifest, which also led to an increased autonomy for the BoZ. The government could still create a deficit, but it could no longer hide the consequences.

At this time an internal discussion about the future role of the Central Bank had started. Together with a number of other Sida consultants I participated in an evaluation of the first two year project. During the evaluation we had several discussions with the Governor (from 1992 a Zambian economist) and the Bank Secretary about a concentration on "the core functions" of the bank. Our evaluation report commented: "Through these measures and developments it should be possible to reduce the staff by 30–40 per cents over the next two to three years". It was by then clear to them that the bank was unmanageable in its prevailing state, and that something had to be done. There was, however, very little support for these ideas from other managers in the bank.

During 1993, the planning for a new and modern central bank started in the BoZ, under the leadership of the Bank Secretary, Mr. M.M. Mupunda with strong support from the Governor Mr. D. Mulaisho. By now, the Kwacha was for all practical purposes convertible, with a floating rate of exchange. The foreign exchange control was abolished, and about 100 employees were made redundant. A number of studies of the internal organization were now done in order to identify areas that were not part of the "core functions". Some of these studies were financed directly by Sida in Lusaka at the request of the Bank Secretary. They revealed a gross overstaffing in all areas, and pointed out a number of peripheral service areas that did not need to be part of the bank, or that were simply producing no output. It was agreed that a large, diverse organization requires too much of scarce management capacity just to keep it running, and that for this reason the BoZ should aim towards a small, specialized and highly professional organization.

The organizational structure of the bank was also examined. It was found to be designed for an organization based on manual work and a bureaucratic work style. Given the smaller size of the future bank, and given that it would operate as a modern bank with largely automatic, computerized production facilities, a more functional organization structure was envisaged.

Apart from the inputs and support given by the consultants from time to time, the entire restructuring process was driven from within the bank itself. I did several short term consultancies at the bank during this time, and could note how a group of change-oriented younger managers—informally—took form under the leadership of the Bank Secretary. The group had a focus, and it gradually developed a manpower base for the transformation.

Reconstruction

By mid-1994 the ground work was done. 1993 had been spent paving the way for the reconstruction that was now to begin. The bank had a mission statement approved by the board, a new Bank of Zambia Act was being processed, and the "hiving off" of several peripheral functions had been prepared and accepted by the board. At this stage, the donors pledged continued support for 1994–96, thereby allowing for continued development projects in several areas—computer systems, accounting, bank supervision, and management training and development. A number of personnel changes had also taken place. Several division and department managers who had been less than enthusiastic about the changes had been retired and replaced by mainly younger and well qualified Zambians. Everything was now prepared for the big change.

The reconstruction was going to be a massive one. Several hundred people were going to be removed from the bank, and naturally this could not be done without regard for their welfare. This problem was addressed with a great deal of ingenuity in two different ways. The key was in the words "hive off", as bees do when a hive becomes too crowded. For a number of service functions the bank helped the employees in those areas to form their own private service companies. These companies had a contract with the BoZ to purchase their services for a limited period of time. Through this, a large part of the entrepreneurial risk was eliminated, and separate companies were formed for refuse collection, office cleaning, the BoZ canteen and catering, the BoZ Club House, office maintenance and repair, private security and a florist business. Many former employees found employment in these companies, some of which are now doing well.

The other way was a more traditional retirement or retrenchment package. The conditions were very favourable for Zambian conditions, and they were made open to all employees of the bank. The packages were accepted by a large number of people, and on the whole the process seems to have been fairly smooth. As always in a situation like this, the bank lost a number of managers who preferred to take the package and go into early retirement or to other occupations. This did leave a leadership vacuum in some places, but it has since been dealt with through external recruitment.

Another action taken after the retrenchment was that the bank sold nearly all bank owned staff houses to the people who lived in them. The bank arranged the financing of the purchases on favourable terms, and in this way another managerial problem was removed.

According to one of the managers involved, it was a massive exercise, like a "tidal wave" that swept through the bank. The number of employees went down from 1,250 in 1993 to about 600 in 1996.

The next step was to fill some of the vacancies and to restructure those posts that were to remain. A new organizational structure had been planned earlier. A number of external recruitments were made, and new managers were appointed all round. New salary scales and conditions of employment were worked out. The budget for personnel costs was retained and increased although the staff had been cut by half. The average personnel cost per person has increased from US$ 4,000 in 1993 to US$19,000 in 1996. Employment in the BoZ was now very competitive, and the average professional qualifications of the staff had increased enormously.

As soon as the restructuring was finished, an extensive management training programme was initiated by the newly appointed Director of Personnel. This project "The BoZ way" involved all organization units in a management training and identification exercise. Departmental objectives and codes of conduct were formulated in seminars where all staff participated. The exercise was financed by Sida and supported by a UK management consultant.[1]

The restructuring process has all the time been controlled and "owned" by the BoZ management, under the leadership of Mr. M.M. Mupunda, who was the Bank Secretary until his retirement in 1995. There was a team of younger officers who did the hard work, and who later took on different management posts in the bank. The consultants were used in a very constructive way, to reinforce directions, to investigate facts and to formulate opinions. A great deal of vision and encouragement from the two most recent governors has supported the process.

Sida's involvement has been important. The long-term nature of the cooperation between Sida and the BoZ, and the continuity of the persons involved, has in my opinion been instrumental in carrying the project forward. The same consultants have returned to the bank year after year, and this has increased the trust and confidence between the parties. Trust is an important word in this context. It takes great courage to embark on a restructuring of the scope and size that we have witnessed at the bank. The price of failure is heavy in the Zambian context, and I think that the constructive dialogue between the BoZ, Sida and the consultants helped to remove a great deal of the uncertainty about whether this was the right thing to do.

In addition to Sida, several other donors have contributed substantial resources to the bank. During the whole period, the IMF has financed a senior economist as an advisor to the Governor and contributed substantial resources for legal matters, foreign exchange matters and general management. IDA and CIDA have been involved in accounting and bank supervision. UNDP has supported activities related to debt management, information systems and foreign exchange management. Donor coordination has rarely been an issue in the projects, since the objectives of the reconstruction have been well founded in the bank's own management. The coordination was done within the bank itself.

The Bank of Zambia is now well on the way to becoming a modern central bank. There are still things to do—the basic information and accounting systems are obsolete and need to be replaced, the training of managers and staff is never finished, there is still over-

---

[1] Private communication with Mr. M.M. Mupunda and Mr. M. Mwalie in Lusaka, June and December 1997.

staffing, and some functional areas are not functioning well. But these are normal problems in any organization, and no revolution is needed to rectify them. This is a success story, if not without parallel in Africa, then at least remarkable enough to receive a good deal of attention and praise.

Summary—some lessons learned

The successful restructuring of the Bank of Zambia is remarkable in the Zambian context. There are a number of general observations worth pointing out.

–   *Autonomy.* The BoZ already had legal autonomy as a central bank from the 1985 Bank of Zambia Act. However, the autonomy was circumscribed by the government in several ways, and the reality was that the BoZ was very much controlled. This changed abruptly with the removal of the foreign exchange control, and later with the introduction of treasury bills instead of a government controlled overdraft to finance the budget deficit. After this, the government had neither the need nor the mechanisms to exercise a detailed control of the bank. The bank management then took upon itself to make the necessary changes in the internal organization. They did not have to ask the government for permission.

–   *Ownership.* The change process was owned by the Bank of Zambia. There was substantial support and encouragement from the outside—mainly the donors—but the driving forces were employees of the bank. This case strongly supports the idea that internal ownership is essential for the success of all cooperation that involves public institutions.

–   *Continuity.* All the major donors involved in the support to the BoZ have participated for a long time. Long-term relationships were created between the institutions, and at least in the case of Sida, a very trusting relationship has been built up over the years. The driving force within the bank, the Bank Secretary, had been in the bank for many years, having survived a great many Governors. The continuity within the bank matched that of the external parties.

- *Acceptance* from the donors that the BoZ took charge of the change process. This is related to the issue of ownership, but it is worth a separate point. It has happened in many cases that donors have been reluctant to hand over the control of a change process to the cooperating partner. There is a contradiction between the call for ownership and the holding back on the control of a project. In this case, it seems that the mutual trust between the competent team in the BoZ and the donors had a positive effect.

- *Personnel.* No change process is successful without the right people. The Bank Secretary assembled a team of mainly young and well educated people around him. This highly motivated group of people made up the "critical mass" necessary to make an impact.

It is difficult to select just one of the above issues as the most important factor explaining the success in this case. They are all important and necessary. One could speculate on the effects of removing them one by one, and try to see if the overall effect would still remain the same. To some extent I think all these conditions have to be fulfilled simultaneously. They are each and every one necessary conditions for success.

Olof Hesselmark is a Swedish economist. He has lived for nine years in different countries in Eastern and Southern Africa, working in different management positions and as a consultant. He is currently working in Sweden as a private consultant, specializing in IT, financial software and management.

References

Andersson, G. and J. Solheim, 1990, *Appraisal of the Plan of Operation.* Stockholm: Sida.

Andersson, G., O. Hesselmark and O. Strømme, 1993, *Continued Support to the Bank of Zambia. Report from a Project Identification Mission.* Lusaka: Sida.

Andersson, G., O. Hesselmark and T. Grung Moe, 1992, *Change and Opportunity—Challenges for the Bank of Zambia.* Lusaka: Sida.

Andersson, G., O. Hesselmark and T. Ögren, 1994, *Project Proposals for Sida Support to the Bank of Zambia.* Stockholm: Sida.

Borg, M. and B. Portén, 1989, *Management Consultancy at the Bank of Zambia.* Lusaka: Sida.

Christian Michelsen Institute, 1986, *Zambia—Country Study and Norwegian Aid Review*. Bergen: CMI.

Hesselmark, O., 1993, *Bank of Zambia. The Bank's Organization. A Scenario for Change*. Lusaka: Sida.

Sida, 1997, *Landstrategi Zambia*. Stockholm: Sida.

UNDP, 1994, *Capacity Building Program for Economic Management. Modernization and Restructuring of the Bank of Zambia*. Lusaka: UNDP.

Winai, P. and O. Hesselmark, 1997, *The Bank of Zambia Way forward. Project Evaluation*. Stockholm: Sida.

Support for Building Institutions and Civil Service in Zimbabwe

Andreas Bengtsson

Introduction

Sweden and Zimbabwe have co-operated around the development of the civil service since 1982. The primary goals are to help Zimbabwe create an efficient national and municipal administration to serve as a basis for growth and implement the ongoing reform programmes, mainly the economic structural adjustment and the Civil Service Reform (CSR).

The experiences of several cases in Zimbabwe reveal conditions similar to those highlighted in previous chapters. The country's civil service has many of the characteristics described there. As pointed out in the Public Service Review commissioned by the Zimbabwe government "the corps of civil servants maintains, often with professionalism and steadfast principles, a strict system of regulations, where problem solving demands skilled manoeuvring between paragraphs, and errands are often referred to more senior personnel. At the same time the administration is characterized by centralization, slowness, lack of transparency, poor accessibility, lack of competence, inability to take decisions, a strong hierarchical order, complicated and circuitous procedures for dealing with staff and generally low service-mindedness. Thus it is often regarded with scepticism and dissatisfaction, both by the civil servants themselves and by the public" (PSRC Report, 1994).

In addition, Zimbabwe is in the midst of an economic reform programme, and it suffers from recurring periods of drought which affect large population groups very badly. Thus there are good reasons to make the civil service more efficient. Swedish development co-operation plays an important role, even if it only encompasses a limited section of the sector.

After a short presentation of the Zimbabwean reform work, Swedish support to the public administration sector is presented followed by a discussion of experiences and results. Finally I attempt to summarize and draw conclusions.

The Zimbabwean reform process

The Public Service Review Commission (PSRC)

At independence, Zimbabwe had an administrative apparatus that was characterized by both its colonial heritage and apartheid. Some important decisions on principles form the background to today's reform work. One of these was the decision to reform local government. Another was the decision, in 1989, to appoint an independent commission to review the entire civil service, The Public Service Review Commission (PSRC). The aim was to make the civil service more efficient so that it could improve its service to the public. The intention was to decentralize responsibility, simplify administrative routines and reinforce managerial capacity. The review and its recommendations are a cornerstone in the work of reform in Zimbabwe.

The (PSRC) was done before the introduction of the structural adjustment programme and since then macro-economic developments have substantially changed the conditions. The government must adapt itself to the difficult combination of shrinking budgets and increasing needs.

The Economic Structural Adjustment Programme (ESAP)

In 1990 Zimbabwe embarked on a five year Economic Structural Adjustment Programme. Market-oriented reforms and deregulation were introduced into the economy to stimulate growth and macro-economic stability. This would also help clear the way for modernized management thinking in the civil service, which in turn would exert an influence on the managers in their work and change the demands made upon them.

One target identified in ESAP was to reduce the number of civil servants by 23,000 from 192,000 in 1991. This aim has been achieved, even surpassed. It is unclear, however, if there were any short term savings since the generous retrenchment packages were a severe drain on the national budget. The cut-backs were also vaguely formulated as it was neither clarified by how much wage costs were to be reduced, nor clearly specified which categories of staff were to be retrenched.

Civil Service Reform (CSR)

Parallel with the economic reforms being introduced by ESAP, there is rethinking on the role of the state and a restructuring of the administrative apparatus. In the so-called Civil Service Reform, the intention is to reorganize the state, to reinvigorate its institutions, and to make it more efficient. The state's role should be to advise and facilitate rather than implement. The wider term Public Service Reform is being increasingly used for this and elements of the economic reforms.

In 1994 an attempt was made to summarize the aims and methods of the reform in a document called Framework for Civil Service Reform, which is being reviewed and updated during 1997/98. Although certain contexts are unclear in the original version, the document gives an overall picture of the various components. As it has been interpreted by the Public Service Commission (PSC), the reform encompasses, among other things, performance management, subcontracting, commercialization and decentralization to local government. There will also be a need to review the government's entire financial management system not least as regards performance management, and delegation of functions to local government. In the document itself, however, the most thoroughly described proposals concern personnel management.

The picture is further complicated, as the Ministry of Finance and the Public Service Commission each have their respective responsibility for the most important resources in the public administration: money and staff. A struggle for increased influence is going on, in which both parties assert their particular position. It is of major importance to deal with this issue and create mechanisms for concrete and mutual co-operation. Currently, efforts are under way to establish some form of reform co-ordination committee. Its success will of course depend on the importance attached to it by the various key stakeholders.

This lack of co-ordination and communication increases the risk of the work of reform stagnating. It is not clear in which order things should happen and what should be given priority. There may be a justified unwillingness to share sensitive parts of the reform with outsiders before they have been agreed upon internally, but this does not totally explain the apparent lack of a clear plan of action. Work with developing such a plan, as part of the revised Framework, is however ongoing. One underlying difficulty may have been the ideological aspects of changing systems. By now, however, all major stakeholders and decision-makers in government seem to be in agreement. The question is no longer *if*, but *how*?

The ongoing introduction of performance management will be another complicated part of the Civil Service Reform. It will require that each manager, together with his subordinate, identifies objectives and targets for the work ahead. At the present time, however, few managers can undertake to achieve a particular result, since power and resources (not least staff) are allocated from above and cannot be guaranteed in advance.

Finally, it should be added that a civil service reform is a complicated process. It should be comprehensive and all-embracing, and implemented in a decisive and systematic way. It is easy to take too much upon oneself in relation to the resources available. Regardless of the quality of planning and strategy, the most essential ingredient in any reform will be total political commitment.

Swedish assistance to the civil service — the examples of ZIPAM and the Department of Taxes (DoT) at the Ministry of Finance

Swedish development assistance aimed primarily at supporting economic structural adjustment encompasses taxes, auditing and (until recently) statistics. It is directed at the three key institutions: Department of Taxes (DoT), Office of the Comptroller and Auditor General and Central Statistics Office (CSO). All of these bodies are involved in institutional co-operation with Swedish sister authorities (twinning).

It is impossible to give a comprehensive picture of Swedish assistance and its results and conclusions here. Two examples will thus serve to illustrate some important experiences, ZIPAM and the Department of Taxes.

ZIPAM— from government training institution to commercialized consultancy

Swedish support to the Zimbabwe Institute of Public Administration and Management (ZIPAM) was introduced in 1988 in the form of Sida financed co-operation between the institute and Swedish SIPU (formerly the National Institute for Personnel Development, now a private company).

The Swedish assistance has primarily been directed towards supporting the process of transition from a government institution to a parastatal business. In parallel, there has been partial but decreasing financing of the production of selected courses to keep operations running while the process of change is under way.

ZIPAM has been regarded as an important actor in the work of implementing the recommendations of the Public Service Commission. The demands are high, both individually and organizationally. At the same time, ZIPAM's position has been controversial. The quality of the training offered has been called into question by participants, and by outsiders in evaluations. In the past there has been difficulty in recruiting qualified staff. After being reconstructured as a parastatal in 1993, ZIPAM can now employ professional trainers and pay them salaries that are virtually the same as in the private sector. There is, however, more to do with regard to individual and result-based remuneration.

At the moment the work is meant to be run on a cost recovery basis and ZIPAM is expected in time to survive without state subsidies. The transformation from a government training institution to an income-earning parastatal is a process to which Swedish support has contributed through, amongst other things, technical assistance. Yet the government is still responsible for a diminishing part of ZIPAM's running costs.

Judging from the results to date, ZIPAM has reasonable possibilities of supplying the civil service's needs for relevant and qualified training for managers. The transformation to a parastatal has, however, been sluggish. It is taking time to improve its reputation and to remove the scepticism of potential users. In addition, the concept of marketing its services is new to ZIPAM. Previously it was not necessary to make an effort to attract participants to the courses; with larger spending budgets and a seemingly endless need of training, the state supplied the institute with a steady stream of candidates.

Now ZIPAM is trying to sell its services through brochures and even television commercials. Former civil servants are to become businessmen and the supply of courses must be adapted to offer what the market wants. Yet more than a superficial change is required; a thorough-going change in attitude is necessary so that the institute accepts that the clients' needs and desires must guide the design of the products. The staff has to improve the quality of the training and become better at marketing. At the same time, the government, the major client, must become better at ordering, and paying for, courses.

The Ministry of Public Service and the Public Service Commission have both been sceptical about ZIPAM. The feeling is that private companies sometimes give better value for money. Cynically, it may not simply be a matter of quality, but also the fact that a diploma from ZIPAM has lower status than one from abroad or from a reputable domestic company. In practice, however, the organization ought to have quite good prerequisites to train civil servants. ZIPAM knows both the work and the culture. With its roots in the past, it ought to be able to combine the best experiences from the civil service with credible new ideas and in this way improve its competitiveness.

ZIPAM has also been contracted to assist in key areas of the introduction of performance management in the entire civil service. This is a major task including the development of materials and training of trainers, who will in turn train more than 100,000 people. If this is carried out with reasonable results it could mean a break-through for ZIPAM. If they fail, which may actually depend on factors outside ZIPAM's control, the company's credibility will again be at stake.

The above example indicates how thinking more in terms of the market has affected ZIPAM. The state no longer takes economic responsibility for the institute, but it had initial problems in accepting that its former institution was trying to act as an independent consultancy. The state wanted to eat its cake and still have it. At ZIPAM, on the other hand, some staff members, the ones expected to implement the reforms, were under the impression that they could continue working as in the past. If no one wants to take the courses, they ought to be made compulsory, as someone put it!

The Department of Taxes—a question of sustainability

Sweden has supported capacity building within the Department of Taxes (DoT) since 1988. The support is implemented through institutional co-operation with the Swedish National Tax Board (RSV) and the goal is to develop DoT's capacity to ensure that taxes are paid on time and in accordance with the law. It is extremely important to improve efficiency in tax collection. Taxes represent the largest portion of government revenue and this income offers a possibility of partial compensation for structural adjustment's demands for cut-backs by increasing income.

Co-operation between RSV and DoT has been very successful. By providing efficient service, tax revenues can be increased. In brief, the more rapid and better service one gives, the greater is the chance that those who are liable for tax will take the trouble to come up to the office to pay it. Through more efficient investigative work, revenues can increase. It is believed, for instance, that a large number of companies have still not been registered in the tax registers. In comparison with the relatively small Swedish inputs the volume of tax collected has nevertheless increased considerably, particularly after TaxNet, a successful large scale collection exercise in Harare and Bulawayo during 1997.

During 1994/95, some of the most highly qualified staff at the computer and inspection sections resigned with retrenchment packages. Several vacancies also arose at leadership levels. DoT's management has dealt with the problem by recruiting new staff and has thus to some extent had to start again from the beginning. What took several years to build up was largely demolished in less than 12 months. Needless to say this led to tax revenues being temporarily far below estimates. Apparently, no one who saw what the impact would be in critical areas, was able to prevent the effects of the scheme.

The retrenchment packages were introduced as a part of CSR to reduce the size of the civil service. Many were tempted to resign — but not, in the first place, those who were no longer needed. Instead those with the best prospects of finding work in the private sector, not least in the fields of computers and economics, were the first to accept the offer. Although (or perhaps because) DoT's personnel is highly trained and is part of a very efficient tax administration, the department's work is weakened by external factors. Notwithstanding the strength of DoT, it has neither competed successfully with the attraction of the private sector, nor with the government's own campaign to tempt staff to resign!

Swedish support has, by and large, been focused on the handling and management of information and consequently it has been primarily concerned with data development. The conditions for the partners have differed substantially in important areas. DoT has not had the opportunity of independently promoting or financially rewarding its staff itself and the traditional pattern in the public administration, with strong centralization, poor spread of information and a reluctance to take independent initiatives, has also left its mark. Even organizationally, in common with the entire ministry of finance in Zimbabwe, DoT has had less independence than Sweden's RSV.

It has thus been difficult to build up an ability to handle external pressures, such as the retrenchments. At a critical time when management was needed to stand up for the work and encourage the staff, there was hardly any management left! Those who remained were primarily concerned with trying to repair the damage and keep as much as possible of the work going. At that time, it was therefore difficult for RSV to carry through more systematic work on management and policy questions in DoT.

Nonetheless, during 1996 and 1997, DoT showed remarkable internal strength and largely managed to recover. New managers were promoted, increased training in management was introduced in co-operation with RSV and a process of corporate planning was initiated. The prospect of being transformed into a more independent revenue authority, along with the Department of Customs, has greatly boosted morale.

Lessons and conclusions

This area is highly politicized, which makes the dialogue on policies both complicated and sensitive. There has been an unwillingness among civil servants to really discuss different programmes of action, although signs of change are now increasingly evident. The wider context of the reform process does, of course, make the capacity building work even harder. The institutions that are being developed are not only expected to be sustainable and capable of executing their designated tasks, but also flexible enough to cope with both pressure to change and the unpredictability of a changing society. The significance of genuine political will and courage at the highest levels, to implement the complex of reforms, should, therefore, not be underestimated.

Good results

In spite of an uncertain future, and thinking about what could have been done better, it must be remembered that a good deal has been achieved! Despite all the difficulties, significant changes have taken place. ZIPAM has been transformed into a parastatal, a demanding and painful process that requires a great deal of all those involved.

The long-term results must not be taken for granted, but there have been changes!

DoT has improved its capacity dramatically, and the volume of taxes collected has increased. Despite this, it is obvious how vulnerable the institution is when retrenchments have taken their toll and that it may take time to replace the skills of those who have disappeared. Nevertheless, the organization is decidedly, and sustainably, stronger today than when co-operation with RSV began about ten years ago.

Another area supported by Sweden, namely, the Central Statistics Office has built up impressive competence within several specific fields. A population census has been conducted that is regarded as a good example for the region and the office has also been engaged in development work with its sister office in Namibia. There are difficulties, for instance in the production of national accounts, but the institution is standing on its own two feet, even if somewhat shakily.

Co-operation between the Office of the Comptroller and Auditor General and the Swedish National Audit Office (RRV) only began in 1991. It has produced good results in most areas, and the plans are that it will be phased out by the end of 1999, since the parties feel that by then there will be an increasingly diminishing rate of returns. This co-operation has also demonstrated the value of having a sister institution as a partner in the capacity building process. It is unlikely that a private audit firm could have established the same close relations with the management that RRV, as a national audit office, has done.

Leadership/organization

Reforms demand a new leadership culture. On the part of foreign consultants, they require increased knowledge about management functions in the local context and about what can be done to increase sustained efficiency on the basis of existing conditions. A "western" management culture (whatever that may be) will not make a major break-through in Zimbabwe, just as Japanese management culture, for instance, will have little effect in the United States. One must identify the specifics of the environment and let development occur in line with domestic conditions.

The retrenchment packages and their consequences for the Department of Taxes, for instance, show the importance of co-ordination and information before crucial changes are implemented. With a clearer process of consultation and with greater willingness to listen to signals from lower down in the administration, the programme might have been implemented more efficiently. Perhaps the staff it was desirable to retain could have been dealt with in a better way.

In general, the public sector would probably fare better through a more organized interchange of staff with the private sector. Decision makers in the private sector need to meet officials from the public sector to get more information on rules, government policies and future plans that affect the work of the companies. Public sector managers need, in a corresponding way, to learn more about private sector management. The ongoing changes in the civil service place very great demands on the public administration in general and there is a great deal of knowledge and experience to gain from the private sector. In practice, there is today virtually no exchange at senior management level between the public and private sectors, including parastatals.

Professional competence and management

The institutional twinning projects have shown relatively good results, but they also require time and must be seen in the long-term. When looking more closely at this kind of co-operation, a tendency emerges, not only in Zimbabwe. Major progress is evident in the technical field. With regard to development of professional competence and information technology, for instance, employees have acquired great knowledge which they also apply in their daily work. At the same time, there are often gaps in planning and management. It is as if institutional co-operation does not function as well when it comes to transfer of knowledge and competence in the management field. For instance, problems are experienced in analysis and allowing for external factors outside the control of both the institution and the consultant. This makes long-term planning more difficult. One such factor is of course the high staff turn-over, often associated with un-competitive employment conditions.

The Civil Service Reform and its retrenchment packages have indicated how vulnerable an organization is to external influences at a time of great changes. The authorities must not only develop so that they succeed in managing their tasks independently, but they must also be so flexible that they manage to introduce internal changes in response to external ones.

With reference to the development steps presented by Andersson and Winai elsewhere in this book, the institutions discussed above are still somewhere on the first three steps. In the main they do not yet have the capacity to develop through their own power. Both the statistics and the audit offices on the whole deliver products which are in demand and of a reasonable standard. Gaps in production remain and thus both CSO in respect of national accounts and the audit office as regards parastatal auditing are still on the first step.

We may also need to review goal formulation and the expectations of what could be achieved. The development of institutions has its own dynamics and is more demanding than superficial appearances might indicate. It is necessary to involve the entire institution, create understanding and bridge cultural differences as well as, from the start, daring and being able to identify the problem in its entirety. (Cf. Anton Johnston's contribution to this anthology, *On Developing Institutions in Africa*.) What we are faced with is an extremely authoritarian and centralized organization which will not be able to function unless attitudes undergo a radical change. There may be a lot at stake for those who have the final say in formulating goals.

Leadership and management may be areas where capacity building is particularly difficult. It is easier to open the door to a foreign consultant if it is a matter of technical capacity rather than managerial ability. This latter type of consultant may mean to a manager that he (and it is most often a man) has to face consequences which affect his prestige in relation to close colleagues, subordinates and/or senior staff. Consequently, help is often requested on the technical side, not least with equipment. In addition, for some managers, regardless of nationality, the very fact that they have an executive position must by definition mean that they are good managers—otherwise they would not be there in the first place!

It is possible that institutional co-operation with sister institutions should be further developed. Perhaps the idea of hiring management consultants specifically to assist in that part of the capacity building should be re-explored. Perhaps it is possible to retain the traditional institutions (generally Swedish) as the main entrepreneur, but encourage them to sub-contract consultants for advice and training on management and planning. This is already happening in individual cases, but it is as yet too early to express an opinion on the results. There is room for creative new thinking where the best of what has already been done is used while allowing new methods to evolve to improve on what is still faulty.

Ideas which were already touched on in the sector study done in 1990 (Gustafsson, Blunt et al., 1991) still appear to be relevant. Institutional co-operation involves both technology and management. Technical professional capacity alone is inadequate. Change must also be pursued in an organization. Even external factors have an influence, and committed managers, who have the power and authority to recruit, promote and give a fair salary to their staff, are a fundamental precondition to enable an organization to improve its performance. This cannot be better than what personal commitment and management roles permit. One can also look at it from another perspective and return to Jerker Carlsson: a changed management role is not possible unless the organizational and institutional environments undergo a fundamental change. It is in such work of change that public administration development co-operation has a given and very important role.

Andreas Bengtsson is a political scientist. He is working at present for Sida at the Swedish Embassy in Harare.

References

"Compensation Survey of Senior Management in the Public Service of Zimbabwe", May 1994, ARA-TECHTOP (UNDP/MDP Project Zim 90/008).

Gustafsson, L., P. Blunt et al., 1991, "Keeping the Goals in Sight. An Evaluation of Swedish Support to Public Administration in Zimbabwe", *Sida Evaluation Report*, 1991/4.